SLAYERS

AND THEIR

VAMPIRES

SLAYERS

AND

THEIR

VAMPIRES

A CULTURAL HISTORY
OF KILLING THE DEAD

BRUCE A. MCCLELLAND

THE UNIVERSITY OF MICHIGAN PRESS / ANN ARBOR

Copyright © by the University of Michigan 2006
All rights reserved
Published in the United States of America by
The University of Michigan Press
Manufactured in the United States of America
♾ Printed on acid-free paper

2009   2008   4   3   2

A CIP catalog record for this book is available from the British Library.

Library of Congress Cataloging-in-Publication Data

McClelland, Bruce.
    Slayers and their vampires : a cultural history of killing the
dead / Bruce A. McClelland.
        p.   cm.
    Includes bibliographical references and index.
    ISBN-13: 978-0-472-09923-8 (cloth : alk. paper)
    ISBN-10: 0-472-09923-X (cloth : alk. paper)
    ISBN-13: 978-0-472-06923-1 (pbk. : alk. paper)
    ISBN-10: 0-472-06923-3 (pbk. : alk. paper)   1. Vampires—History.
    I. Title.

GR830.V3M23   2006
398'.45—dc22   2005033820

Contents

Illustrations

Preface

Almost three centuries have passed since a curious rash of hysterical vampire epidemics at the fringes of the Habsburg Empire first brought this type of oral folklore from the mysterious Balkans and the Transylvanian region into Western consciousness. Although there had previously been no precisely equivalent folklore about the ambulatory dead in the Roman Catholic and Protestant countries of Western Europe, the Inquisition's prosecutions of people denounced as witches were still fresh in the public memory. In fact, it was the possible recrudescence of such intolerable social injustice that prompted Empress Maria Theresa to send a noted scientist to a Slavic region on the northeastern frontier to learn what these epidemics were all about and then to advise her on how to prevent a new round of witch hunts from emerging.

Here, then, from the very beginning of the incorporation of the vampire motif into the European literary tradition, a loose equation was established between the witch and the vampire. Subsequently, these two incarnate vectors of evil have continued to compel the attention of artists, scientists, clergy, and scholars of various disciplines, as well as the general populace. As Western society has become more secular, furthermore, these figures have increasingly been used to ground the negative pole of historical (and military) Christianity, insofar as both are represented as enemies of all that is good and, in some cases, as being in league with Satan or the Devil. The witch, for example, is portrayed as indulging in total, corrupt inversions of Christian ritual and behavior, while the vampire can be destroyed by implicitly sacred implements of Christian magic (the cross, holy water, etc.).

The concept of evil, in the West at least, thus continues to be linked to a fundamental belief in the apostasy of anything that inherently subverts canonical Christian theology, especially with regard to healing and mystical knowledge. (The linking of witches and vampires to Satan serves to incorporate Judaic belief as Christian prehistory while denying Judaism any status in the argument about the nature of evil.) The threat posed by both the witch and the vampire has to do with their special knowledge, acquired through contact with the dead: the witch has the ability to foretell and thus control the future, while the unholy vampire is somehow able to return from the dead without the permission of Jesus or his clergy. This threat, ultimately, goes to the very foundation of Christian eschatology. Such knowledge also directly challenges the uniqueness and absolute power of Christ. It would appear that however rational the post-Enlightenment societies of Europe and the Americas consider themselves, there persists a broad concept of evil as whatever is taken at the time to be anti-Christian.

At the time of this writing, the term *evil* has been applied more publicly not so much to individual folkloric or literary/cinematic horror figures as to large groups of people whose political agendas threaten to undermine the very foundation of some "way of life." Thus, where once the Soviet Union was labeled an "evil empire," when that atheistic and politically opposing force went underground only to be replaced by non-Western opposition to the imperatives of late international capitalism, certain countries that now dare challenge Western nuclear hegemony have been publicly labeled the "axis of evil," a wonderful phrase that even manages to invoke associations with the long-reigning symbol of absolute evil, Nazism. Furthermore, so-called Islamic extremism/fundamentalism/terrorism is now quite obviously emerging to replace the Soviet Union as the central sponsor of evil in the world. And lest we imagine that this labeling goes eastward only, the United States has found itself proclaimed by these same infidels to be a hypostasis of the Great Satan.

There is, of course, a presumption in all this that those groups who are calling the others evil should somehow be, if not above reproach, at least immune from reciprocal accusations. There is a cohering aspect to the word that binds its utterers ever more irrevocably to evil's antithesis (as if evil itself could never say its own name) and thus permits a restoration of well-being and order. To label something evil is to magically circumscribe it and to effectively push the obligation of proof of goodness onto the thing so designated. To define what constitutes anathema, to excommunicate *ex officio,* is of course to assert or reassert, with full authority, one's own unquestionable status as good. From the appropriate pulpit, to label something evil loudly enough is to provide perfect cover for any previous or subsequent actions that otherwise might be seen as unjust, intolerable, or even evil.

Alas, not all incarnations of evil are as identifiable as Osama bin Laden. There are evil effects that are not so well documented as the attacks on the World Trade Center. In some ways, these vaguer effects may induce a stronger, albeit subtler, sense of chaos than obvious (violent) aggression. For there is always the possibility that any violence and destruction leveled at us—or, as we now see, merely intended for us—is not necessarily evil but, rather, a form of retributive justice, whether human or divine. Against the ambiguously evil, embodied folklorically by simulacra of the human, such as the witch or the vampire, we desire heroes that are not bound by the mundane and banal perceptions of the politician or the soldier. If the magnetic needle indicating true evil can swing to any point on our relativistic moral compass, we need a force—a special person—who can be called on to orient it away from us, lest we be forced to look inward and see how we might not live up to the values we claim to uphold.

In the history of both Western and Eastern Europe—a political division that may be disputable on nationalistic grounds, but one that I hope is provisionally tolerable for all the evident historical and cultural differences between the two regions—there is a tradition with respect to vampires and witches of endowing select, marked individuals with the mystical power to identify, to actually see, the ambulatory evil that is resident within our community. These seers, who perhaps had provided something of a healing function in earlier millennia, over time used their powers, often for personal gain, to uncover the insidious evil carried by those members of the community that represented a threat to the common order and that were even more evil than most because they seemed to have so little real social power: witches, after all, were usually women, while vampires were always dead.

While there does seem to be some similarity in the way witches and vampires have been regarded, these two figures in fact underwent quite different vicissitudes in the history of Europe, regardless of whether or not they had any sort of common religious ancestry. There is, however, a distinct and important historical flex point when the vampire moved from its natural ecology—Balkan, Orthodox, Slavic, and preliterate— into an adapted environment (a new host, if you will) whose characteristics are (Western) European, Catholic or Protestant, non-Slavic, and literate. As Gábor Klaniczay has pointed out, what seems to happen in the early eighteenth century is the replacement of a pattern of actual witch persecution with episodes of vampire hysteria and then the subsequent reportage, the transfer of the vampire from a folkloric entity to a symbolic literary type, capable of embodying metaphorically a host of shifting contemporary concepts of social evil.

We might hope that in the transfer of the image of the vampire from that of a dead excommunicated villager to that of an undead, urbane, if castle-dwelling, nobleman, the borrowers of this motif would have understood quite well the "scapegoat" nature of the vampire, such that they might then have used the vampire narrative to lay bare the modalities of injustice and blindness that pervade the scapegoat dynamic. But this did not happen at all. In fact, these otherwise learned borrowers of the vampire motif were themselves ignorant of the broader cultural system of which the folkloric vampire was but one not terribly significant part. Consequently, they tended to take the vampire's presumed evil as authentic, not the result of a social compact in which an insentient corpse was reimagined as alive so that it could bear the projection of guilt and withstand the violence and humiliation enacted on it. It is almost as if, once the mechanism for projecting evil onto the figure of the witch had been suppressed in the name of antiimaginal rationalism, the vampire came to stand in as the perfect defenseless target of collective violence, because the vampire's evil—tied so permanently to the abject horror (adapting Kristeva's notion) of the unholy returning corpse—would remain unquestionable.

This incessantly repeated victory over the simulacrum of the dead vampire, often engineered or initiated by a seer or slayer who has been granted special knowledge of the vampire's true identity, is a complex mechanism that intentionally obscures the absence of certain values inherited from the Enlightenment, such as due process and the separation of church and state. This obscuration, I argue in these pages, is itself part of the mechanism by which ordinarily just or humane persons can come to subscribe to the collective attribution of evil in order to act out vengeance and rage on the abject body. The obscuring process continually recurs and may be accompanied by a translation of its essential features to a new object, a new land (e.g., across the Danube or across the narrative gulf from literature to film), where an imbalance in the system of social justice can once more go unrecognized for what it is. To further protect the perennial need to perform violence on a victim whose guilt must be unquestionable, a hero with special skills must come along, at least once into every age.

Acknowledgments

This book wraps up an investigation that began over thirty years ago, when I first naively became aware there were historical and folkloric antecedents to the vampires I had previously known only from literature and the movies. Only when my interests in both Slavic languages and vampires found their common justification in Jan Perkowski's works on Slavic vampirism did I realize that I should be looking not in Transylvania or Romania for the answers to my questions about this myth but, rather, in the Balkans. So it is first to "Mr. Perkowski" that I owe my gratitude, since without his insights, I could never have known what I did not know. It was at the University of Virginia that I met other Slavic scholars whose breadth and seriousness I would need to emulate, especially Natalie Kononenko and David Herman.

It was in Bulgaria, however, that I knew I was finally on to something, and there my interest in vampire research was always taken very seriously. Anisava Miltenova and her colleagues at the Institute for Bulgarian Literature arranged my visits to archives and institutes and helped me find what I needed. Evgenija Miceva and Račko Popov allowed me to mine their enormous knowledge of the Bulgarian oral vampire tradition, while Margi Karamihova even offered to provide me with the phone numbers of current vampires, and Ivan Marazov and the Russian Scythianist Dmitri Raevskii enchanted me with their erudition. For me, though, the highest place of all Bulgarian scholars will always be reserved for Sabina Pavlova, whose love of her country she managed to infect me with and whose knowledge of the language was critical for my understanding.

The most valuable combination of psychological and intellectual support with persistent reminders to remain subversive in my thinking was provided by Bruce Lincoln, in whose honor this book was written. Those who read and commented on earlier drafts of portions of the manuscript or who listened and discussed its ideas or gave encouragement also performed a valuable service for me: Arthur Chapin, Michael Kaufman, Mary McClelland, Paul Moruza, Peter Ronayne, Cathleen Shattuck, and Lisa Stoffer (Lesy). Several people provided me with materials or ideas that in some way influenced the direction of my research and thinking, especially Paul Kahn and Eric Keathley. The long-lasting enthusiasm for this project shown by two editors at the University of Michigan Press, Ellen McCarthy and Raphael Allen, was essential for getting this book into print.

Finally, the members of my family—Cynthia, Amy, and Jay—have lived with this vampire, now become a slayer, for many decades. To them I say, we have found his where.

I

INTRODUCTION

E vil—wherever belief in it is held—tends to be thought of in one of two ways. It is either a force equal to or slightly inferior to an opposing force or, as in Orthodox Christianity, the absence, withdrawal, perversion, or deflection of a universal inclination called "good." Cosmological narratives usually give it both a body and a name and situate it in a separate dark, turbulent, or alien realm. In the so-called natural world, evil may become manifest through the agency of demons or spirits. Whether such demons take on the imaginal form of beasts or humans (even when their form is not always humanly visible), the consequences of their actions are always encountered in the human sphere; that is, even when evil directs itself against animals or vegetation, it is always with an eye toward disrupting the social order (e.g., husbandry, agriculture) and the dependencies of humankind on these areas of human ecology and economy. At its base, evil is a pernicious threat to human survival above all else, and it is essentially different from death itself. Whereas death is universal, evil is selective.

There are countless representations and personifications of evil across history and religious and cultural systems, just as there are many images of the good and the heroic. These various images are depicted in the narratives of both official and folk religions, mythology and folk-lore, as well as, even quite recently, in the secular metaphors of political and ideological discourse. In virtually all these narratives, at some point the physical representatives of good and evil become direct, often violent, antagonists. The outcome of their struggle for domination over the moral direction of the community holds a central place in its value system.

Perhaps the most dangerous form that evil takes is the visibly human, since when it is ambulatory and mimetic of the individual, it is difficult to distinguish the evil being from a fellow member of the community. This is especially true if there are no obvious markers, such as a tail and horns, to call attention to its difference. When the average person cannot definitely identify another individual as evil, yet some inexplicable adversity suggests malevolence that has gone beyond mere temper, it is critical that the threatened individual or collective immediately locate evil's nexus—even if it is found to be the heart of a neighbor and there is no confirming evidence aside from belief. Once evil is found, it must be destroyed or, at the very least, banished far beyond the possibility of return.

In contemporary Western European and North American popular culture, the vampire has become one of the most pervasive and recognizable symbols of insidious evil. Though, according to some notions, the vampire can shift his shape into that of a wolf or bat or other animal and perhaps possesses other supernatural powers, he[1] is different from monstrous beasts or even from Satan in that he possesses a single human body. Furthermore, in both folklore and literature/cinema, in his humanlike, untransformed state, he is not easily recognized as a different order of being. The vampire, as we shall see in chapter 7, thus has very much in common with the European witch, with one critically important difference: whereas witches are alive at the time they are tortured or ritually executed, vampires are by definition dead or at least undead (whatever that means). But both witches and vampires are held to be evil, for reasons that have much in common.

A great deal, naturally, has been written about vampires, and though I hope to add to that discourse, I do not intend here to place the vampire at the exact center of my discussion. Like evil, the vampire is a force that must be struggled with and overcome, and he thus represents only a single pole in a moral dyad. Whether or not we choose to label the vampire's antagonist "good," there is not much of a story if the violence and destruction wrought by the vampire goes unchecked. While it is rare that a vampire tale or a treatment of the vampire legend does not include an episode in which the vampire is destroyed or banished by some agency, little attention has been paid to the history and character of the vampire's personal nemesis, now popularly known as the vampire slayer.

In the elaborate heroic tales found in epics, the central theme is ordinarily the hero's transformation in the struggle against evil (in the form, say, of a dragon) or oppression. In most vampire motifs, however, the ostensible forces of good who would identify, oppose, and destroy vampires tend to be nameless and often incidental to the narrative. In fact, it is only fairly recently that the vampire slayer has had anything like a leading role: Abraham van Helsing, in *Dracula* (1897), is arguably the first significant self-professed vampire slayer in a tradition that culminates in the television series *Buffy the Vampire Slayer* (1997–2003).

Ever since the publication of *Dracula,* or at least since movies adapted that novel's central characters and narrative points in 1922 (*Nosferatu*) and 1931 (*Dracula*), the nature, origin, and meaning of the vampire have been frequent subjects of inquiry by European and American scholars. Historical, literary, cultural, political, and even psychoanalytic discussions of the nature and role of the vampire have abounded since the vampire became widely known in Western Europe in the early eighteenth century. But the tradition of the vampire and, indeed, of the word *vampire* itself, which also had a prefolkloric meaning, goes back several centuries before Europeans living north and west of the Danube had ever heard of such things. As we ought to expect, the meaning of the Slavic term *vampir* changed considerably over a millennium, yet most writers on the subject have ignored both the cultural context in which the term arose and the possible changes in the nature of the thing designated by the word across time.

Among the more significant causes of this inattention to the broader development of the vampire motif is the understandable, if Orientalistic, cultural ignorance on the part of Europeans living far from those areas of Europe—in particular, the Balkans and the Carpathians—that were dominated for so long by the Ottoman Turks. Toward the end of the seventeenth century, as the power of the Ottoman Empire began to wane in southeastern Europe, scientists and journalists who were curious about rumors of strange vampire phenomena ventured more intrepidly into such places as Serbia, Croatia, and other areas around the borders of the Habsburg Empire.[2] Their noble intention was first to record and then explain the exotic and perhaps supernatural goings-on at the boundaries of the civilized world. This they did with a vengeance, writing reports and learned treatises to explain away the very possibility of the ambulatory dead. To prevent a resurgence of the extreme and irrational religious persecution that characterized the Inquisition, these journalists and scientists drew on the scientific methods that were emerging during the Enlightenment.

Thus, the conception of the vampire on which virtually all subsequent vampire literature (and, by technological extension, cinema) was based derived from a handful of notorious episodes. These "epidemics" occurred over the span of only a couple of decades at the fringes of Western Europe, where Balkan folklore had come into direct contact with and had thus been contaminated by contemporary ideas about witches and witchcraft. Though a few reports by seventeenth-century travelers accurately described the Greek vampire, or revenant, known by the borrowed Slavic name *broukolakos,*[3] there was no understanding at the time of the vampire's role within a much broader demonological or lower mythological system. The phenomenology of the vampire was appropriated in its entirety into a new, Enlightenment worldview, while the semantics and cultural history of the Old Slavic term *vampir* were almost completely ignored.

Perhaps the most profound consequence of this appropriation was that important, structural aspects of the vampire motif went unrecognized. The significance of the vampire hunter, for example, was for a long while overshadowed by a natural fascination—which preoccupied early Western writers on the subject—with the vampire's appearance, powers, and behavior. Until quite recently, even scholarly discussions of famous outbreaks of vampirism, such as those involving Arnod Paole and others near Belgrade between 1727 and 1732, were often blind to the folkloric patterning beneath the reports and thus tended to take the basic events of the reportage as fact.[4] This may occur because the structure of a certain type of Balkan vampire tale is

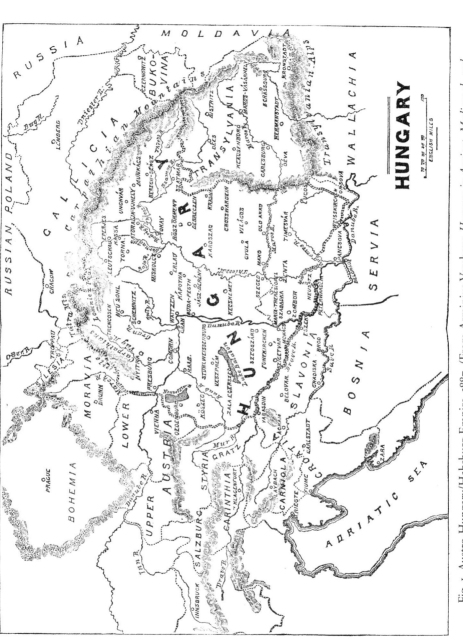

Fig. 1. Austro-Hungary/Habsburg Empire, 1887. (From Arminius Vambery, *Hungary in Ancient, Mediaeval, and Modern Times* [London: T. Fisher Unwin, 1887]).

not recognizable to anyone who has not previously encountered a large number of oral tales (not always about vampires per se) with similar structures. The dynamic of the vampire report, in which the real focus is on the methods used to identify and thereby dispatch the evil vampire, is missed as a consequence. What remains misunderstood is how the appearance of evil always seems to require counteraction or expiation at the hands of someone possessing both the necessary insight to recognize a vampire and the knowledge of the necessary rituals to destroy one. The meaning of the symbols in the original folkloric system is not carried over into the new, literary adaptation of the vampire theme.

The present work, then, attempts to restore the balance—between the vampire and his heroic adversary—that was disturbed with the transfer of the vampire from his home within Slavic lands, especially the South Slavic cultures of the Balkans. In particular, it is important to recognize first that the vampire hunter or slayer is not at all a modern phenomenon, dreamed up by Gothic writers for dramatic or literary purposes. More likely, this character is a reflex of an ancient shamanic figure possessing the healing power to peer into the world of the dead. As a matter of speculation, I would even propose that as the spiritual power of shamans was denigrated with the ascendancy of Christianity and its priestly classes,[5] the role of shamans as healers was eventually suppressed. This left the residual incarnation of evil in the form of the reanimated dead as the more complex and interesting figure. Indeed, we might view the vampiric figure of the empty ambulatory corpse as merely the derelict spiritual housing abandoned by a disempowered religious healer who is no longer able to move freely in both directions across the boundary between life and death.

In addition to trying to understand the deep history of the vampire seer (seeing, not slaying, was the primary objective), it is also important to understand how the vampire cannot exist without some sort of prescription for identifying or eliminating him. While a seer is not always required—there are times when the identity of the vampire is obvious to everyone in the community—there nevertheless must be a prescribed pattern for handling the vampire so that his destructive actions cease and he never returns. In such cases, a specially designated individual or group must take the heroic action of killing a corpse. In the earliest folklore about vampires, that person or group was the equivalent of the spiritual hero, since his or their actions were undertaken on behalf of the entire community.[6]

The heroic nature of the vampire slayer is predicated on his ability to identify the force that saps the energy from the life of the community. Something unnatural, unholy, invades and disturbs the natural order of things, and through this puncture in the tissue of everyday existence, something—is it a certain trust in the impermeability of that which separates us from the dead?—drains out. Yet because this intruder is invisible or, at the very least, unnoticeable—he is one of us, after all—only those with a special understanding of his nature are able to intervene and stop the hemorrhage. Like the vampire, the slayer must be marked—externally, by some sign of birth or accident; internally, by his symbolic connection to the world of the dead.

The nature of this bipolar relationship between the vampire and his adversary, the hunter or slayer, and the ways in which this connection becomes manifest and changes over several hundred years have not been adequately investigated. An examination of early Balkan folklore reveals that the vampire slayer, whose perceptive powers transcend those permitted ordinary Christian villagers, is the vampire's true mirror image. The slayer is the heroic and opposing reflection that is curiously, but necessarily, generated by the presence of evil, and he is as closely bound to evil as a reflection is to its original. If the vampire is a dangerous and antihuman replica of the human, the seer or slayer is the rejector or suppressor of the replica, who restores order by allowing the community to differentiate the authentic from the false.[7] This critical difficulty in distinguishing the true from the false, the beneficent from the treacherous, is, as we shall see, also the basis of the conflict between early Christianity and paganism and heresy. Historically, it was out of that conflict as it was played out in the Balkans that the folkloric meaning of the vampire arose.

Contemporary culture-based interpretations of the vampire "myth" have great value in explaining our apparent need to continually retell the vampire story, with all its attendant variations. Clearly, some limits must be placed around the definitions of vampires (and, I suppose, slayers) and the sorts of events and problems that are encountered in vampire narratives—whether folklore, literature, or film—so that the vampire motif is identifiable as such. Much scholarship has been devoted to identifying the essence of this motif, in order to get at its meaning. Hence, for example, much popularity accompanies such monographs as Nina Auerbach's *Our Vampires, Ourselves* (1995) and the various essays—in such compendia as *Blood Read: The Vampire as Metaphor in Contemporary Culture* (1997)—that take on not only the vampires of nineteenth-century European literature but also the popular cultural images of the vampire in everything from cartoons to movies to cereal boxes to video games to long-running television shows. But, again, to survey and analyze these cultural phenomena without reference to the context from which they were originally drawn is to run the risk of missing something that is persistent in this myth but that escapes our notice if we are aware only of the modern phenomenology of the vampire. (With respect to the development of the vampire theme, "modern" here means after around 1732, that is, toward the beginning of the Enlightenment.) In particular, since, in modern times, the public significance of abjection that is symbolized by excommunication has been greatly reduced, the fact that the first vampires were excommunicates tends to be ignored or to lie outside the bounds of interpretation. Yet apostasy was once a status of serious consequence for life in an Orthodox community, ambiguously defining the excommunicate as both a physical member of the community and a spiritual persona non grata. This ecclesiastical designation is a prerequisite for the emergence of vampire folklore, for it defines the consequences after life for one who is ejected from the Church and prevented from undergoing funerary rituals to ensure the proper path of the soul into the otherworld after death. It also implicitly defines the qualifications of those who would prevent the return of the banished after their death.

There have certainly been attempts to understand the significance of the vampire with reference to historical events and social movements. Franco Moretti, for example, has pointed to the influence of Marx's famous analogy between capitalism and vampirism upon the uptake of this theme in Europe prior to Stoker.[8] More recently, vampires have been linked to the contemporary "culture of consumption."[9] However, cultural metaphors that involve the vampire motif, which are an entirely Western phenomenon,[10] tend not to extend to the methods of perceiving them or slaying them. (If they did, we might have expected Marx to point out that capitalism can only be destroyed by someone who either has been a capitalist or else has had close contact with capitalists.) The linkage between the literary vampire and the folkloric one is a topic beginning to receive a great deal of attention. However, most scholars in this area take the modern vampire, especially as it has been configured since *Dracula* and its immediate precursors, as their starting point. They then go back into the folklore only as far as the literature itself allows, glossing over the significance of the enormous lacunae in the knowledge of vampire folklore drawn on by those earliest investigators into the subject.

The current study differs in two ways from others that attempt to draw a line between the modern vampire tale and various hypothetical points of origin. First, I take the "original" vampire—who I believe was neither folkloric nor supernatural—as the primary manifestation of a deep religious and social conflict. From this point of view, the modern (and even postmodern) tale, in whatever medium, is a culturally informed derivative, capable of adaptation as the role of religious belief in society has risen and fallen. I presume and will attempt to prove that despite the changes in the "manifest content" of the vampire narrative as it is used in various social metaphors, the fundamental role of the vampire within the societies and periods that have adopted him remains invariant. Second, as I have already implied, I propose that the vampire only became a protagonist with the demise of his natural antagonist at the hands of proselytizing Christian polemicists. This individual would have been a magician or healer or, in other words, a holy person from a pre-Christian religion with a much different idea about the afterlife.[11]

It is understandable that the vampire might acquire a certain narrative status due to his identification with a formerly living member of the community, which would tend to provide him with something of a personality. But since the vampire must be identified and destroyed ritually, we are obliged to conclude that his original adversary must have possessed the power to perform such rituals in a manner that would be efficacious. His adversary, whose contemporary manifestation is Van Helsing or Buffy, might once have been a hero able to cure magic-induced illness. Eventually, as such heroes were either incorporated into Christian hagiography or reduced to fools, they lost their proper place in the narrative. This left the evil, excommunicate vampire at the center of speculation concerning the eschatological consequences of unnatural death or burial. At some point, the vampire seer, which is the shaman's healing aspect,[12] had to reemerge, in the heroic role of restorer of order.

One of the more obvious advantages of dealing with the modern vampire is that many of one's assertions can be tested against extant documentation, since the Western European vampire is by definition a literary phenomenon. Alas, in the following pages, where we must consider as well the premodern vampire, the *terra* on which the investigation must trek from ancient Bulgaria all the way to twenty-first-century southern California is not always quite so *firma*. The reasons for this are both manifold and widely known, often having to do with the slow spread of vernacular literacy and, therefore, secular literature in the Slavic Balkans. More significant, we are attempting to deal in large part with what has been for many centuries an oral tradition. This tradition survived and spread in a region that was located at the crossroads between the East and the West, where, over the centuries, commerce brought into close contact ethnic groups ranging geographically from Iran and Central Asia to northern Europe.[13] Meanwhile, the names of both the vampire and the vampire slayer in this region are numerous and even quite dissimilar. As Jan Perkowski reminds us, it is imperative to make sure, when comparing putative vampires from different areas, that we are talking about the same fundamental phenomenon.[14] So despite the lack of unambiguous evidence to support various assertions along the way, I would like to encourage the reader to occasionally be willing to join me in leaps of argumentation that are founded more on surmise and likelihood than certainty and that are open to challenge by any new testimony that was not available to me previously.

Likewise, the reader who stays with this project will be subjected to ideas and information from a number of disciplines and areas of specialization, not all of which have been mastered equally. I suspect it would take more lives than I expect to live to control all of the necessary data in such diverse areas as early church history, Slavic and Indo-European comparative linguistics, Central European and Bulgarian prehistory and history, Old Bulgarian literature, Balkan ethnography, Slavic mythology and folklore, the geopolitics of the Habsburg Empire and the principles of the Enlightenment and its philosophical aftermath, nineteenth-century European literature and social movements, twentieth-century cinema, and twenty-first-century television—among, most likely, several others. Yet that is what the topic at hand demands: we shall cross at least a thousand years and several thousand miles in the attempt to determine how the earliest known vampire, a defrocked priest who condemned himself for having been so weak as to allow himself to be initiated into a pagan ritual, reemerges eight hundred years later in monstrous form under the suburban California streets patrolled by Buffy and her Scooby Gang (named after the group of teenaged ghost hunters in the long-running animated television series *Scooby-Doo*).

It might appear, on the basis of the foregoing discussion, that we are about to embark on a history of the belief system surrounding the vampire and the vampire seer. Although chronology is loosely used here as an organizing principle, the task of covering in a single volume the millennium or so that the Slavic word *vampir* has been in existence prohibits the sort of narrow (and logical) sequencing that would constitute a true history of the vampire. Instead, this study begins closer to the end of the process, by examining and elaborating on a claim made by Perkowski—and further amplified in my doctoral dissertation[15]—that the folkloric vampire serves primarily as a kind of scapegoat. In addition to outlining the scapegoat process (following René Girard), this study describes at the very outset the mimetic nature of the threat posed by the vampire at its most abstract level. I contend that we must both differentiate vampire tales from other tales of horror or the demonic and trace how this essential characteristic leads to the emergence of a seer to counteract the evil that is embodied in the vampire.

Chapters 3 and 4 do indeed go back to the Slavic period when the term *vampir* likely arose—namely, the period of Christianization of the Balkans by the Byzantine Orthodox Church. During this time, the proselytizers encountered a resistant indigenous agrarian population—a mix of Slavs, their Bulgar overlords, and ethnic Thracians—whose willingness to abandon their non-Christian beliefs and rituals was not by any means universal. Complicating the picture, as the last vestiges of paganism died out and went underground, the missionaries had to contend with another political force, a growing sect of dualist heretics known as Bogomils. The first vampires were connected, it appears, with a refusal to abandon beliefs and practices that were considered anathema by the Eastern Church. Sections of chapters 3 and 4 may be difficult going for the reader with no background in Slavic languages, but the view of the vampire as a target of the wrath of the church from the very beginning is established there. The patient reader will be rewarded later on, when I show how this historical aspect of the vampire is still present, albeit not explicit, in contemporary conceptions. Chapter 5 continues with the development of the Slavic vampire up into the early eighteenth century, when Balkan culture was finally directly encountered by travelers from the nonoccupied countries of Western Europe.

Before this study moves on to discuss how the vampire narrative became a topic of great interest in Western Europe in the mid-eighteenth century, chapters 6 and 7 introduce the various manifestations of the Balkan vampire slayer, known by such strange names as *vampirdžia, glog, dhampir,* or *sâbotnik,* among others. These chapters show how folkloric seers and slayers may have been connected with similar seers in Hungary and northeastern Italy who represented survivals of Central European shamanism. Here, I show that the earliest vampire hunters were most likely healers who were believed to possess the power to identify vampires because they were able to enter the world of the dead and to transfer the knowledge they gained there back into the world of the living. In terms of social power, identifying a vampire was akin to determining the cause of an epidemic.

The original interest shown in various episodes of vampire hysteria that began to occur in the second quarter of the eighteenth century was due in large part to the growth, in Western Europe, of the rationalist philosophy of the Enlightenment. Though there were several investigators that attempted to explain vampires from either a purely scientific (i.e., Protestant) or purely Catholic perspective, chapter 8 is devoted to one investigator in particular (for reasons that will become clear in chapter 9), the erudite Dutch physician, librarian, and medical historian Gerard van Swieten. Dr. Van Swieten was sent by the empress of Hungary, Maria Theresa, in 1755 to document supernatural events occurring in Silesia and to debunk in scientific (i.e., medical) terms the very possibility of a vampire. His treatise, here quoted in English translation for the first time, is a literary touchstone for the origin of the vampire hunter in non-Orthodox Europe.

Fig. 2. Hugh Jackman as the new Van Helsing. (© 2004 Universal Studios. Courtesy of Universal Studios Licensing LLLP.)

Jumping straight from the Enlightenment to the end of the Victorian period and the Industrial Revolution, chapters 9 and 10 are devoted to the two most famous representatives of the motif of vampire and vampire slayer, Bram Stoker's *Dracula* and *Buffy the Vampire Slayer*. Both of these extended narratives have received their share of attention from scholars of literature and contemporary culture. Not only would it be redundant to attempt here a discussion of the reasons for their appeal or their cultural significance, but it would also lie beyond the boundaries of my topic, which specifically concerns the link between the vampire and the vampire seer with regard to their shared connection to the world of the dead. Instead, I shall confine my readings of both *Buffy* and *Dracula* to those areas in the texts where this ancient underlying link is manifest. In both stories, the scapegoat aspect of the vampire is still present, but, I will argue, it has been obscured by the dynamics of the scapegoat process itself. One important aspect of this process is that those who would designate an innocent member of the community as a scapegoat must remain blind to the injustice they are carrying out.[16]

While folklore about vampires seems to be dying out in the Balkans as a result of the inexorable processes of westernization and urbanization, it is not clear whether the literary and cinematic vampire theme is likewise cooling down. More precisely, it is not yet clear, as of this writing, whether we are witnessing a return of the hero within the popular vampire narrative. Certainly, the success of *Buffy*, which makes of the slayer a complicated superhero in a fantastic suburban universe, would seem to indicate that we are becoming more interested in making the heroic primary and vampiric evil secondary. (In *Buffy*, for example, almost all of the vampires and demons that are killed are more or less nameless and unsympathetic.) But the low U.S. attendance figures for Universal's high-budget *Van Helsing* (Universal Pictures, 2004) suggest that stories of monolithic, violent vanquishers of one-dimensional monsters cannot sustain interest and in fact miss the central point of the dual nature of the vampire-slayer pair. These days, the evil that walks among us unrecognized is more often played by the sociopathic serial or mass killer, while the hero who is intuitively connected to that disturbed orientation takes the form of a forensic psychologist, or profiler. It may be that solving the problem of real evil with real (human) agents in today's world has surpassed any need to dally with the purely imaginary.

2

Back from the Dead

Monsters and Violence

How then are we to begin our strife to destroy him? How shall
we find his where, and having found it, how can we destroy?
> —*Dr. Van Helsing, Mina Harker's journal,*
> *30 September, Bram Stoker,* Dracula

Oh, my friend John, but it was butcher work.
> —*Dr. Van Helsing's memorandum,*
> *5 November, afternoon, Bram Stoker,* Dracula

Over a hundred years ago, a Dublin civil servant turned London theatrical manager concocted the story of Count Dracula, and since then, the vampire tale has been retold, with variations, in hundreds of novels, short stories, plays, and, most significantly, films. For the background of his narrative, Bram Stoker drew on folklore and history compiled from several sources: an English-language literary tradition about vampires dating back to around 1800;[1] stories about Central Europe possibly passed on by the Hungarian agent provocateur and adventurer Arminius Vambery;[2] and Stoker's own researches into travelogues, Transylvanian and Carpathian ethnography,[3] and Romanian history, requiring many hours at the British Museum. The eventual and long-lasting success of this engaging novel, which forms the basis for a myth that has seemingly found a deeper resonance in America than in England or Europe, is of course independent of how accurately it might represent Carpathian or Balkan folklore.

In recent years, the history and data of vampire folklore have been studied in the West from a more scholarly and less chauvinistic perspective, and it is now commonly accepted that much of the detail about vampires that is found in *Dracula* is not to be found in primary Transylvanian or Balkan demonic folklore.[4] The imaginative Stoker was the first to yoke the epithet of a fifteenth-century Wallachian warlord to received notions about vampires. Now, thanks to several popularizing monographs about the origin of the vampire and the history of the family of Vlad III, "the Impaler," also known as Dracula, most casual vampirophiles today still mistakenly believe vampire lore to be primarily a Romanian phenomenon, despite the 1989 publication of Jan Perkowski's *The Darkling*, which demonstrates that the vampire is of Slavic and Bulgarian—or, more generally, Balkan—provenance.

Whether they concur with the East European ethnographic data or not, the many literary readings of the *Dracula* tale and the wide variety of popular Euro-American beliefs about vampires are now part of a still-emerging myth. As with any mythic story that grips a large community over a significant period of time, changes in the emphasis or details of the story and in the characters that populate it may reflect distinct cultural shifts. It is even possible that the longevity of the vampire motif is due partly to Stoker's distortion of the anthropological facts to please a contemporary urban audience. Certainly none of the often illiterate or semiliterate farmworkers of the East European agrarian communities where vampire stories were, until fairly recently,[5] part of the fabric of daily existence could ever have admixed Romantic notions about the evil of an exhausted aristocracy into their more banal tales about the return from the dead of suicides, murder or drowning victims, alcoholics, or simply deceased men who had the misfortune of having a cat jump over their corpse during an all-night preburial vigil.

Furthermore, the overriding theme of *Dracula* is bound up with an unmistakable Anglocentric Orientalism that would never have made sense to a Bulgarian farmer living under the "Ottoman yoke" (as the Bulgarians refer to the long occupation of their land that officially ended in 1878). The evil Count Dracula as a monstrous invader—a subversive, destructive threat to British imperial order—is a motif that seemed to find peculiar resonance between the twentieth century's world wars.[6] This view of a socially or politically powerful vampire (never found in Balkan lore) was later adapted to the realities of the cold war, and Dracula's Eastern European origins took on a new significance as the political center of the West moved west. As Nina Auerbach succinctly puts it, "Vampires go where power is."[7] This ability of the vampire motif to take on new symbolic shapes according to shifts in political circumstances attests to its vitality as a contemporary myth. It also suggests that the story itself encodes some central belief or perception that is, if not universal, at least more or less constant from the vampire's very beginnings.

Despite the superficial changes in the popularized vampire story (whose form in the Americas and Western Europe has tended to remain connected to the basic *Dracula* narrative), an essential mythical core within the original conception of the vampire remains discernible through all its variations. If the popular image of the vampire can metamorphose from a prematurely deceased Balkan villager, to a vicious nobleman from Transylvania, to a sympathetic narrator in old New Orleans, to a parasite of adipose tissue[8] or the half-breed paramilitary hero of a futuristic postapocalypse, there is beneath all these shifts of the popular vampire's shape an idea that is not merely politically metaphoric and tendentious (or even specifically cultural) and a meaning that goes beyond whatever one might be inclined to attach to the idea of returning from the dead.

MONSTERS AND THE VIOLENCE OF RETURN

Physical return from the dead is not only aberrant—even in modern societies where the definition of medical death has lately become somewhat unstable and where the possibility of resuscitation from medical stasis is no longer entirely laughable—but also violent (at least as violent as birth) and dangerous. In the Christian tradition, for example, Christ's imperative "Noli me tangere" (John 20:17) upon his return from hell can be read as a warning to the awed living that he was still charged with a dangerous shamanic power acquired from having been in the world of the dead. In Greco-Thracian mythology, the inability of Orpheus (also a shaman) to bring Eurydice back into the world of the living is more than a failure of will; it is an acknowledgment that images encountered in the underworld cannot withstand the violence of return without distortion.[9] The reversal of the usually irreversible process of bodily decay, meanwhile, constitutes such a violent upending of natural laws that the idea of an animated corpse is frequently associated with monstrosity.[10] This monstrosity may be physical repulsiveness, or it may be a kind of social monstrosity, often associated with aggressive or vengeful violence. The literary folktale *The Monkey's Paw* (W. W. Jacobs 1902) and, more recently, Stephen King's book *Pet Sematary* (1983) warn us of the danger of even wishing that the dead would return. The will to bring a being back from the dead is itself a violent or aggressive urge. In both folklore and the literary/cinematic tradition, the desire that the dead return usually originates among the living and is almost always accompanied by nefarious, sorcerous intent.

In American consciousness, the most commonly held image of the undead vampire does not come directly from Stoker's novel or even from Murnau's silent, illicit adaptation, *Nosferatu*, but, rather, from Tod Browning's 1931 film version of *Dracula*. On the basis of the success of that film, starring Bela Lugosi as Count Dracula and Edward van Sloan as his eminent adversary, Abraham van Helsing, Universal Pictures in Hollywood went on to make a series of films that became the progenitors of the American horror genre. Also in 1931, another eerie British novel with monstrous violence as its theme was converted to film: *Frankenstein* starred Boris Karloff. The following year saw the release of *The Mummy*, again starring Boris Karloff in the role of the monster. Along with the somewhat later *The Wolf Man* (1941), these horror movies from Universal had an interesting feature in common. In each case, there is some contact with Central or Eastern Europe or (as in the case of *The Mummy*) the exotic Near East. Dracula, of course, comes from Transylvania (the region around the southern Danube was generally considered by citizens of more northern European countries to be culturally closer to "the Orient" than to the West,

Fig. 3. Van Helsing (Edward van Sloan) finds Count Dracula's "where." (© 1931 Universal Pictures Corporation. Courtesy of Universal Studios Licensing LLLP.)

presumably because of the five-century occupation of the Balkan region and parts of the Carpathians by the Ottoman Empire).[11] The Mummy, meanwhile, is a cursed and resuscitated Egyptian priest. The Wolf Man is infected through (violent) contact with Gypsies (so-called because of the incorrect presumption of their Egyptian origin). Although the original film version of *Frankenstein* is set in Germany, much of the action takes place among villagers who look and behave exactly like the Hollywood villagers in both *Dracula* and *The Wolf Man;* that is, they are made out to be both foreign and superstitious. They are also, by the way, agrarian.

The archetypal monster in each case is also associated with legend, superstition, and folk belief in the possibility of return from the dead. The Wolf Man has been attacked by a wolf and would have died from his wounds had the attacker not been in reality a deathless Gypsy sorcerer transmitting his curse through violent contact with the victim's blood. In *Frankenstein,* although the doctor-baron represents the most advanced type of post-Enlightenment medical materialist, it is from the body parts of deceased local villagers, including, unfortunately, a violent one, that a living being, the monster, is created. The Mummy is reactivated by a fanatical archeologist who is conversant with hieroglyphics and ancient magical spells and who is not content to permit a funerary seal to remain unbroken. Finally, Dracula, at least as Browning's film frames the story, is forced to leave his mountain homeland, where the local villagers despise and fear him, believing him to be among the undead and to be a murderer as well.

In subsequent decades, these four films collectively spawned hundreds of sequels, remakes, and imitations around the globe. In the 1950s, Hammer Studios in England produced Technicolor updates of the Universal archetypes. As a group, the original Universal Pictures monsters are deeply enough ingrained in American consciousness that a series of monster-commemorating postage stamps was released by the U.S. Postal Service in 1997. Surrounding each of these monster types is a fear of reanimation of the dead as a threat and embodiment of violence. Not only do the reanimated dead have supernatural powers; being dead, they are beyond any natural threat of retribution or punishment, whether by legal or extralegal means.

The linking of this fear to notions of foreignness is revealing both historically and culturally, insofar as the deeper conflict in each of the four cases seems to be between a vision of civil order and the disruption of that order by an un-Christian or anti-Christian belief system. For example, the symbolically isolated and blind old Jew in *Bride of Frankenstein* (1935) encounters the monster and tries, unsuccessfully, to quell his violent nature and bring him into the human community with music and the camaraderie of talk and smoking, with unhappy consequence. As regards their religious status, the Mummy is polytheistic and pagan, the Frankenstein monster is a creature of scientific hubris, the Wolf Man is a product of Gypsy animism, and Dracula abhors the cross. In none of these genres does the person or spirit who has the misfortune to live outside of the time of the normal human life span choose his own aberrant condition. He is portrayed in each case as a sympathetic, or perhaps pathetic, victim as well as a monster. He has either been infected (the Wolf Man, Dracula) by some preexisting evil being or sorcerer, animated by arrogance and hubris (Frankenstein), or brought back by a magical act (the Mummy). Sorcery and megalomaniacal science are deemed morally equivalent.[12] The will to bring the dead to life is presumed evil in essence, not only because it violently disrupts the natural order, but because the combination of evil intention and the violence of reconstituting the dead (a huge bolt of lightning is required to animate Frankenstein's monster; breaking the crypt seal frees the mummy) can lead to nothing but a cycle of violence. The monster is, from the very point of his reincarnation, outside any social order in which he could survive without violence, and therefore he must be put to death by (ritual) violence. He is outside of reason, and rational methods of dispatching him are ineffective. Furthermore, the inevitable violent destruction of the monster compensates for the violence done to the social order through the creation or instantiation of the monster.

THE REAL FEAR

Another significant thing these famous monsters have in common is that they are all essentially human, albeit with superhuman powers. The violence they inflict occurs at the individual, rather than the group, level, and the retribution envisioned by the community under attack is directed at the individual (usually the monster rather than the monster's creator or summoner). These reanimated people are mimetic replicas, insofar as they are human in shape but animated by evil or some force different from that which inhabits the truly human.[13] Possessing both human form and language, but not subject to the same primary existential law as mortal beings (i.e., death), these creatures can be neither redeemed nor reasoned with, since they are possessed of no moral purpose beyond vengeful rage.[14] The idea of a walking dead simulacrum as a serious threat to the social order is of course much older than any of the monsters that caught the public imagination in American cinema in the early 1930s or even than their literary antecedents from a century before. Ideas about animated corpses are widespread and ancient. In the European tradition, the Greek folkloric revenant (commonly referred to by a borrowed Slavic name, *broukolakos*), an animated corpse, is in all likelihood the model on which the oldest of these unholy creatures, the vampire, is based.[15] Though, in Greek folklore, revenants were not thought to be as hostile toward human society as the vampire eventually came to be, the classical revenant poses a threat nonetheless: the artificial humanness, the capacity for mimesis, is intrinsically powerful, in part because it blurs the boundaries around the category "human" and therefore around morality.[16]

Notions of mimetic copies as powerful and dangerous to social organization are evident in much folklore. The magic of the mimetic is found in so-called voodoo dolls; it is the central problem of Johann Wolfgang von Goethe's 1797 ballad "The Sorcerer's Apprentice" (where the magically animated copy goes out of control because it is not rational), and of such cold war fantasies as *Invasion of the Body Snatchers* (1956) (where the doppelgänger[17] invaders are indistinguishable from one's family and neighbors, except for their inability to exhibit compassion or emotion); and it seems to lie behind the contemporary technophobia surrounding popular attitudes toward genetic cloning.[18] Discussing the potential power of mimesis and its threatening aspect, Michael Taussig points to such repressive social responses to it as fascism (and we might have no trouble linking it to other forms of totalitarian repression, including religious fanaticism), which he says is an accentuated form of modern civilization which is itself to be read as the history of repression of mimesis—the ban on graven images, gypsies, actors; the love-hate relationship with the body; the cessation of Carnival; and finally the kind of teaching which does not allow children to be children.

Taussig continues:

> But above all, fascism is more than outright repression of the mimetic; it is a return of the repressed, based on the "organized control of mimesis." Thus fascism, through mimesis of mimesis, "seeks to make the rebellion of suppressed nature against domination directly useful to domination."[19]

This urge to repress mimetic expressions, which are central to that form of the imagination known as magic, is at the very heart of the vampire tale. The vampire, I will show, is always an anathematized being, a heretic, who must be destroyed within the context of a moral system (Christianity) that cannot tolerate a dualistic worldview. Dualism posits that the authors of good and evil, or light and darkness, are essentially independent and mythologically opposed. As a philosophy or theology, it manifests the problem of the mimetic in such supposedly anti-Christian claims as that the material world itself is a copy;[20] that the author of evil is a mirror image of, but at least equal in authorial power to, the author of good; or even that the physical Jesus himself is unreal or without worth.[21]

The economic problem posed by the existence of a simulacrum (e.g., the vampire) who resembles too closely the living without actually being alive is that he, as all doubles do, destabilizes the value of the living, which is based on discrimination and differentiation. For example, in some Balkan folklore (as well as in *Dracula*), the vampire is capable of seducing or absconding with the local women. Here, a social resource (mothers) is surreptitiously siphoned off by a parasite, a bloodsucker who is a nonproducing rival of the local men. The vampire thus interrupts the process of sexual selection. This is possible, we must assume, because the women are unable to distinguish between the vampire suitor and the other men in the village. What might this say, then, about those other men?

The invisibility of the vampire—or, in some tales, the lack of any simple way to distinguish a vampire from other people—has an interesting consequence: ordinary systems of justice and authority provide no method for preventing or reversing the harm done by the vampire. Not only is the vampire effectively unpunishable; he is also impossible to identify. Because he is in fact a mimetic double, he has no valid identity, no evident social position. (In this sense, because he—or, more rarely, she—is dead, he has a value different from the witch, who is always alive and has a clear social status.) This lack, of course, provokes serious anxiety in a society that wishes to assign blame but does not know where to assign it. Where there is mischief or inexplicable disease, the double, the heretic, the vampire, might be to blame, functioning as a scapegoat for free-floating disturbances. But the vampire, who either walks about looking like everyone else or does his business at night (*negotium perambulans in tenebris*), cannot properly serve as a scapegoat until he has been identified.

HUNTERS AND SLAYERS

The presence of a humanlike threat that is either not visible or generally not detectable naturally brings about the need to locate an individual who possesses the unique power to identify and hence accuse the duplicitous aggressor. It might be claimed that the entire Inquisition was dedicated to the problem of identifying witches and sorcerers and heretics, who had in common the fact that, aside from their erroneous beliefs and unholy actions, they looked more or less like ordinary people.[22] Self-accusation (i.e., confession, usually obtained by torture or threat) was an effective method of certifying a witch, but sometimes lack of confession necessitated an accusation backed up by someone possessing more firsthand knowledge or evidence. Those who could identify witches were presumed to have sorcerous or at least special powers themselves, under the principle that it takes one to know one. Thus, the role of witch accuser was fraught with real danger: while it could indemnify the accuser as being on the right side of the moral law, it only insulated the accuser by a hair's breadth from the reciprocal accusation of witchcraft.

Witch hunts of just about any sort rely on designated individuals willing to confirm the identity of those who are to be persecuted, and these people tend to be marked either by some physical marker or by a circumstantial one (e.g., being born on a particular day). In the fifteenth century, for example, the *benandanti* were said to have been born with a caul.[23] The *benandanti* claimed to be able to identify witches and to leave their physical bodies during sleep and fight witches on their own turf, at the witches' nocturnal sabbats. Over several decades, however, these farmers became too closely associated with witchcraft; their testimony against witches became tantamount to an admission of participation in orgiastic sabbats, and they no longer served as effective witch-hunters.

As with European witchcraft, in vampire lore there is a similar need to identify vampires, but the class of individuals who are thought to possess such powers is not so well defined as the group of *benandanti.* People born on a Saturday or thought to be the offspring of a vampire and a live mother are among those presumed to have the power to detect vampires. In *Dracula,* Van Helsing is marked by being a foreigner (like Dracula himself) and a credentialed vampire specialist, who is called on by the Londoners to link various misfortunes to the immigrant count.

I have demonstrated elsewhere,[24] as has Perkowski,[25] that the vampire functions in the Balkan folkloric context as a type of scapegoat. The mechanism by which this type of scapegoat is instantiated is complex[26] and involves the designation not only of an aggressor but also of a counteracting force, someone who is saddled by the will of the community with the obligation to detect and perhaps even destroy the otherwise unknowable intruder. The counteractor—for example, the vampire hunter or slayer—is usually linked in some symbolic way with the scapegoat, who will become the slayer's victim. The group's designation of the slayer, or seer, or hunter[27] serves to absolve the group from any accusation of injustice (since the ritual actions taken against the vampire will ultimately have to take place outside the law). This power dynamic, in which aggressive violence is projected by the community onto a mimetic replica who is in turn destroyed by retributive collective violence, is the abstract basis of the vampire myth.

The meanings of the vampire story have more often than not been derived from an examination of the vampire alone, his behavior and features. But the common characterization of the vampire as simply an evil monster who preys on innocent victims[28] and is therefore worthy of destruction obscures the subtler process by which an individual becomes known as a vampire and thus a focal point of group retribution. In order to see around this blind spot, it is useful to examine the myth through the lens of the vampire's opponents: the set of living individuals who, thanks to some special mark that links them to vampires (or other demonic beings), are thought capable of unmasking the false human (or antihuman) and of stating aloud what everyone knows but no one else wants to say—namely, who the vampire really is. In so doing, they implicitly acknowledge their own position outside society.

BLIND SPOTS

As I claimed earlier, in the twentieth century and now in the twenty-first, the basic popular conception of the vampire turns out to be based not so much on Stoker's *Dracula* as on the subsequent film versions of the story. The differences between the novel and its cinematic derivatives, which will be examined in more detail later on, underscore what they have in common. The structure of Stoker's novel is epistolary: everything the reader comes to believe about Count Dracula is based on a composite sketch of letters, diary entries, newspaper clippings, ships' logs, and the like. There is no omniscient point of view in the narrative, and, in fact, the pathway to the collective conclusion that the transplanted Centralian nobleman is a supernatural vampire begins inside an evidentiary frame supplied by the foreigner Van Helsing. The novel is so compellingly organized around coincidence, misperception, and ambiguity that Stoker is able to take the reader along the same pseudological path of reasoning that eventually persuades the main characters of Dracula's guilt. The ambiguity of Count Dracula's role in London society is conveniently obscured by the inexorable mounting of evidence that points ever more convincingly at Dracula as an unhuman serial criminal.

Stoker, well versed in the Gothic tradition, is quite careful to leave the door open to the possibility that Dracula is not necessarily what Van Helsing or Jonathan Harker says he is, and a close reading of the novel opens that door even wider. When, however, the movies came along twenty-five years later, they of necessity narrowed the novel's structure to a much-simplified narrative line focused on Count Dracula as an unambiguously supernatural threat from the uncivilized and violent East.[29] Suddenly missing from the story is any question about the validity or cohesiveness of the evidence implicating Dracula as a shape-shifting vampire. In Tod Browning's film, the tale is flattened into a black-and-white struggle of good against evil: the mesmeric, undead Dracula is quite definitely monstrous and supernatural, and any sympathy the viewer might have for him as a character can only be based on the dramatic pathos of his self-proclaimed inability to die.[30]

The moral simplification that occurs in the shift from the printed to the cinematic version is, I would argue, of the same nature as the simplification that allows a mob, without compunction and where there is no evidentiary proceeding (as there is not in Dracula's case), to perceive a targeted scapegoat as guilty.[31] In other words, in one sense, the novel is as much about the nature of the blind spot of the jealous, but polite, Englishmen (and one American) who fail to understand or even examine their own irrational reasons for fearing Dracula as it is about Dracula as an evil monster. A major reason the novel is still in print over a hundred years after its publication is not the quality of the writing, which is only slightly better than mediocre, but, rather, because this ambiguity of evidence is fascinating and tantalizing in its subtlety. In part thanks to the technical difficulty of executing an epistolary structure on film, but perhaps more because the 1931 version of *Dracula* encoded a growing xenophobia surrounding the political dangers brewing in Central Europe after World War I, the cinematic versions unwittingly reproduce the blind spot that occurs with a monocular reading of the novel.

As a result, it has become virtually impossible for anyone steeped in the Western vampire film tradition to see through to the ambiguity of Count Dracula as both monster and victim—viewers are always persecutors. Even later films that purport to restore the lost integrity of the novel—Francis Ford Coppola's 1992 version, for example, is titled *Bram Stoker's Dracula,* thus claiming to be a closer retelling of the literary version[32]—fail to capture the circumstantial ambiguity of Stoker's novel. This failure is a compounding form of complicity in a misreading of *Dracula.* The perennial reproductions of that misreading successfully obscure the more persistent meaning of the original vampire tale, which involves community violence that is not always just in its execution.

To see the vampire as unambiguously evil and, consequently, to side with the hero(es) is what we are supposed to do. The novels of Anne Rice, although they intentionally amplify the sexual threat of the vampire, thus picking up on a much earlier, Romantic variant of the vampire theme after it moved from Balkan into Western culture, do not ultimately succeed in transforming the demon into a hero.[33] For example, in her first book, *Interview with the Vampire,* the idea of the vampire hunter is not discarded but is rather curiously inverted: it is the vampire protagonist who must tell the vampire hunter (in this case, the reporter-narrator-interlocutor) of his actions and therefore his evil identity. From this self-conscious change in focus, we might infer that, as far as Rice's vampires are concerned, the postcolonial condition is one in which condemnation of the marginalized or abject Other is not an automatic moral good and has thus resulted in the loss of the magical power to identify vampires. Interesting as this proposition might be, Rice nonetheless also implicitly buys into the monocular reading of the vampire myth insofar as she merely inverts the good-evil value scale, somewhat mechanically, by glorifying or romanticizing the vampire's corruption and does not recognize the contingency of the vampire's so-called evil on those who would be afraid of him.

Were it not for Anne Rice, however, we probably never could have gotten to the camp postmodern approach to vampires seen in the television series *Buffy the Vampire Slayer. Buffy* restores some sense of the original power relationship between vampires and vampire slayers by establishing a fairly simple superhero who acts outside the rule of law.[34] The general absence of legitimate or effective urban authority figures, such as policemen, in the average *Buffy* narrative of course appeals to an adolescent urge for independence from parental authority, but the structure also mimics the centuries-old folkloric idea that only someone who possesses special powers can see or destroy a vampire. It should be evident to anyone who has seen a few episodes of the program that the "demons" in *Buffy* intentionally extend the boundaries of the traditional vampire; in fact, the images and plots would seem to have much closer links with Western witchcraft and Inquisitional demonology than with Balkan folklore. Still, the notion of a vampire slayer has a very ancient precedent, which existed in a time and place where it was socially more useful to produce a vampire as a guilty criminal than to incriminate one's friends and neighbors. Buffy, in the original movie *Buffy the Vampire Slayer* (1992) and to some extent also in the television show, is, like the vampire slayers of eighteenth-century Bulgaria or Serbia,[35] marked. She is chosen; she does not particularly want to be a vampire slayer, and this superimposed identity understandably interferes with the business of trying to be a popular high school cheerleader.[36] Whether the show's creators were aware of it or not, the social position of Buffy in her solo late-adolescent struggle against Sunnydale's supernatural vampires and demons is quite homologous to that of the Balkan *sâbotnik* or *vampirdžia,* who were chosen or marked and obliged by the local villagers to unambiguously identify an otherwise invisible evil being in their midst.

Perhaps one reason for the success of *Buffy the Vampire Slayer* is that it allows us to perceive something about the vampire dynamic that has been obscured for almost a century now—at least since the stage and then the cinematic versions of the Dracula story intentionally blinded us to an ambiguity about the vampire that Stoker sensed and that is certainly evident in the folkloric tradition. *Buffy's* weekly presentation of a society where adolescent outsiders (e.g., creeps, losers, and the like) are perceived, perhaps out of collective guilt, as violent and vengeful "demons" is not all that distant from a Bulgarian village.[37] In the village setting, a suicide or a heretic who has been buried in unhallowed ground outside the town's boundaries is imaginally reanimated and likewise envisioned as full of desire to harm his former tormentors. In order to quell the dead intruder without reinforcing the deceased's alienation, a special person is identified to take care of the social problem. That person becomes a vampire hunter or slayer, a surrogate and mediator who battles violence with counteractive violence.

The path from the coinage of the Slavic term *vampir* to today's pop-cultural vampires and their counterparts, the slayers, is a millennial journey. Certainly, the shape of the mythological vampire, who, like Dracula himself, has moved his center from Eastern Europe to the West, has undergone significant change. Nevertheless, over the course of centuries, the category "vampire" has maintained a cohesive semantic center that allows us to begin to seek its meaning in the homologies between the earliest meaning of the term and what we see in contemporary readings of the vampire in books, movies, Internet and video games, and television. Whatever other themes they may address, tales about vampires are on some level always about the relationship between violence, social cohesion, and justice. In order to see more clearly what lies at the base of the contemporary vampire, we will do well to see what the term *vampire* has meant over time. Also, in order to understand the vampire, we should look at him as we would a witch, who plays a role in Western lore and, unfortunately, history that is quite similar to that of the vampire to the east and south of the Danube. The sex difference (witches in the West are more often women, while vampires in the East are more often men), though significant in the socioeconomic equation, is probably not as significant as the living/dead gender split[38] for understanding the relationship between witches and vampires, witch hunts and vampire slayings. In the latter case—and we have historical records of such actions taken by villagers in the middle of the night—what is done locally to restore social order is tantamount to killing the dead.

3

CONVERSION IN THE BALKANS

A *Thousand Years of the Vampire*

I f it is hard to imagine the fictional Dracula as anything but an evil, sharp-toothed, shape-shifting, undead monster, it is even more difficult to consider that the term *vampire* did not always refer to a supernatural or folkloric being. But if the word did not originally denote the sort of being that comes to mind whenever we hear it now, can it be legitimately claimed that there is some essence or constant characteristic of the vampire that has persisted from the word's inception to the present day? While the origin of the term—most likely in the eastern Balkans (present-day Bulgaria) somewhere between eight hundred and a thousand years ago—cannot be pinpointed with certainty, there is evidence that the Slavic word *vampir,* which first appears in written form around the eleventh century,[1] was a shorthand (and probably pejorative) label for an individual who either belonged to a specific group or practiced a particular belief or ritual. Contrary to most proposed etymologies, which unfortunately reconstruct for the term an original meaning that is based more or less on its contemporary range of meanings, the original vampire was nothing or no one supernatural. Solid testimony may be lacking as to what that group or its beliefs and practices might have been, but it is possible to make some inferences. Armed with a sense of what *vampire* designated when it first came into circulation, it will be somewhat easier to determine whether there is some underlying semantic core that will help us understand the nuances of the word as it is used today.

EARLY CHRISTIANITY IN THE BALKANS
Pagans, Heretics, and the First Vampires

In the centuries from late antiquity to the medieval period, the Balkan region was the locus of a good deal of political and religious turmoil, situated as it was between Rome and Byzantium, which gradually became opposed centers of different interpretations of Christianity. Furthermore, the land was the home not only of pre-Christian Slavs, agrarian tribes who had migrated there in the sixth century, but also of a dwindling number of displaced indigenous Thracians, who tried to maintain their culture and rituals as they were pushed from the cities to the mountain villages in the Rhodope and Balkan mountain ranges. During this period, which witnessed a significant number of struggles between the competing forms of Christianity, other religious groups were also attempting to survive or establish themselves all the way from the Near East to Western Europe. As a result, even today the main religion of Bulgaria, Serbia, and Macedonia, Orthodox Christianity, is in fact highly syncretic in form.

Judaism, Christianity, late forms of Gnosticism, and the passing polytheistic religions of the Roman Empire (collectively referred to as paganism) were all involved in the struggle between the two centers of political power. Byzantium, furthermore, had to deal with increasing military threats after the seventh century from Iran and the Arab world, which were tied to the emergence of another universalist religion, Islam. Thus, for Christianity, the difficulties of establishing a stable *ecclesia* did not abate in the early Middle Ages, despite Christianity's broad official acceptance from Russia to Spain and France. On the contrary, dissident cults and sects began to take on even greater political significance, and strife between religious groups was rampant. Often, this strife took the form merely of verbal polemic, but it occa-

sionally led to physical destruction and even legislation for capital punishment. For example, in the seventh century, under Emperor Justinian II, Manichaeans[2] were ordered to be burned at the stake, although
this sentence was not frequently carried out. Paganism—primarily in
the form of Mithraism, a Romanized version of a Persian religion that
was widespread within the Roman military—had its last gasp as a state-
supported religion under Emperor Julian the Apostate (361–63), but
that does not mean that religious rites and beliefs of a pagan nature
ceased to exist. The Balkans played a significant role in keeping both
paganism and dualism alive.

Christianity had actually come to the Balkans quite early. The
Thracians had accepted Christianity during Saint Paul's first voyage to
Macedonia and Illyria, around AD 51–52. This was about the same
time that the Thracians lost their independence to Rome, one consequence of which was that many Thracian people were subjected to slavery. The Thracian acceptance of Christianity was far from universal,
however, and once-Thracian lands were still home to tribes that maintained their allegiance to Orphism[3] or practiced other forms of worship. The Romans were less interested in devastating the remnants of
Thracian religion than in using the populace to increase the empire's
manpower. However, beginning in the mid-fourth century, a series of
invasions into the Balkans by marauding tribes—Goths, Gepids, Sar-
matians, and Huns—resulted in a shift of the population of the countryside. Thracian peasants were forced to move either into the mountains and other areas where they would be protected from the invaders
or into the urban centers, bringing with them, in either case, their
practices and beliefs.[4]

For a while, then, many of the autochthonous pagans overtly resisted Christianization, insisting on their right to perform their rituals
and conduct their festivals. The forces of Christianity, meanwhile, attempted to convert the heathens by using both polemic and military
might. Within a century, the portion of Thrace south of the Balkan
mountain range was almost entirely Christianized. By the end of the
sixth century, the Balkan territory was primarily Christian, to the extent that there was any cohesiveness or religious identity at all. But another wave of barbarians, this time the Slavs, once more disrupted the
slow process of conversion of the local inhabitants. An early attempt

was made under Emperor Heraclius (610–41) to convert the Balkan Slavs, whose migrations had reached as far south as the Peloponnesus, but this more or less failed. Although the Slavs were eventually pushed back out of the Greek mainland, from their settling until the arrival of the Bulgars, the Balkans were firmly in Slavic hands.

It is tempting, when looking at the picture of the early medieval Balkans, to perceive a higher resolution than is actually possible. While we now may comfortably trace the histories and accidents that led to the philosophical distinctions between various pagan religions, say, or between various shades of dualism that had spread from the Near East, and while we may even trace the underground connections between Gnosticism and Judaism,[5] the fact of the matter is that much of the tension between Christians and non-Christians arose on the basis of political defensiveness and gross misunderstanding. Virtually all dualists, of any stripe, were originally referred to as Manichaean.[6] Pagans and heretics were sometimes distinguished from each other according to their supposed ritual practices, but the distinction was just as often ignored. The triad of Jews, heretics, and pagans effectively represented, for practicing Christians, the political Other, the totality of the non-Christian world in the days before Muhammad's ideas had spread westward. In short, ethnic, philosophical, and demographic distinctions that can be reconstructed from the modern vantage point were often neither visible nor desirable for those embroiled in ideological conflict.

The conflict between Christians and non-Christians in the Balkans did not really become overt until after the conversion of the Bulgarian khan Boris in 864. Christianity had been slowly spreading among the Slavs in the early ninth century and probably before, and Boris's predecessor, Omurtag (r. 815–31), was clearly hostile to the "new" religion invading from Byzantium. The ruling classes of Bulgaria (Boyars), comprising mostly Bulgars but increasingly Slavs, objected to the threat posed by Christianity to the old order of privileges. The dualist Paulicians had been transplanted to Thrace from Armenia by Emperor Constantine V Copronymus in 745 and 757, but as heretics whose philosophy was somewhat sparse, they were hardly inclined to object to pagan practices. The conversion of Boris effectively meant the Christianization of the entire Bulgarian state, which was tied to and meant to reinforce a less inimical relationship between the Bulgarian and Byzantine empires. It also meant that the form of Christianity that would become predominant in the Balkans was the Eastern Orthodox sort, as opposed to Western (Roman) Catholicism, which had effectively lost the battle for hegemony in the eastern regions. As a consequence, most of the documents against paganism and heresy in the Balkans are written from the point of view of Orthodox apologists and were produced either in Greek or—after the late ninth-century mission of Constantine-Cyril and Methodius to convert the Slavs and provide a writing system for the Slavic language—in Slavic.

DEMONS AND PAGANS

Although medieval Christianity ultimately became more concerned with rooting out heresy, there was a double-pronged threat in the Balkans, where pagan practices had been able to persist underground thanks to the turmoil of successive invasions. Greco-Roman mystery religions, the remnants of Thracian religions, and some brand of shamanistic religion brought by the Bulgars coexisted in varying degrees of syncretism over the very centuries that Orthodox Christianity was extending its push into the Balkans. We unfortunately know as little about proto-Bulgar religion as we do of the Bulgar language, of which only a few solid pieces of evidence remain. Yuri Stoyanov claims that the Bulgars had a "well developed astronomo-astrological system, based on the Central Asian 'animal cycle' calendar, along with an array of shamanistic beliefs and practices."7 However, given the rapidity with which the Bulgars assimilated themselves to Slavic culture in the Balkans, it would appear that their desire to cling to their religious practices was not all that strong. Among the Bulgars, Christianization encountered opposition of a more political than religious nature.

Thus, Christianity had to contend with the existence of a variety of gods (and cults) before it could attend to the subtler problems of dualism qua heresy. From its earliest efforts to go forth and multiply, Christianity had used a strategy of accommodating itself to local folk practices to the degree possible, so long as these beliefs, styles, and ritual practices did not absolutely undercut fundamental Christian precepts. It is quite arguable that such adaptability is partially responsible for the success of Christianity in supplanting paganism. Wherever possible, rather than overtly attack such practices as sacrifices or funeral services or festivals, Christianizers generally tried to reinterpret folk rites and beliefs so they would be more in accord with Orthodox belief. Since most of the pre-Christian world held polytheistic beliefs of one sort or another, a primary strategy of Christianity, which had defined itself as a "trinitarian monotheism,"[8] was always to find an acceptable place for the divinities of polytheistic religions.

That picture might actually be somewhat misleading, since it implies an organized hierarchy of supernatural beings worthy of some sort of worship. In the Balkans, polytheism was more an artifact of the merger of a multiplicity of cults, often reflecting different ethnic or tribal beliefs—Slavic being prominent among them. Since Christianity could acknowledge only one God (irrespective of its own internal arguments about the nature of the Trinity), all other gods were relegated to the status of demons or, in some cases, admitted into the company of saints.[9] As a by-product of this ontological reassignment, residual practice of worship devoted to pagan divinities became, by definition, anathema—effectively, demon worship—and had to be eliminated. The Christian encounter with pagan divinities after the fourth century resulted in an almost systematic approach to incorporation of the offending religious beliefs. Nevertheless, there were some aspects of paganism that needed to be destroyed altogether.

THE ATTACK ON SACRIFICE

Blood sacrifice, a ritual practice that was at the center of many pre-Christian religions, epitomized paganism for the early and medieval Christians. Sacrifice was always addressed to a divinity or demon or perhaps to a king who was identified with such, but in any case, the victims of sacrifice were not intended for the one God. According to Christian belief, since God was the creator of all things, he was not in need of sacrifices performed by men. Offerings, to be sure, could be made by men on behalf of other men, living or departed,[10] but Christians objected vehemently to the act of destroying life and handing it over to a demon.

Furthermore, in Christianity, sacrifice had taken on a transferred meaning, pertaining no longer to the taking of life (or in Bataille's sense, expenditure of excess)[11] for the sake of procuring some benefit (the so-called *do ut des* motivation) but, rather, to the surrender of one's personal desires to the will of God.[12] In this sense of sublimation, sacrifice was perceived as creative rather than destructive (from the pagan point of view, too, sacrifice was creative, ensuring the continuance of the created world and its order). Georges Florovsky points out that "the decisive line drawn by Christian ontology was not that between natural and supernatural, nor ultimately that between good and evil, but that between the Creator and his creatures, be they good or evil."[13] This firm boundary is homologous to the one separating the pagan and Christian concepts of sacrifice.

The Christian encounter with sacrifice is recorded early in the era of the Bulgarian Empire. Perhaps the earliest mention of the hostility toward sacrifice is contained in a tale extolling the marvels of Saint George, "The Miracle of St. George and the Bulgarian."[14] This tale—which describes events from the Bulgarian ninth century but which probably dates, according to Teodorov, from the tenth—contains the following passage:

> I am of the newly Christianized Bulgarian people, whom God blessed with holy baptism in those days through his chosen one Boris, . . . who . . . turned them away from the dark and deceitful and stinking sacrifices, hated by God, . . . and they rejected stinking and unclean sacrificial food.[15]

Lest we imagine that the unknown author of this tale, being a good Christian, rejects all forms of sacrifice, we ought to read a little further.

> And when the day came to set off to war, I summoned the priest and performed a holy mass; I slaughtered my best ox and gave to the poor the meat from ten sheep and ten pigs.[16]

Teodorov concludes from these two passages that "the church quite soon legalized blood sacrifices as 'church rituals.'"[17] This would seem to reveal a contradiction, within the same text, in attitudes toward sacrifice: in one case, sacrifice is "stinking and hated by God," while in another, it receives the blessing of a priest. The contradiction, however, does not really exist: in the second case, the "sacrifice" is not really a sacrifice; it is the offering of an ox and ten each of sheep and pigs for the benefit of the poor. The meat is not consumed by any gods, nor is the event consecrated to them. While the author has indeed provided for the poor a feast, it is different in nature from the sacrifices he refers to in the first passage. In the first part, ritual sacrifices are explicitly condemned, while in the second, no reference is made to sacrifice. Rather, the author admits to slaughtering a number of animals, which refers not to a ritual but merely to a certain type of killing. The presence of the priest was required, no doubt, to bless the act or the meat or the victims, but hardly to offer a sacrifice to the Lord.

Unfortunately, this tale leaves us with few details about the pagan sacrifices that Khan Boris, by being christened, helped the Bulgarian people to reject. We can infer that there was already a conceptual distinction between animal sacrifice offered to the pagan gods and what we might call the prototype of the modern Turco-Bulgarian feast known as *kurban*.[18] Perhaps the contrast between the two passages in this tale was intentional, highlighting for the listener an important difference between *sacrifice to* and *offering for*. It is unlikely, however, that this distinction was always heeded by early converts to Christianity or even by those urging the conversion.

VAMPIRES AND SACRIFICE

The context for condemnation of pagan sacrifice is more often to be found in "instructions," or lectures, by Orthodox Christians, which sought to clarify for the masses exactly which behaviors were to be tolerated by Christianity and which were not. Implicit in these teachings are links between behaviors and cultural identity, although racism—the attachment of culture-bound behavioral stereotypes to ethnicity—is certainly not present. Since ethnicity was far from being well defined in early Bulgaria, and since, in any case, many of the Slavonic instructions were shallow translations from the much earlier Greek of Byzantine models, it was more effective to point to a particular belief or ritual than to single out a particular ethnic group for chastisement. The result is that these documents tend, over their several recensions, to not distinguish carefully between religions, either. Thus, for example, condemnations of Thracian Dionysiac practices are interspersed freely among those of Slavic ones, while various offenses are ascribed to heretics and Jews willy-nilly. Still, because of their repetitious nature, a pattern of intentional persecution emerges. The underlying intent of these instructions is as much about eliminating the attractiveness of alternative beliefs as about promoting the Christian worldview.

Among the most well known of these monuments of church literature against paganism and popular beliefs is a compilation generally known as the "Oration of Saint Gregory the Theologian concerning How the Pagans Worshiped Idols."[19] Various versions of the text are included in several late medieval collections, which differ from each other in significant ways, each having been amended in the centuries after the original text was written.[20] The most comprehensive redaction is included in the *Paisievskij sbornik* (*PS*),[21] which dates from the fourteenth century; the manuscript from the Sofia cathedral of Novgorod, *Novgorodskij sofijskij sobor* (*NS*)[22] was produced at the end of the fifteenth century, and a manuscript housed at the Kirillo-Belozerskij monastery (*KB*)[23] has been dated from the seventeenth century.[24]

The dating of the recensions of the sermon is not indisputable.[25] The available texts are written in Old Russian and are therefore East Slavic. It is possible that the original text was written in the latter half of the eleventh century, when the Russian church's battle against pagan priests (*volxvy*) was just beginning. This uncertainty regarding dating—plus the fact that the texts are of East Slavic, rather than South Slavic, provenance—poses a bit of an obstacle. However, the issues confronting Slavic Orthodoxy, which originated in the Balkans (the conversion of Boris preceded that of Vladimir of Novgorod by roughly twenty years), would not differ substantially between the two Slavic regions. This obstacle is further reduced when we observe that the basis for the text is, in any case, Greek (Byzantine), purportedly written by Gregory of Nazianzus (nicknamed "the Theologian"), who died in 389.[26]

Although idol worship (in the form of sacrifice) is the specific target of the lecture, one motif stands out above the others in this oration—namely, the struggle not against sacrifice per se but, rather, against feasts and games, which from the very beginning occupied the attention of Christian educators. The connection between sacrifices and feasting can be traced back at least to the time of Homer, so what is important in this connection is the shift in emphasis. True, the pagan worship of false gods is implicitly condemned, but the author of the oration is concerned more with the behavior exhibited by those pagans than with their beliefs. This suggests that since the Christianized Slavs had taken up sacrifice in modified form, the criticism of sacrificial rituals here must refer to some aspect other than the mere slaughter of animals. The distinction (noted earlier) between pagan sacrificial feasting and whatever might be called the Christian equivalent of sacrifice was important to maintain. From a moral perspective, the Orthodox Christians found it better to participate in feasting "in the pagan fashion" (i.e., treating it as an event having for them no religious significance) than to contaminate the Christian act of prayer by means of blood sacrifice.[27]

By the eleventh century, when sacrifice was forbidden by the Orthodox church, the feasting that generally accompanied sacrifice was seen as an excuse for revelry and abandonment. This perceived rejection of personal responsibility, which the Christian clergy viewed with dead seriousness, was a more critical threat to the Christian mission than was devotion to pagan gods per se.[28] After all, the pagan gods no longer had either the religious or the political significance they possessed at the height of the Roman Empire. Though pagan rituals continued to be performed, especially among the peasants, this was more likely due to a reluctance to give up traditional practices than to any insistence on the powers of cult deities. From the agrarian peasant's point of view, the order of life, as well as survival itself, was still strongly dependent on natural or supernatural forces beyond human control. By the Middle Ages, traditional practices had become more or less superstitious—that is, divorced from a coherent and active belief system. What the Christians saw from the outside were simply rituals, particularly wedding feasts, that were characterized by abandonment of self-control in the form of drinking, dancing, and music making—in short, the orgiastic. Sexual abandonment was noticed as well, though it is often hard to tell whether such practices were observed in fact or only imagined to take place. The imputation of sexual licentiousness to religious gatherings and rites was common even between rival Christian groups. According to Peter Brown, "by the year 200, every Christian group had accused its own Christian rivals of bizarre sexual practices."[29] We may gather that the habit of such accusations was ingrained by the Middle Ages.

This was probably even more the case in Bulgaria than in Russia, since many of the rituals encountered in the post-Thracian Balkans would have been distant survivals of Dionysiac beliefs.[30] In the *Paisievskij sbornik,*

Dionysus is mentioned by name—along with Aphrodite and another Thracian divinity, Artemis—in a list of divinities deserving of contempt as objects of sacrifice: ". . . praying [sacrificing] to the mother of the beasts, the goddess Aphrodite, and Korun, and Artemis, and accursed Dionysus." Earlier in the same text, it is proclaimed that "foul services" are performed by "polluted pagans" who conduct "sacrifices taught by the devil." Alongside these formulaic denunciations of sacrifice—the inclusion of the Thraco-Hellenic divinities in this roll call was a consequence of borrowing from the Greek[31]—are allegations of debauchery and, of all things, music and dancing: "Greek love, tambourine slapping, (reed-)pipe and *gusli* [a stringed instrument] music."[32]

The picture that emerges from this section of *PS* is complex. Orations against heretics and paganism by Gregory the Theologian in the fourth century were conserved by translation and modification in the earliest days of Slavonic literature. The author of the oration that formed the basis for the texts that exist in later variations translated it in a quite literal way but emended the Greek text to suit the ecclesiastical purposes of Byzantine Orthodoxy as it spread into Slavic areas. Though sacrifice still represented the archetypal pagan ritual, the emphasis of the translated texts was more on behavior at the feasts that followed the sacrifice. The depiction of extreme behavior intended to marginalize pagans or even support their persecution—at this point, the persecution of virtually any organized group that was reluctant to adopt Orthodoxy—was extended to include the crimes of demon worship and sexual licentiousness. Later versions further amplified this theme in the attempt to root out the last vestiges of pagan religion in Russia and the Balkans. Among the notable additions to the later recensions is mention of the vampire.

WORSHIP OF VAMPIRES

A fragment of text that is often cited in etymological discussions of the word *vampir* (Russ. *upyr'*) is to be found as an insertion into the manuscript of the "Oration of Saint Gregory" from the Sofia cathedral. The passage reads as follows:

> to the same gods the Slavic people make fires and perform sacrifice, and
> to *vilas* [a type of demon] and Mokoš and the *diva* [another, unseen

she-demon] and Perun and Rod and Rožanica [spirits of ancestors].
And to vampires and *bereginas.* And dancing to Pereplut [god of seafar-
ers], they drink to him in horns.[33]

Since this reference to the vampire and the collection of Slavic gods is
not included in the *Paisievskij sbornik,* it is likely a relatively late (fifteenth-century) insertion.[34] Consequently, its usefulness for understanding the original sense of the term is limited. Nevertheless, it is
quite significant that the vampire is enumerated among demons to
whom the (Eastern) Slavs brought sacrifices.

In his article "Heretics as Vampires and Demons in Russia,"[35] Felix
Oinas follows Mansikka in dating the encyclical around the eleventh
century. The early dating is based on the date of the original text, not
on that of the *Novgorodskij sofijskij sobor* manuscript. This has an unfortunate consequence, which I am obliged to rectify here.

In *NS,* the claim that the Slavs worshiped, in addition to their gods,
both vampires and *beregyni*—the latter being some type of "unquiet
dead," riverbank spirits[36] about which we know very little—provides a
misleading connection between the vampire and the supernatural.
While it is probable that by the fifteenth century, the word *vampir/upyr'*
most likely designated a demonic entity, in all likelihood the word had
no such metaphysical connotations four hundred years earlier. Virtually
all etymologies of *vampir* except those proposed by Perkowski[37] suggest
directly or indirectly that the earliest meaning of the term referred to a
supernatural entity, a demon, a walking corpse. This assertion is either
based directly on or supported by the evidence of a fifteenth-century
manuscript insertion (the text fragment previously cited), since earlier
occurrences of the word provide very little useful context. Nevertheless,
it is far from certain that the supernatural meaning that can be attached
to the term *vampir* on the basis of the *NS* context was available in the
tenth or eleventh century.[38] The problematic etymology of the word
vampire is brought up again in chapter 4.

BOGOMILS AND VAMPIRES

The earliest vampire has been linked with the heretical sect known
as the Bogomils, whose dualistic beliefs challenged Orthodox

Christianity from the tenth through the fourteenth centuries.[39] By the time of the postmedieval Russian versions of the teachings based on the works of Gregory the Theologian and John Chrysostom, heretics among the Eastern Slavs were definitively associated with vampirelike creatures. Oinas claims that "beliefs pertaining to vampires were transferred to heretics" and thus that "the term 'heretic' was extended to also include vampire."[40] This would mean not only that the vampire became associated with heresy fairly late but also that the South Slavic meanings of the term, which are often associated with excommunication, were derived by the Bulgarians from the Russians, rather than the other way around.

It is more probable, however, that *vampir* became associated with heresy much earlier, but indirectly—after the Bogomils began to represent a major politico-religious threat in the Balkans. Vampires probably originally belonged to some group (of pagans) that was thought to engage in any number of offensive acts: sacrifice, idol worship, "magic," feasting, and generally abandoned, even orgiastic, behavior. Sacrifice and feasting were the major ritual characteristics of these early *vampiri*.

Indeed, the feature now most commonly associated with vampires, blood drinking, is traceable directly to these behaviors. Drinking the blood of a sacrificed animal in order to obtain immortality or secure the other benefits of ritual sacrifice was a practice among the pagans (Slavs) described by the Arab chronicler Ibn Masudi in 950,[41] only a few decades before the Slavs began to be converted to Christianity. It is only logical that members of this group (which may have been loosely defined, and thus members may not have had a specific name for themselves) would have been labeled according to their involvement with a practice that contradicted the Christian attitude toward sacrifice. This tendency to condemn the literal drinking of blood would have been amplified, since Christian writers were disturbed that heretics would not admit the symbolic nature of the Eucharist.[42]

Heresy and pagan practice were not carefully distinguished, nor were Christian polemicists above accusing the heretics of engaging in rituals generally associated with pagans. Accusations by early Christian apologists against paganism were as little grounded in fact as were the earlier pagan accusations against the Christians. The outlandish accusations were intended to magnify the perception of paganism as tantamount to antihuman barbarism, thus effectively scaring Christians away from any temptation to drift away from the church. In the Balkans, the task of conversion was halting and difficult, partly for social and political reasons and partly for geographical ones. Exaggeration and condemnation therefore became common tools of propaganda in the struggle against, first, pagans and, later, heretics, in a land whose internal and external politics were for a long time quite unstable.

COSMAS THE PRESBYTER

We are fortunate to possess a tract against the Bogomils, written by Cosmas the Presbyter,[43] in which are laid out in detail the reasons why heretics are in fact worse than pagans. In this treatise, idol worship and sacrifice, practices of the pagans, are considered almost minor offenses in comparison to the dualist heresy that had sprung up in Bulgaria and attracted a substantial following in a brief period. Cosmas was a tenth-century Orthodox priest writing in Slavonic, who was nevertheless highly critical of the Bulgarian Orthodox church, which he saw as lax and corrupt. The earliest manuscript with the text of Cosmas's tract dates from the fifteenth century, but it is generally agreed that he wrote it not long after the death of the Bulgarian Tsar Peter in 969. Although Cosmas is principally concerned with halting the spread of Bogomilism in Bulgaria, his *Discourse* in general attempts to show the waywardness of any but canonical Orthodox beliefs and practices.

Cosmas is well aware of the practice of sacrificing to pagan gods, a practice that is initiated by the Devil, who wishes to deceive humankind.

> Our enemy the devil . . . has never ceased to lead mankind astray; beginning with Adam, the first man, until today, he has not ceased to try to entice all men from the faith, so that a large number of men might be with him in torment; his deceptions have led some to worship idols, others to kill their brothers, yet others to commit fornication and other sins. But . . . all these sins cannot be compared with heresy.[44]

Judging from this passage, it would seem that at the time of Cosmas, idol worship (and, by extension, sacrifice) had already receded into the background. Paganism, no longer officially supported and therefore no longer representing an active threat to the church, could be regarded as an erroneous belief, but one that was understandable, since those sinful polytheistic beliefs preceded Christianity.

Alongside the shift in the perception of the greater threat as coming from the outside to one coming from the inside (heretics passing themselves off as Christians), there is a parallel change that is of great relevance to the argument that the earliest vampires were not Bogomils. Early Bogomilism, as described by Cosmas, was not a highly structured religion. Rather, Bogomils seemed to have been content to call little attention to themselves, and they shunned ritual in principle and in practice.

It was not their obvious difference but, rather, their insidiousness that made Bogomils so threatening. Whereas pagans could be easily identified by their sacrifices and other public acts, the Bogomils engaged in no such rituals and in fact considered themselves to be true Christians, believing, however, in neither the Crucifixion nor baptism. They thus could not be dealt with symbolically: the power of the Cross had no effect on them, since they had no regard for it and in fact held that the Crucifixion, if not an illusion, had no religious significance.

> Shall I compare [the heretics] to demons? They are worse than the demons themselves, for the demons are afraid of the cross of Christ, while the heretics chop up crosses and make tools of them. The demons are afraid of the image of the Lord painted on a wooden panel, but the heretics do not venerate icons, but call them idols. The demons are afraid of the relics of God's just.[45]

Demons are simply easier to deal with. Christianity, after the peace of Constantine, was quite victorious over other religions in the greater empire, effectively driving "paganism" underground, if not totally obliterating it, by AD 800. The demons became "afraid of the cross," inasmuch as people holding onto pagan beliefs were persecuted. (It is perhaps more correct to say that demons became "personalized," representing the capacity for individual corruption rather than misplaced religious belief.)[46] But heretics were another story: not only were they more persistent (a "neo-Manichaean" movement arose in the Balkans in the tenth century); they were also harder to eliminate. The Bogomil movement in particular attracted a number of Bulgarian peasants who had reason to resist the onslaught of economic hardships and military threats coming from Byzantium. The movement was in many ways politically dissident,[47] if only because its very philosophy was opposed to the imperialism of Byzantium and the underlying universalism. Orthodoxy's incompletely resolved monotheism, meanwhile, had led to the rise of a professional priesthood, which was responsible for doctrinal rigidification.[48]

The worldview of the Bogomils represented a conscious rejection of all that Byzantine Orthodoxy was attempting to establish. It was therefore substantially worse than paganism, whose objections to Christianity were easier to dismiss once paganism no longer had a solid political foothold. But the accusations against the Bogomils (and, before them, the Paulicians) grew out of the rhetoric used against paganism and its rituals. In one of the tenth-century abjuration formulae directed against dualist heretics, listing the *anathemata* that any repentant heretics would have to confess, we find accusations that are more than a little reminiscent of the back-and-forth accusations of child sacrifice, incest, and sacrifice several centuries earlier.

> Anathema to all those . . . who reject the communion of the holy mysteries, but use the burnt umbilical cords of children for the purification (but rather the pollution) of their souls, and with them defile their food . . .
>
> Anathema to those who pollute themselves by eating the flesh of dead animals, and to those who reject all Christian fasts, and at the season of what they think is Lent enjoy cheese and milk . . .
>
> Anathema to those who are polluted with their sister or mother-in-law or sister-in-law, and those who gather to celebrate a feast on the first of January, and after the evening drinking-session put out the lights and have an orgy, sparing no one on the grounds of age or sex or relationship.[49]

It is with these early abjuration formulae, along with the *Discourse* of Cosmas, that the emphasis shifts from paganism to dualism as the object of Orthodoxy's hostility. On the one hand, the Paulician dualists are accused of engaging in incestuous orgies around the time of

New Years' feasts,[50] while, on the other, they are accused of having no regard for the reality of the Christian mystery.

> Anathema . . . to those who despise the holy cross, although they pretend to honor it, and think instead of Christ, who (they say) extended his arms and so made the sign of the cross; and to those who turn away from the communion of the precious body and blood of Christ.[51]

Later, Cosmas states that because the heretics deny the actuality of Christ's divinity, they are worse even than Jews.

> For all sin is less serious than heresy. Even Jews did not spit on anything but the Lord's flesh, while heretics spit on His divinity, but this rebounds on their own face. So heretics are greater sinners than the very Jews who crucified Christ.[52]

This attitude perfectly echoes that held by the Greek theologian John of Damascus (d. 749), who claimed, "it is better to be converted to Judaism and to die a Jew than to have any fellowship with the Manichaeans."[53]

By the time of Cosmas, it is presumed that Christian rites have triumphed over pagan ones, that the symbol of the cross has replaced that of sacrifice.

> Indeed, what Christian has not been enlightened by the Lord's cross? Who has not rejoiced to see crosses set up in high places, where once men sacrificed to demons, immolating their sons and daughters?[54]

Thus, from the triad of Jews, pagans, and heretics that together coalesced into the image of the enemy of Christianity from its very beginnings, heretics emerged in late antiquity as representing the utmost evil. Whereas Judaism and paganism in some sense "had an excuse," there was no excusing heresy, because it claimed to represent Christianity. Its falseness was proof enough of its connection with the Devil.

So far as the vampire is concerned, we may conclude that the explicit association between heretics and vampires in fifteenth-century Russia can be traced to the Bogomils, who were generally confused with Bulgarians. The accusations against the Bogomils, who abstained from virtually all rituals,[55] were subtler than those brought without much foundation against the earlier sect of dualists in the Balkans, the

Paulicians. Descriptions of Paulicians were still grounded in the early Christian rhetoric against pagans and Manichaean heretics, continuing the tradition of tying them to barbarian practices: (child) sacrifice, sexual licentiousness and orgiasm, incest, and so on. The original vampire, we may surmise, was affiliated in some way with one or all of the groups whose beliefs the church tried to eradicate: Jews, pagans, and heretics.

4

SCAPEGOATS AND DEMONS

A Thousand Years of the Vampire, Continued

The meaning of the Greek ecclesiastical term used by Cosmas and others in their attacks on heretics and pagans, *anathema,* is "anything accursed." *Anathema* means literally that which must be removed, taken out (not unlike a cancer), and hence accursed. This notion of cursing by removing—that is, banishing to some place outside the community—is of course quite critical to understanding the earliest significance of the vampire.

The disease of untruth carried by heretics and pagans—and, to some extent, Jews—had to be destroyed, eliminated, according to medieval Christian theologians in both the West and the East. The beliefs and behavior of these enemy religions—their philosophies and rituals—were considered destructive, false, and insidious. Insofar as they were sponsored by the Devil, by Satan himself, they were evil and potentially contaminating.

The earliest accusations against the pagans concerned their worship, in the form of sacrificial offerings, of pagan gods, which came to be generally referred to by Christians as demons (*daimones*). This worship had to stop, because it represented a deviation from the worship of the one God and Creator. Furthermore, the practice of sacrifice represented a form of collective violence to which Christianity strenuously objected, at least in theory. Christianity purports to put an end to vengeful collective violence by exposing the injustice of it.[1] This essentially political process, however, whereby earlier religious systems are characterized as barbaric or evil, is hardly unique to Christianity. As cultures attempt to move away from sanctioned violence, they often attribute its practice "to an older mythological generation and to a religious system now seen to be 'barbarous' and 'primitive.'"[2]

Such an attribution naturally serves to reinforce the ideological boundary between the more and the less civilized groups. Less civilized groups, in turn, may be held responsible for certain adversities befalling the more civilized. This may be because the more barbaric groups have inflicted actual punishment (warfare, punitive legislation, economic hardship) on the group that despises their barbarism or because the behavior (in the form of rituals) and beliefs of the ostensible barbarians represent such violations of sanctity and propriety that they can only produce negative consequences. These accusations against enemies become exaggerated as they are further removed from any factual center, and as the exaggerations become more pronounced, the boundary between the real and the supernatural is crossed. Prayers to cult gods, when seen through a hostile lens, become invocations of supernatural demons.

The imputation of magic or outrageous demonic behavior to groups that are perceived as threatening frequently characterizes the scapegoating phenomenon.

> In reality magical thought does not originate in disinterested curiosity. It is usually the last resort in a time of disaster, and provides principally a system of accusation. It is always the *other* who plays the role of the sorcerer and acts in an unnatural fashion to harm his neighbor . . . Magical thought seeks "a significant cause on the level of social relations," in other words a human being, a victim, a scapegoat.[3]

Whereas at first there might be well-reasoned arguments against beliefs held by other groups, intended to set apart and reinforce the coherence of a group that is not yet entirely confident or stable (e.g., Christianity in late antiquity), under certain circumstances the polemical reasoning is supplanted by imagery of a stereotypical nature. Behavior that is at first considered merely transgressive or immoral comes to be viewed as perverse or unnatural; the label "unnatural" may then soon be replaced by the label "supernatural" when the need to hold another group responsible for some adversity (including actual or potential attrition of membership) is desperate.

Mary Douglas points out that this exaggeration of powers ascribed to an individual who is to be accused of bringing down adverse effects is common, for example, in societies where witchcraft has an important place and where certain structural conditions exist.

> [T]he body politic tends to have a clear external boundary, and a confused internal state in which envy and favouritism flourish and continually confound the expectations of the members. So the body of the witch, normal-seeming and apparently carrying the normal human limitations, is equipped with hidden and extraordinarily malevolent powers.[4]

The vampire is thus very witchlike.

> [T]he witch . . . is someone whose inside is corrupt and who works harm on his victims by attacking their pure, innocent insides . . . Sometimes he sucks out their soul . . . [and] sometimes he needs access to their inner bodily juices.[5]

Perhaps the primary difference, then, between a vampire and a so-called witch is that the former is dead. It would be difficult to assert that the vampire is, like the witch, "normal-seeming," but perhaps the vampire's mimetic resemblance or linkage to a formerly living person qualifies the vampire as possessing "normal human limitations." However, the form of the vampire in folklore is not always so ordinary: sometimes the vampire is unseen; at other times, he has an anomalous shape; at other times still, he is virtually indistinguishable from the person whose demise led to vampirization. This multiplicity of forms constitutes an important difference from the witch, a difference that must be accounted for.

In any case, it is by such a process that a member of an actual social group gradually becomes demonized and, in the process, acquires supernatural powers. In the case of the vampire, there seems to be a progression over the course of several centuries, from pagan to heretic to demon. The leap from a perverse violator of taboos (child sacrifice, incest) to a supernatural demon who rises from the dead and attacks the living and who tends to function as a scapegoat during inexplicable adversity is not a small one. It requires, first, the acquisition of mythological features. For the vampire to become a supernatural being, it must absorb appropriate attributes from existing concepts about the supernatural. The attributes it takes on must express symbolically the underlying anathema it represents. The early misconceptions about the qualities and beliefs of precisely those groups that the church could not accept or incorporate were transformed over time into folkloric notions about the vampire's features and (ritualized) activities, along with the means of blocking or destroying these evil beings.

WHO BECOMES A VAMPIRE?

In its folkloric sense, the term *vampire,* as far as I can make out, has always referred to a specific, known (deceased) individual within or just outside of a particular community. The means of determining which members of a given group may become vampires and under which circumstances cannot be arbitrary, since the primary function of a scapegoat is to restore order to a community.[6] Arbitrariness in the operation of such a mechanism would have the opposite effect—namely, to make all members of the group insecure. If anyone in a community may be turned against at random and held responsible for some adversity that has no clearly definable cause, the result is an increase in social disorder (which in turn may justify further repression). In such cases, the group coherence promised by focusing on a single individual or representative of a group is never restored, since members of the community then begin to redirect their energies toward attaining invisibility to or immunity from the forces of accusation. They strive to remain unmarked; they go underground.

Sacrificial victims are always marked in some way:[7] by animal category, by color, by physical marking, by astronomical or calendrical synchronicity, by gender, by age—in short, victims are selected on the basis of their position within a ritually reinforced hierarchy of power. Generally agreed-on markers symbolize the boundaries separating the levels in this complex hierarchy. Scapegoats, too, are selected according to social parameters, although the value ascribed to the scapegoat is usually different from that ascribed to the sacrificial victim.[8] Unlike sacrificial victims, scapegoats are not ritually purified or consecrated before they are expelled. On the contrary, it is their status as unclean, dirty, polluted, or transgressive that marks them as suitable candidates to bear collective sin.[9] They are considered dangerous in any case, so expelling them does not constitute any great loss. Thus, the methods of becoming a vampire should correspond to value assignments, in particular to transgressions and methods of contamination. Some of these methods, such as excommunication, are quite obvious, while others are more obscure.

In Bulgaria, by far the most common event by which a corpse is turned into a vampire is through violation of the space around the body. Curiously, this etiology is not encountered in Western Europe, where the literary vampire is predominant and where the folkloric one is almost unknown. In a good deal of Balkan folklore from the nineteenth century to recent times, if a cat should happen to jump over a corpse as it lies in state before burial, the deceased is destined to become a vampire immediately after burial. Although the cat is most commonly cited, dogs are also implicated. In addition, if a chicken should fly over a corpse, a similar result occurs.

This taboo against something passing over the deceased prior to burial must be extended to include transactions. Giving someone an object or even shaking someone's hand in the space above the corpse produces a result identical to that caused by a cat jumping over it.[10] Even the falling of a living person's shadow on a dead body can produce a vampire. The nature of the space around and especially above a dead person, it would appear, is more critical than the type of object that invades it.

It is of great importance that nothing impede the journey of the soul to the otherworld once a person has died. According to Orthodox belief as it is encountered in Slavic areas, the soul is separable from the body but is required to stay around the body for forty days. Thus, the separation of soul and body is not complete even after burial. Until that separation is final, there is the risk of disturbing the process of detachment by failing to observe certain precautions, such as those already outlined.

The space around the body is therefore in some sense sacred or at the very least charged, dangerous. This notion about the space around the deceased being sacred occurs frequently in Indo-European mythology.[11] Van Gennep, furthermore, claims that the time after death is often "transitional" for both survivors and deceased and, consequently, a period of danger.[12] In certain Slavic societies today, there is still observed a precaution concerning shaking hands or conducting any transaction across a threshold. From these facts, we may infer that the deceased, being neither wholly in the world of the living nor yet outside it, represents a sort of threshold. Indeed, the whole concept of liminality, as described by structural anthropologists, is based on a spatial metaphor: the area occupied by that which is between categorical boundaries is a place of transition, a threshold, which has peculiar properties.

The dead body in a sense acts as or occupies a liminal area. In order for the soul of the deceased to depart properly on its journey, it is critical not to violate that space or otherwise risk reanimation by the spirit of an animal. From a purely functional point of view, however, the taboo against animals jumping over a corpse is a means of ensuring attention to a corpse during the vigil prior to burial. The need for this postmortem care arises because there is high susceptibility to the influence of evil spirits, that is, incursion into the area around the body where the soul dwells, a disruption of the sacred space between this world and the other.

RITUAL INFELICITIES

Vampirization caused by a cat or other animal or even by a shadow moving across the corpse has the least restricted distribution of all causes: virtually anyone is capable, through no fault of his or her own, of becoming a vampire after death.[13] In terms of the scapegoat mechanism, this effective operation of chance is very convenient. Times of crisis in a small community do not always coincide with the demise of the sort of person who might be easily blamed because of some obvious physical or behavioral characteristic. Logically, it would seem that such a generalized process came into existence in a later period, almost as a guarantee that a vampire could be found who could be held responsible in case of any unforeseen catastrophic eventuality. Earlier constraints on vampirization—which is essentially a process of selecting a scapegoat—had no doubt been tighter.

The accusation of vampirism against people who, during their lifetimes, were not otherwise outcast represents a unique variation of the scapegoat process. The marker of suitability is reduced, quite simply, to deadness (the inability to pose an objection); ultimately, no other characteristic is necessary to be blamed for some inexplicable adversity. In such cases, the vampire comes into being simply because the taboo concerning contact with the dead has been inadvertently broken by a member of the household, even if only a domestic animal.

Vampires originally came into existence thanks to their actions or status during their lives. From the earliest recorded times, vampires were the result of excommunication, anathema, or other ritual infelicity separating them from the rest of the Christian community. According to the earliest attestation of a general belief in vampires from seventeenth-century Macedonia, vampires were dead persons who had been excommunicated.[14] According to Serbian belief, those whose souls were sinful were destined for torment after death, and they often became vampires.[15] Even children who had not been baptized before premature death became vampirelike *nekrštenici,* who threatened harm to newborns and young mothers.[16] In Bulgaria, those who were not honored with proper burial rites—either by accidental omission or, more commonly, because church law forbade it (as in the case of suicide)—became vampires. For example, if the actual burial is unaccompanied by a priest reading the mass for the dead or if the body of the deceased is not anointed with wine and oil forming the sign of the cross, the person will become a vampire.[17] A sixteenth-century reference states that unbelievers, excommunicates, and godless and anathematized people become vampires after death.[18]

Taken as a whole, this class of individuals whose actions forced them to be separated from the church and from salvation is in all likelihood the oldest category of vampires. The boundaries of this class are not clear-cut, since it may be desirable to include those who were believed to be witches or magicians—that is to say, those who practiced rites that from the church's point of view were pagan or satanic. Certain types of criminals and people of dubious morality also become vampires,[19] even though their crimes were secular rather than religious.

The early attitude toward the vampire was that it threatened the salvation of the soul, insofar as it came into being as a result either of moral insufficiency or of failure to make certain observances.

It is not difficult to see the connection between vampirism as a consequence of excommunication and the earlier attacks on pagans and heretics that were common in late antiquity and the Middle Ages. But the Christian worldview embedded in vampire folklore cannot be separated entirely from traces of pre-Christian belief. Listed alongside etiologies that quite clearly reflect Christian hostility toward paganism are causes that do not exhibit any obvious connection with commonly accepted Christian belief. The general Slavic belief that the incarnated soul must abide on the earth for a specified period of time and that any curtailment of that time produces undesirable results is evident in Balkan vampire lore. In South Slavic folklore, the prematurely dead—including those killed by natural forces (lightning, fire, etc.) and by animals or other men, as well as suicides, mothers dying in childbirth, drowned people, and so forth—become vampires.[20]

In the broadest terms, the vampire represents the consequence of succumbing to forces that remove the individual from the ordered, productive life of the community. Weakness of will, evidenced by participation in un-Christian behavior, is viewed as a form of selfishness that is punished by the soul's being prevented from journeying to the otherworld. The notion that individuals should stay alive for a particular time, certainly long enough to participate in all the basic life-cycle rituals (birth, baptism, marriage), reinforces the sense of usefulness of the individual to the community—as a source of labor, if nothing else. In Slavic agrarian communities, where labor was not so highly differentiated as in urban communities, the labor contribution of the individual, especially in farm and household matters, was critical to the well-being of the group. Thus, there were strong taboos against ignoring the communal good. From an abstract point of view, suicide may be considered the ultimate affront to the society, representing an aggressive and violent means of preempting the society from placing further constraints or making further demands on the individual. The suicide is often a person who feels marginalized, persecuted, or otherwise mistreated and who thus acts out passive-aggressively and effectively "punishes" the society by removing himself from the pool. The automatic "vampirization" of suicides not only reinforces the taboo against suicide but does so by promising violent retribution against those who have elected, in an ultimate way, to avoid further participation in the hostile community.

Making vampires—scapegoats—of those whose time on earth is abbreviated by violence of course supports the will to live but also supports the will to participate in the society. In Bulgarian, as in Greek, mythology, the individual's time on earth is established at birth by divine forces,[21] so any inexplicable modification of that time constitutes either demonic intervention or evil intention on the part of the individual. In any case, those who die at the wrong age or under the wrong circumstances have the advantage of being socially marked and are therefore suitable candidates for vampirization. Sometimes, the wrong circumstances were nothing more than being born at the wrong time of year.

THE "UNCLEAN DAYS"

Vampires, along with other nocturnal demons (in particular, one known as *karakondžol*), are also associated with certain calendrical periods. In Bulgaria, the "twelve days of Christmas," from Christmas Eve through Epiphany, or Jordan's Day (January 6), are known as the "Unclean Days." Other names for this period are quite revealing: they include "Pagan Days," "Ember Days," "Unbaptized Days," and even "Vampire Days."[22] This brief midwinter period represents a time when, it is believed, evil spirits are able to roam the earth. Consequently, taboos against certain behaviors are stronger and more elaborate during this period than usual.

The period known as the "Unclean Days" represents a bounded time when the pre-Christian substratum of Bulgarian folk belief is permitted expression. Indeed, the very name "Pagan Days" conveys this, and the emergence onto the earth of demons during this time corresponds to the reemergence of suppressed pagan divinities.[23] Rituals performed during and at the end of this period strongly suggest purification and a need to reintegrate into the community those who have been obliged to have contact with the dangerous forces of pagan religion. During the Pagan Days, it is claimed, performing Christian rites actually strengthens the fatal influence of evil forces. Consequently, birthdays, weddings, and baptisms are never performed during this time, and if someone should die, he or she is buried, but the Christian burial service is reserved for after Epiphany.

The restrictions, practices, and beliefs associated with this period are quite ancient and not merely Slavic. Many Western and Central European cultures possess folklore about pagan activity during this time of year. In fifteenth-century Germany, for example, there is testimony about a band of witches who traveled out of their bodies during the Ember Days, "provoking storms and casting non-fatal spells on men." Similarly, the *benandanti* were said to leave their bodies to fight witches during the Ember Days.[24] For all its importance as a Christian holiday, the time between Christmas and Epiphany is also strongly associated with pre-Christian belief, as if the repression of the pagan gods (or the agrarian worldview those gods might represent) could not be vigorously maintained during this transitional period.

In South Slavic belief, people who die during this period invariably become vampires. Also, children who are born or conceived during this period have special powers and may themselves become vampires. Bulgarian villagers seem to be highly susceptible to contamination during this period and are thus guarded by a plethora of taboos. Banning of sexual intercourse during this period of course eliminates the possibility of conceiving a future vampire, but it also has the implicit (and intended) side effect of blocking indulgence in fleshly pleasures during a holy period. When we recall that fleshly celebrations were condemned as pagan by Orthodox apologists,[25] the link between vampires and paganism becomes unequivocal.

WAYS OF DETECTING A VAMPIRE

The set of signs that reveal to a community that a vampire is afoot is frequently distinguished from the set of behaviors that are ascribed to the vampire by that community. There is some overlap here, since it is often by a vampire's presumed activity (e.g., bloodsucking) that it is realized that a vampire is or has been nearby. But the discovery of a vampire is entirely motivated by evidence of its behavior. The vampire and similar entities in fact serve primarily as nomenclature for pairs of manifestations (activities) and anticipatory or reactionary responses (precautions and cures). Since the vampire is a former member of the community, we may understand the precautions as akin to taboos, insofar as they either proscribe or reinforce certain types of behavior, while curative measures serve the scapegoat mechanism, once a determination has been made that a scapegoat is needed (to offset crisis, disease, catastrophe, etc.). These pairs (activities and collective response) indeed vary from location to location and may exhibit evidence of "demon contamination," but nowhere does a given vampire activity lead to arbitrary selection of a response or to an undefined response. The belief about what to do in the presence of a vampire is inextricably linked to the beliefs regarding how a vampire is detected.

The conditions under which an individual may become a vampire represent, in some sense, a special case of detection. The probability that a given individual will turn into a vampire corresponds to his availability, once dead, as a potential scapegoat. The ability to recognize the marks or status of a potential vampire is a capacity that may be given to anyone as part of a tradition, while the ability to actually recognize a wandering vampire is a gift frequently possessed only by a select group of people. In Bulgarian folklore, some types of vampire are invisible[26] and thus can only be recognized by their traces (sick or dead sheep, exhausted livestock, noises in the roof, etc.). Vampires that have taken on some sort of physical shape usually cannot be recognized as vampires except by animals, especially dogs, and by special people possessing the ability to see vampires. These people are themselves quasi-supernatural and are called by such names as *vampirdžii, sâbotnici,* and *dhampiri.*

THE *VAMPIRDŽIA* AND THE *SÂBOTNIK*

Among the activities that a vampire may engage in is sexual consort with his former wife, and this leads, almost always, to pregnancy. In fact, in the village context, a widow's pregnancy might have no other logical explanation, for her chastity in widowhood goes without question. Thus, a widow's pregnancy can point to no more likely a cause than that her deceased husband has become a vampire—the situation requires a scapegoat. As we might expect, the offspring of such an unnatural union is thought to inherit some features of his supernatural father, particularly the ability to see and therefore to destroy vampires.

These children of vampires are called *glogove* (pl.; sing. *glog*) or *vampirdžii*,[27] the latter especially in western Bulgaria, Macedonia, and areas of the Balkans where Ottoman influence was strong.

Now, in most cultures with a highly paternalistic and firmly Christian religious base, the son of an unmarried widow would ordinarily be marked as illegitimate, a bastard. The social status of such children tends to be marginal at best. The *vampirdžia,* however, although marked, is instead endowed with heroic abilities,[28] almost as if in compensation. The elevation of status produced by reversing the polarity of the *vampirdžia's* "genetic abnormality"[29] first of all offsets the unjust violence collectively performed or contemplated by the community. But more important, it provides a subtle mechanism for future accusations against vampires, a mechanism that frees the villagers as a group from any culpability. Since the *vampirdžia* becomes the only person relied on to identify and kill vampires, he takes on sole responsibility for selecting and destroying a scapegoat. The *vampirdžia,* as a "professional,"[30] is entrusted with the power to act on behalf of the group and thereby guarantees the unquestioning unanimity that is necessary for the scapegoat process to function properly. The willingness of the village bastard son to put on the mantle of *vampirdžia* is heightened not only by social approval and potential financial benefit but also by consideration of the consequences of declining the job. He is protected from becoming a mere murderer by the fact that those whom he kills are already dead.

Like the *vampirdžia,* the *sâbotnik* is also able to detect vampires, as well as other evil demons and diseases, but they are not necessarily half-vampire, at least genetically. Rather, according to folk etymology, a *sâbotnik* is someone who was "born on Saturday" (Bulg. *sâbota*)[31] and acquires his, or rarely her, powers (which include the ability to interpret dreams and to recognize magicians in addition to seeing vampires) merely through that fact. Dogs born on Saturday, which is a day on which the dead are honored, are also considered *sâbotnici,* and vampires and personified diseases are afraid of both the human and canine types.[32]

The Sabbath, by definition, is a day bounded by taboos. Very early in its history, Christianity, to distinguish itself from Judaism, designated Sunday as its Sabbath, rather than Saturday.[33] Violation of taboos brought about undesirable results: in the early centuries of Christianity, it was believed that couples who slept together on Sunday and other days of abstinence "would beget lepers and epileptics."[34] Therefore, the tradition by which the offspring of illicit liaisons are somehow deformed or marked—not unlike the *vampirdžia*—is quite ancient. Folklore about *sâbotnici* suggests that their semisupernatural powers, a consequence of being born on the Jewish, rather than the Christian, Sabbath, are virtually identical to those ascribed to the *vampirdžia,* and we may thus infer that Saturday and vampires are connected in other ways.

Indeed, vampires are not able to leave their graves on Saturday (except on Holy Saturday), when they are reincarnated, at least according to belief in the Banat region of Bulgaria.[35] On the surface, this would seem illogical: if Saturday is so closely associated with the dead that it is known, popularly, as "Dead Day," it would stand to reason that vampires would be more powerful, rather than powerless, on that day. But we must remember that at least part of the "evil time" between sunset and cockcrow actually constitutes what we might usually consider Sunday morning.[36] That Saturday is strongly linked to both the vampire and his adversary, the *sâbotnik,* and that this link constitutes a form of social marking allows us to understand the significance of the *sâbotnik.*

Recalling that vampires were originally linked, in the early Christian Slavic mind, with either a pagan or a heretical sect, it is possible that the specialness of Saturday is based on its identification with the Hebrew Sabbath. Jews, after all, were the third group usually mentioned by Christian polemicists as opponents of Christianity. But of the group comprising pagans, heretics, and Jews, Jews were the least offensive.[37] Recall Cosmas's remark that heretics were greater sinners than Jews and John of Damascus's claim that it is better to die a Jew than to consort with Manichaeans (both statements are discussed in chap. 3). Since the Jews, evidently, were not considered as foul as either pagans or heretics, the *sâbotnik,* being symbolically tied to Judaism through their connection with the Jewish Sabbath, was not imbued with the same degree of evil as the vampire. Marked as an outsider, the *sâbotnik* would share features with the vampire and would consequently be able to identify vampires, but he would not himself be responsible for the same degree of evil that the vampire brings. It may be stretching the point, especially in the absence of any other data supporting this conjectural connection between the *sâbotnik* and the Sabbath,[38] but in light of the *sâbotnik*'s social role, his willingness to identify or kill an innocent scapegoat may be seen as a folkloric analogue to the wish of the Roman Jews to crucify Christ.

The marking of Saturday as a somehow unholy day seems to have other roots than simply the Hebrew Sabbath. According to the Russian Orthodox metropolitan Cyril, on "Saturday evening men and women gather, dance shamelessly, and act foully into the night of holy Sunday, like the Dionysian holiday the unclean heathens celebrate."[39] Thus, the identification of Saturday as an impure day or evening seems to have been widespread and linked not only to notions about the Jews but to rumors about the pagans as well. I have already noted that popular notions about Dionysiac rituals exemplified sacrifice, orgiasm, and in general the most intolerable features of pagan religions—especially fleshly pleasure.

THE VAMPIRE'S EFFECTS

In addition to its recognition by specifically identified individuals in a community, a vampire may be known by the consequences of its activity. Vampires are also associated with particular activities and locations; therefore, people with certain professions or reputations may be easily suspected. In both cases, the vampire is someone known in the community, even if not a resident ("wanderers" often being suspicious), since otherwise there would be no way of telling whether the conditions for vampirization had been met. The expertise of the *vampirdžia* or the *sâbotnik* may allow them to transcend this requirement of local familiarity with the vampire, but most often, a vampire is selected from among the recently dead within a small community.

Catastrophes

Catastrophes, such as epidemics or destructive natural events (weather-related, fire, etc.), may provoke varying responses, depending on the beliefs of those who are affected. In some cases, specific sacrificial rituals are performed to propitiate the powers thought to cause adverse natural phenomena. Thus, in Bulgaria, the rituals known as "Butterfly" and "Gherman" may be performed to end a drought. Highly symbolic, both are clearly sacrificial and undoubtedly pre-Christian in origin.[40]

In the case of Gherman, an ithyphallic clay doll is destroyed, lamented, and placed in a small coffin and buried. According to Račko Popov, "[the effigy] Gherman has never been considered a dead man, but he is rather the personification of the idea of a 'living corpse,' because of whose violent destruction the earth would be fertilized."[41]

Here is an example of an expiatory ritual, since drought in the Bulgarian countryside was considered a divine punishment, as were hail, floods, and epidemics. This punishment is inflicted as a result of illicit pregnancy or a violation of the incest taboo.[42] The remedy for the drought is therefore to appease the Lord (earlier, of course, some divinity, perhaps the Slavic thunder god Perun)[43] by means of an offering. Curiously, the offered object is construed as a "living corpse," reminiscent of the vampire.

More common than natural disasters in the context of vampire lore are adversities or distressing phenomena that are seemingly more directed at an individual or a family. Whereas drought or hail affects everyone simultaneously and equally, an epidemic affecting livestock or people usually starts with an individual case. The epidemiological focus of a highly contagious disease may be seen to be the first victim of a pernicious force, such as a vampire, say, or a personified disease known as *nežit*.[44]

Vampires are thought to be the causes of some epidemics,[45] but not all. The plague, for example, is personified separately and has nothing to do with the vampire in those locations where the contagious disease is conceived as an "old hag." The correlation between a particular catastrophic event and the mythology called on to explain it or deal with it is highly complex, resulting from a number of accidental and syncretic factors, as well as structural ones.[46] Regardless of whether an expiatory sacrificial ritual, such as Gherman, or a scapegoating process, such as the public response to a vampire,[47] is selected to restore social coherence, in either case the action taken serves to assign a reason, "a significant cause on the level of social relations."[48]

Death and Mischief

The assignment of causes for inexplicable events is not limited, in Balkan folklore, to major catastrophes, such as disease or drought. On the contrary, a number of phenomena of day-to-day agrarian life seem to be most easily dismissed by viewing them as the result of some demonic activity. Inexplicable death, especially during sleep, is perhaps the most serious of these, and in such cases, vampires are imagined to press down on the sleeping or to choke them. From our modern perspective, we view panic attacks and coronary events during sleep as resulting from neurological and pathological processes, certainly nothing supernatural. It may be that those who attribute such misfortunes to vampires are nevertheless aware of rational, "scientific" reasons.[49] However, the question that is not answered by medical science when, for example, someone's anxious dreams cause the cardiovascular system to become overworked and perhaps induce thrombosis is why it is that a person's own dreams can kill him or her. It is to this layer of the question that the folkloric response actually addresses itself, not to the explanation of poorly understood physiological processes.[50]

Less serious effects, similar to those of the Germanic poltergeist, are also caused by vampires. These are common and include noises, breakage, and overturning of grain or water barrels. Livestock and horses that seem to be suffering in the morning from exhaustion are thought to have been ridden by vampires during the night. These effects constitute a form of mischief and indeed represent an almost humorous side of vampire folklore. But if the vampire merely did mischief, he would not be so feared. Rather, it is the vampire's tendency to drink blood that has led to the longevity and broad distribution of vampire legends.

Blood Drinking

Blood drinking, although a common feature of vampire lore, is neither sufficient nor necessary to define a vampire, since it is not mentioned at all in a good deal of the reports of vampires. Indeed, some contemporary informants are not even aware that the vampire drinks blood.[51] The vampire's thirst for blood is nevertheless one of its most notable features overall and is perhaps the strongest link between the modern folkloric vampire and pre-Christian mythology.

The symbolism regarding blood is so prevalent in vampire lore as to be almost overwhelming. Not only do vampires drink blood, but red objects (e.g., red thread)[52] are involved in many apotropaic rituals. Alfred Rush notes: "Red was frequently associated with the cult of the dead in pagan antiquity. Red has its origin in the blood sacrifices with which the ancients were wont to appease the spirits of the dead and the gods of the dead."[53] The external appearance of the vampire in Bulgaria is frequently that of a skin filled with blood, whose puncture with a thorn or stake brings about the vampire's demise.

The importance of blood as the life force is universally evident,[54] and the significance of its lack is also well understood. It is the ultimate consequence of blood's draining away—death—that, in Walter Burkert's opinion, leads to sacrifice as a means of interrupting the cycle of ongoing, retaliatory aggression within a society.[55] The need for blood as an animating substance is projected from the human sphere onto the divine, as the life force is "returned" to its source in acts of propitiation.[56] In Greek legends about human sacrifice, "we have a glimpse of deities, especially the earth powers, craving human blood."[57]

At its most primitive level of understanding, then, blood represented both a force and a possession and could be offered, destroyed, or exchanged. In Christian mythology, blood and wine are symbolically bound together, a connection that had been made long before Christ, in the sacramental rituals surrounding Dionysus[58]—a Thracian god. The habit of pouring wine over the grave, a contemporary analogue of which is the Bulgarian burial custom of anointing the dead with wine, was an ancient method of appeasing the dead.[59] In the Balkans, wine played a central role in the feasting that accompanied sacrifice, and its potential to induce ecstasy or at least revelry and abandonment was the reason its consumption was the target of Christian hostility.

Actual blood drinking had been prohibited relatively early in the Jewish tradition, and in Christian times its practice came to symbolize paganism, specifically pagan sacrifice. Drinking blood was first an accusation made by the Romans against the early Christians, whose Eucharist had been interpreted too literally. But as Christianity gained ascendancy, it tried to put as much ritual distance as possible between itself and paganism. Since medieval Orthodox Christians were aware that Jewish law forbade the drinking of blood,[60] and since there is no evidence either that heretical sects ever engaged in blood sacrifice or even that they were accused of doing so,[61] we must conclude that the blood drinking attributed to the vampire is derived from notions about pagans rather than Jews or heretics.

THE VAMPIRE'S APPEARANCE

Although the vampire is usually claimed to be invisible, it is capable of taking on flesh after a certain period,[62] such that it increasingly comes to resemble a human. This "fleshed out" vampire is known in Bulgarian as a *plâtenik, plât* being the Bulgarian word for "flesh."[63] Bulgarian vampires seem to go through a process of "growing up"; that is, they go through definite stages, proceeding from the invisible, through the amorphous, to animal and then to human shape.[64] After death, the vampire begins a process of literal "incarnation," taking on meat but not actual bones[65]—substance without structure and without that part of the body that would remain after decomposition.

Vampires that have roamed the earth undetected or without being destroyed for forty days come to resemble the person they had been before death.[66] In folktales, vampires often marry and move to another city, where they take up the kinds of jobs that vampires frequently occupy, such as butchers, barbers, and tailors. These occupations, naturally, are fraught with danger for the vampire, insofar as the tools of these trades threaten to incise or puncture the vampire's skin, thereby destroying it. (The idea that vampires become barbers and tailors is probably based on an analogy with butchers; the butcher, after all, is the descendant of the sacrifier [Gk. *mageiros*], the person who presided over the slaughter of animal victims of sacrifice.)[67]

The progression from unseen to human is paralleled by an increase in power to do harm; as vampires gradually approximate humans in form, their aggressiveness increases. Younger vampires only drink the blood of animals, and in terms of their shape-shifting ability, they are only able to take on the form of their victim. Early-stage vampires are somewhat narcissistic, thought to feed on their own corpses, until they grow strong enough to attack the human community, when they assume a shape miming the human.

Before it assumes an animal shape, the Bulgarian vampire is characterized most frequently as a "puffed-up bag of blood" that is made of skin. Rather than a nose, he has a sharp snout with a hole through which he sucks blood. Individual reports vary, and the composite image is somewhat contradictory. Sometimes the vampire is like a "buffalo head" or the head of a pig or an ox, which rolls along the countryside. At this point, we should have no difficulty understanding the image of the severed animal head as related to animal sacrifice. More commonly, at this stage of incarnation, the vampire is likened to a *gajda* (a Balkan bagpipe made from a sheep's stomach) that is filled with blood.[68] This puffed-up skin[69] (*mjax*—the same term that is used for the bag of a *gajda*) is highly vulnerable to puncture, an event that causes the blood to flow out and turn into a sort of jellied mass (*pixtija*) resembling coagulating blood. This bag can be easily destroyed by no more than a thorn, specifically a hawthorn, which is thought to have special properties.[70]

The resemblance to the stuffed *gajda* is hardly arbitrary. First of all, this amorphous monster is neither human nor animal but, rather, an incompletely developed simulacrum. Second, the *gajda* is made from the innards of an animal commonly sacrificed at the Turco-Bulgarian feast known as *kurban*. Finally, and most significantly, the *gajda* is a festive instrument, played at weddings and thus symbolizing the feasting component of sacrifice. Music, in late antiquity, had both a necromantic[71] and ecstatic[72] aspect and smacked of paganism.[73] Feasting and sacrifice, it will be recalled, were inextricably linked in the minds of the authors of early Slavic texts against pagans, because of their emphasis on worldly pleasure.[74]

The evolution of the vampire from invisible to amorphous shape to a spitting image[75] of a member of the community also seems to represent a process of "reincorporation." The eventual assumption of human physical characteristics and behavior symbolizes, perhaps, a social-psychological process whereby the blind injustice done to the deceased (insofar as he is held responsible for adversity without due process) is over time rectified, leading to a sort of redemption. The threat to the community posed by the scapegoat's return is offset, in the folklore, by the frequently encountered assertion that the vampire, after he remarries, moves to another town where no one knows him. This is especially true of people who lived good lives but became vampires by accident (e.g., due to a cat jumping over the corpse).

GETTING RID OF VAMPIRES

Apotropaic gestures, including taboos and rituals, are undertaken to prevent someone's becoming a vampire or an "attack" by a vampire, whereas destructive measures may be taken to destroy a vampire. The difference between the two approaches is to be found along the axis ranging from magic to sacrificial ritual. To a certain degree this axis is a continuum, insofar as ritual magic may involve sacrificial activities. There is thus some crossover between "prevention" and "cures." A cure is sought when prevention has failed or has not been considered in time. Prevention, meanwhile, in the case of vampires reduces to a set of ritual observances intended to avoid the incursion of evil into a household or community. Many of the rituals performed around the dead body or immediately around the time of death are intended to eliminate obstacles to the natural departure of the soul from the body. Let us examine in more detail some of the more common ways of destroying a vampire, a task that becomes necessary if precautionary observances are not done or are not done correctly.

Despite the wide variation in technique for destroying a vampire, the methods can be reduced to just a few basic ones: physically incapacitating the vampire, incineration, surrounding the grave with barriers, and transfixing the place of death. The implements and methods vary, and we may consider that incineration is a special and extreme case of incapacitation, while transfixion certainly has things in common with both incapacitation and barrier. These essential techniques cover most of the reports concerning ways of eliminating vampires. Sometimes, the vampire is not destroyed but, rather, led, often by trickery, to another village, which of course is a proper scapegoating procedure. Drowning is akin to incineration and may be seen as a variant of incapacitation. There is some evidence that magical spells (prayers) were used against vampires, but available texts are rare. Special masses may also be said against the vampire.[76]

Physically Incapacitating the Vampire

By far the most common method of disposing of a vampire is mutilation of the corpse. This practice seems to have roots in Balkan prehis-

Fig. 4. Seventeenth-century prayer against the vampire. The text translates: "Immaculate Lordly Mother of God, cleanse the venomous serpent, death, and the witch and the vampire and Satan and all evil force from thy servant of god, now, today, and always." (From "Molitva protiv prokletago vampira," NBKM 273, fol. 72r. Courtesy of Narodna Biblioteka Sv. Kirill i Metodij.)

tory. In Thracian necropolises in northeastern Bulgaria from the second century BC, corpses have been found with amputated limbs, especially with cut-off heels.[77] Additional archeological findings reveal that piercing the heel, forehead, throat, navel, and heart frequently occurred, presumably to eliminate the possibility of the body's return. These actions were taken, in pre-Christian times, not against vampires but against criminals, and it is not clear whether this hobbling was done before or after death, which may have been brought by execution.

Impaling of the body with a wooden or iron stake or spike is the old-est[78] and most widely known method of restraining a vampire, and this action has been interpreted as "separating, pinning and stabbing,"[79] that is, making sure that the body (were it alive) does not have the ability to move from the spot where it has been impaled. We must be careful not to rely too heavily on the meanings associated with the English word *stake,* which do not necessarily translate into a single word in Bulgarian or other languages in the region. In the folklore about vampires, further-more, not only stakes but needles, nails, pins, thorns, and even knives are variously used for essentially the same purpose.[80] Still, one Bulgarian word very commonly used for the device used to kill vampires, *kol,*[81] usu-ally glossed in English as "stake," is the root of the verb *zakolvam,* "to slaughter, kill, butcher." This is the verb most often used in descriptions of *kurbans* and designates the act performed to kill a sheep or pig.[82] The ancient Slavic root shows up in modern Russian in *kolot',* meaning both "to prick" and "to slaughter," and in Old Slavonic in *klati,* which was used to translate the Greek *sphattein,* "to slay by cutting the throat; to slay, slaughter, sacrifice, immolate."[83] Thus, while the denotation of *kol* is clearly that of something for pegging, piercing, or pinning, it is strongly associated with an implement used in slaughter and, in particular, sacri-fice. In some reports, the link between the stake and sacrifice is almost explicit: a red-hot poker can also be used to destroy a vampire.[84]

Amputation, decapitation, and similar violence to the body, while seeming to function as means of preventing the corpse from becoming ambulatory, are also derived from sacrificial practices.[85] Modern Balkan fire-dancing rituals, for example, can be traced to Thracian funerary practices, which involved cremation burials and dismemberment of the corpse.[86] In some folktales about vampires, severed fingers are used as lures for vampires.

> A vampire from Begov was troubling his relations. They took his finger and put it in a sack [*čuval*][87] because vampires like to eat fingers. He went after the person with the finger. They lured him to the river Muresh, where they threw in the sack. The vampire jumped in after the sack and drowned. He was never heard from since.[88]

This vignette of throwing a finger into the water[89] reminds us that vampires are considered very gullible, if not downright stupid, and the willingness of the vampire to jump into the water is a sign of his role as a victim, not unlike an animal victim led to the slaughter.[90] He goes to his death willingly, casting himself into the water and drowning. In Greek religion, following sacrifices dedicated to chthonic divinities, the victim was not eaten (as it was with sacrifices to Ouranian gods) but, rather, disposed of by being thrown into the sea or a river.[91] Curiously, death by drowning constitutes an unnatural death, a bloodless death that can cause the victim to become a vampire. Killing a vampire seems in some cases to require the same methods that are often responsible for producing a vampire: violence or drowning. Incineration, which we shall take up next, may be analogous in this regard to the striking of a grave by lightning, which also causes vampires.[92]

Incineration

The usual view of the practice of incinerating vampires is that it is somehow connected with cremation. To reach such a conclusion, however, it is necessary to view the destruction of the vampire by fire as a sort of second funeral, since cremation is a funerary ritual. Such an assertion must take into account the fact that the official Christian attitude toward cremation was not one of tolerance.[93] Furthermore, it does not explain other methods of eliminating vampires, which do not seem to be connected to funerals or burial per se.

It is certainly true that the practice of cremation, which was common in the Balkans prior to the arrival of the Romans and persisted with the arrival of the Slavs, served to eliminate any traces of the body (except the bones), but it should not be seen as equivalent in function to the sort of incineration that accompanies certain types of sacrifice.[94] In Homeric times, cremation was performed to separate the soul from the body,[95] a motive that is surely not discordant with those of a community attempting to destroy a vampire. Preventing the body from returning, after all, was utmost in the minds of those who set out to stop a vampire from terrorizing the village.

But prevention of the body's literal return must be subordinated to the goal of incineration as it is performed with sacrifice. Destroying the slaughtered victim by fire is a form of both purification and consecration. Immolation by fire is perhaps the central feature of animal sacrifice, having to take place inside a consecrated space so that the act retains its religious character.[96] Indeed, as we turn to the folkloric notions about surrounding the body with barriers, we will see that in fact, these rites serve to consecrate the space where the vampire is "sacrificed."

Surrounding the Grave with Barriers

If a vampire is thought to be frightening a village at night, measures are often taken to inhibit his passage from the grave. Instead of attacking the corpse directly, the space he is presumed to inhabit is confined; barriers of one sort or another circumscribe his movements so that he is in effect neutralized. Such gestures are not the same as destroying the vampire; they are indifferent to the destruction of the body and, from a social point of view, do not involve the same sort of violation of the taboo against digging up corpses. They therefore represent a level of moderation of the scapegoat mechanism.

The most common methods of blocking a vampire's movements involve placing thorns, grains (including grains of sand), or inflammable materials on or near the body or the grave or else pouring various liquids into the grave. These methods are interpreted as having different purposes. The sharp points of thorns are dangerous to vampires because they are capable of rupturing the skin, thereby causing them to leak blood and die. The thorn is selected for use against the vampire not merely because of its ability to prick and draw blood, however, since it is also believed to be efficacious against diseases and evil spirits in general.[97] Not only hawthorn but several other prickly plants, including blackberry and briar, seem to have power against vampires, other demons, magic, and diseases.[98] While the hawthorn has magical properties and in some places is even believed to be the plant from which Jesus' crown of thorns[99] was made, the property of thorniness is in this case valued above the particular species *Crataegus oxyacantha*. The use of hawthorn for apotropaic purposes is widespread in Europe, especially among early Germanic peoples, who threw thorns onto the graves of criminals.[100] Use of thorns to ward off strangers when devils are about is attested even in Bali.[101] However, the significance of hawthorn in particular or of thorns in general in sacrificial ritual is uncertain.[102] Perhaps we should be content with the simplest and most obvious explanation for their use—namely, that hawthorns are perilous and painful.

The sprinkling of grain or sand or similar fine substances around graves is more easily connected to ritual consecration. The folk reasoning behind such actions is that the vampire is obliged—under what compelling force is never stated—to count the grains or seeds before he can emerge from his grave and that by the time he finishes, the sun will have risen, preventing the vampire from climbing out.[103] Again, we see the assumption of the gullibility or stupidity of the vampire.[104] The scattering of grain is a ritual act that was connected with sacrifice in ancient times. A Babylonian text details the sacrifice of a bull, which involved scattering grain and offering breads and libations.[105] We might add, in this regard, that offering bread[106] and pouring libations are both effective techniques for restraining vampires. In one tale, warm bread wrapped in a cloth and put into a red bag was left on the outskirts of town as an offering, to lure the vampire out of the village.[107] Meanwhile, in Bulgarian folklore, libations take the form of pouring hot liquids (usually wine or oil, sometimes water)[108] over or into the grave of the suspected vampire. Among nomadic peoples, who did not build permanent temples and altars where their sacrifices would be performed, sprinkling grain in a circle around a sacrificial victim was a common method of creating a temporary consecrated space. Scattering barley was an obligatory part of Greek *thusia,* a generic animal sacrifice accompanied by feasting, libation, and singing and dancing.[109] The scattering of barley in fact constituted an act of prayer. The notion that the vampire was compulsively obliged to count the grains is in all likelihood a folk etiology, since the religious component of the action had been lost to time.[110]

Thorns of whatever genus placed around the grave are sometimes incinerated with a torch. Other easily inflammable materials (e.g., cotton, hemp, or even matches and gunpowder) can be placed around the vampire as safeguards. (Sometimes these materials are actually placed in the vampire's belt or in the nostrils, eyes, and ears of the corpse.) Red thread is also sometimes used to surround the grave site. These materials are sometimes burned but at other times simply left, "just in case." The pragmatic explanation, naturally, would be that these materials would burn up the vampire and thus constitute a threat of autocremation.

However, there is a clear antecedent for this in ritual sacrifice as well. Fires made from branches were used in Roman sacrifices—for example, during the purificatory Parilia festival in early April.

> Shepherds purified the flocks by sprinkling and sweeping the fold, and by driving the sheep through fires of straw and olive and laurel branches. Millet cakes, baskets of millet, pails of milk, and other food were offered to Pales, a vague, impersonal vegetation power, for aversion of all harm that might come from unwitting sacrilege, such as trespass on sacred ground, disturbing sacred springs, or misuse of boughs of sacred trees. Then milk and heated wine were mixed in a bowl and drunk until the drinkers were intoxicated enough to leap over burning heaps of branches.[111]

In this single ritual—and there are other examples—we encounter grain, libation, and purification by means of brush fires, all strongly analogous to the methods recommended for hedging a vampire in his grave.

Transfixing the Place of Death

Less frequently relied on for eliminating a vampire or preventing his movement are actions taken around the place of death for the person who has become a vampire. These techniques tend to be used when the person has died an unnatural death, outside the house. In some cases, after the body has been moved from the house, a nail is driven into the spot where the deceased's head had been, and above it an ax is placed, "to frighten the soul that it won't return to the house."[112] The location of death has special properties, as if the soul is somehow still attached or attracted to it. In addition to the nail and ax, also placed at the location of death are stones and the now familiar ball of red thread.[113] Sometimes an egg is broken above the place of death, which seems to be a sort of libation and offering.

SUMMARY

The folklore about the vampire in the Balkans and surrounding areas is varied and highly syncretic. Elements of Christian, Islamic, and Judaic beliefs have merged with atavistic beliefs carried over from pre-

Christian times. The history of the Balkans is such that invasion and migration over many centuries have yielded a rich tradition of materials concerning notions about those dead who, by accident or by moral stature, return to life and intrude on the living. The Bulgarian vampire lies at the center, both in time and space, of a complex of similar or equivalent demons with various names in the former Yugoslavia, Albania, Romania, Greece, Hungary, and parts of southern Russia and Ukraine.

Despite the wide variation in the details of the ethnographic reports, vampire folklore across the Balkan and Carpathian region is fairly consistent in its depiction of the vampire as an entity around which are performed various apotropaic and destructive rituals. Even more consistent is the idea that the vampire's presence in a community is detectable by his effects and that he is invariably a threat. The vampire serves as an etiological factor behind visible events requiring an explanation, and ritualized group aggression against the vampire serves to alleviate collective anxiety by making of the vampirized corpse a scapegoat.

Various means have been devised for naming and categorizing the various types of mythological beings that are similar to vampires. It has long been suspected that the vampire embodies many pre-Christian elements, but in the search for those, researchers have been led to posit such vague origins for the vampire as that it is simply "Indo-European,"[114] a conclusion that is in some ways true but that adds nothing to the discussion. Etymologically inclined researchers, meanwhile, have grappled with the strange word *vampir* and its cognates, wrongly projecting onto reconstructed phonological prototypes semantic content derived from the modern (and indeed literary) understanding of the vampire. It has apparently been difficult for those interested in the vampire to interpret the scant early data without reference to the contemporary notion of the vampire as a supernatural entity, a demon.

Starting from the premise that the vampire serves primarily as a cause that can be attached to certain anomalous phenomena, and taking a cue from the evident relationship between vampires and such persecuted groups as witches and magicians, we are led to the conclusion that the early history of the vampire was a by-product of the more general process of selecting and incorporating certain beliefs into the canon of Orthodoxy, while rejecting those that undermined either the theological or economic basis of Christianity and its ecclesiastical hierarchy.

Orthodox Christianity from late antiquity through the Middle Ages expressed open hostility to any group that opposed or subverted its teachings and political thrust.

There is little doubt that early in the history of the word *vampir,* its meaning was tied closely to heresy. Because of this, we expect to find dualistic elements in the folklore. However, the preponderance of ritual elements in the folklore—apotropaics, methods of destruction, ways of becoming a vampire—cannot be explained simply by reference to the Bogomils, Paulicians, or other heretical dualist groups in the Balkans. These groups were ideologically and philosophically opposed to formal ritual.

We have seen that blood sacrifice, which was practiced by the ancient Thracians and in all likelihood by the Slavs, survives in modern Bulgaria and among other Orthodox Balkan groups, in the form of a type of feast known as *kurban.* Sacrifice has been retained there despite official and long-lived Christian hostility, in part due to Islamic religious practice over five hundred years of the Ottoman occupation of Bulgaria. Its continuing importance suggests an unresolved conflict between canonical Orthodoxy and the "traditional religion" based on earlier pagan beliefs and rituals. Out of this conflict, in turn, has emerged a large body of folklore expressing great ambivalence about opposite notions of the afterlife and about divine retribution. The folklore about the vampire also reveals ambivalence about the social injustice of marginalizing or pejoratively labeling certain groups or the practices belonging to those groups. The selection of an unfeeling corpse for a scapegoat is nevertheless an attempt to attenuate the sort of cruelty that occurred in the West during the Inquisition against witches.

I have now examined in some detail many of the more common ritual elements that appear in vampire folklore, dating back at least to the sixteenth century. The working assumption has been that the symbolic elements that have previously been so resistant to interpretation in fact form a more or less coherent system, if looked at through the lens of Christian opposition to certain beliefs and practices. Antecedents for many gestures and objects mentioned in the ethnographic data may be found by looking at ancient customs surrounding blood sacrifice in the Balkans and nearby regions (especially Greece). Notions about heretics and Jews and about other individual apostates, such as suicides and criminals, also make a contribution to the system of folkloric details, but sacrificial ritual clearly predominates as the epitome of pagan and, by extension, anti-Christian behavior.

What, if anything, does this tell us about the essence of the vampire? First, it shows that the scapegoat function of the vampire is traceable to Christian hostility toward pagans before heretics. The link between the vampire and heresy is a later phenomenon, resulting from an extension of the semantic range of the word *vampir,* provoked by the displacement of pagans by heretics as targets of Christian polemic. But beyond that, by understanding that many of the ritual elements in vampire folklore are of a "pagan" nature, we can understand a kind of reparation through which the Bulgarian peasants might pay respect to those who had been outcast for holding on to their traditional beliefs. They paid this respect by conferring on the abject vampires the benefits of their own rituals: performance of sacrifice as a form of consecration was the Christianized Bulgarian's way of sending those who did not subscribe to Christian eschatology into the otherworld.

5

INTO THE WEST

From Folklore to Literature

The early history of the vampire concept is both complex and vague, in part because the term *vampir* itself goes back to a time when a Slavic writing system had only been codified for less than one or two hundred years and was used primarily for biblical texts and Orthodox Christian teachings. The earliest surviving written use of the term appears in a context no more revealing than a marginal annotation to an eleventh-century East Slavic translation of Old Testament prophetic books. Any evidence we have for earlier use appears in later transcriptions of earlier documents and is thus already suspect.[1] The etymology of the term, meanwhile, remains of necessity fairly speculative, even though it has hopefully now been rescued from a tendency on the part of linguists to erroneously project contemporary semantics onto an ancient word (or, more likely, phrase [see the appendix]).

While there can be no certain claim regarding what or whom the word *vampir* originally designated, it should at this point be clear that the first "vampires" were not at all supernatural entities, shape-shifters, or any sort of mythological or demonic beings. Over the long history of the vampire, there has been an evolution in the meaning of the term, from an epithet, to a folkloric figure, to, finally, the familiar literary and cinematic character. Does this shift mean that the vampire of today has nothing in common with its ancient Slavic ancestor, or, on the contrary, can we say that despite the external changes in the vampire's "personal characteristics," there is a basic functional meaning that survives the external cultural changes from a primarily agrarian religious society to a primarily urban and secular one? In order to answer this question, it is important to understand what cultural and historical factors might have motivated the processes of folklorization and, later, literary and cinematic adaptation of folklore.

THE EVOLUTION OF *VAMPIR*

Although it has been ignored in virtually all discussions of the vampire's history, the fact is that the word *vampir* emerged in a context of religious conflict in the Balkans. As I indicated in the last chapter, its meaning at the time reflected the attitudes of one religious group, Orthodox Christians, toward another, so-called pagans—namely, those indigenous adherents of agrarian polytheism (so-called animism, a now deprecated term) who refused to relinquish easily their beliefs and, more important, their rituals, in the face of the advancing hegemony of Byzantine Orthodoxy. Put simply, *vampir* was at first a pejorative label for certain people, perhaps settled Slavs, who continued to practice initiatory or sacrificial rites that were deemed by the Christian proselytizers during the time of the first Bulgarian Empire to be worthy of condemnation. I have suggested elsewhere[2] that the rituals in question may have been associated with a belief in reincarnation (which was a central tenet of Thracian shamanism),[3] but such an assertion is admittedly highly speculative. Still, the eventual connection of the vampire with literal reincarnation, in the form of folklore about people who have returned from the dead and been reanimated, becomes easier to understand if we consider the intolerance of Christianity toward those who would not accept the Orthodox view of time, the afterlife, and the nature of the soul's journey.[4]

In any case, the essential behavioral qualification of the first vampires was ritual practice that was unacceptable to Christians. Whereas private religious beliefs are not themselves visible, performance of particular rituals is generally an outward sign of membership in a particular group, and in the case of the vampire, that group—however loosely defined—was inherently opposed to and by Orthodox Christianity. It is this otherness, seen politically as resistance to a powerful universalizing force sweeping the Balkans from the end of the ninth century, that represents all we really know about the first "vampires." Such information as what these people (as a group in the broadest possible sense) actually believed, what they practiced, how many of them there were, or even how they might have defined themselves ethnically is for now lost or at least not unequivocally clear. It is probably the case that the term *vampir* was originally not very widespread, for otherwise its frequency in written documents from around the tenth or eleventh century or even later would be much greater. It is also likely that the term did not refer to members of a well-defined cult or group; rather, it may have been a shorthand way of designating certain types of people, who had in common merely the fact that they were not easily persuaded of the benefits of adopting the expanding Christian worldview (political as well as religious). Thus, vampires were at the lower end of the social power scale as Christianity became the dominant and official religion of the Bulgarians. This lower social position of the vampire is retained in most Balkan folklore even into the twentieth century, but with the absorption, in the West, of the vampire as a literary symbol in the early nineteenth century, when the vampire became associated with corrupt nobility,[5] the relative social position of the vampire appears to change.

Polytheism, as we know, was eventually obliterated throughout Europe with the expansion of Christianity. The mechanisms for accomplishing this political feat, which began as early as the conversion of Constantine, ranged from outright persecution and even execution of those refusing to acknowledge the one Christian God to a remodeling of pagan religious beliefs and practices in terms that were less offensive to Christian theologians and clergy. Thus, according to a very widespread and well-known process, cult gods tended to be either absorbed into the company of saints or else associated with the host of satanic demons, while seasonally defined agrarian holidays were recast in a Christian frame.

After the last vestiges of the indigenous and transferred pre-Christian religions disappeared throughout Europe, dualist heretical groups emerged as an even greater threat to the stability of Christianity. Meanwhile, the accusation of vampirism, earlier directed at pagans, was now redirected at the heretics, who, I have already noted, were in many ways more insidious and potentially more subversive. Since the dualist sects in the Balkans in the tenth century and later had no ideological commitment to a ritual canon—they viewed ritual as materialistic and therefore false and, unlike the pagans, claimed at the same time to be Christians—their anti-imperial and anti-ecclesiastical message represented a source of potentially subversive confusion for illiterate Balkan villagers.

The later association of vampirism with heresy is somewhat less obscure than its association with paganism. As was mentioned in chapter 3, in medieval Russia a synonym of the Russian word *eretik* was *upyr'*, "vampire." The South Slavic designation *vampir*, meanwhile, became increasingly pejorative: it seems to have begun as just an epithet for a particular anathematized group, but with the expansion of the term to include heretics, it picked up an attributive connotation of "evil." However, since heretics were not thought to be supernatural—they were certainly real enough, perhaps too real—the name *vampire* still did not refer to anything folkloric.

Several of the general accusations brought against heretics were similar in substance to those leveled earlier against pagans, which, not so ironically, were in turn the same as the outrageous accusations against early Christians by pagans prior to the conversion of the Roman Empire to Christianity. The claims included such horrific accusations as orgiastic child murder and infant sacrifice and blood drinking (a fantasy that shows up even in Bram Stoker's *Dracula*). So while the term was still being applied to living humans whose beliefs were not at all well understood by the local Orthodox clergy, its meaning was subtly being modified to suggest a connection with Satan and with evil. Then, as the term *vampir* began to lose its connection to actual religious practice, the mooring of the word to definable groups with particular religious beliefs was being loosened as well. Concomitantly, the word became stabilized in its broadest definition as someone for whom the church held enmity.

The Vampire as Symbol

The historical-semantic stepping-stones I have just used to cross rather quickly from the putative first uses of the word *vampir* in ancient Bulgaria to the contemporary interpretations of the vampire are widely spaced and somewhat slippery. For evidence to support this reasoning about a hypothesized process of folklorization, I have brought forth only a handful of citations of the word *vampire* in a handful of vague (at best) contexts spread out over centuries.[6] Nevertheless, it is indisputable not only that the common meaning of the word *vampire* has changed significantly between the endpoints of its origin and today but also that the semantic changes occurred gradually, over the course of centuries, and took place alongside major cultural and historical shifts of which some record persists. Whereas the details of this argument are perhaps open to challenge, it is reasonable to suppose that the mutation of the meaning of the simple attributive term *vampire* into a folkloric *nomina agentis* was prompted by the gradual disappearance of the original referents and contexts.

This is effectively a process of symbolization, occurring after the term *vampire* no longer possessed any definable social referent, and precisely this strong vector of the vampire as a symbol leads all the way to such recent attempts to explain or decipher the contemporary vampire phenomenon as Auerbach's *Our Bodies, Ourselves* (1995) or Rob Latham's *Consuming Youth* (2001). It might not be so critical to insist on this process of symbolization were it not for such incessant absurd claims as that the vampire is some lower mythological archetype from ancient Egypt or, worse, a proto-Indo-European demon. Failure to recognize the politico-religious roots of the term is a serious blind spot obscuring the deepest sense of the ambiguous role of the vampire across its long history. While Western scholars have gradually been able to articulate the power politics lurking beneath centuries of Western European witchcraft and its persecution at the hands of the clergy, there has been no similar attempt to understand the East European vampire as functionally, perhaps even economically, homologous.

Until the early eighteenth century, the domain of the vampire was restricted for all practical purposes to East and South Slavic regions,[7] primarily the Balkans—an area that from the late fourteenth century

had been under the yoke of the Ottoman Empire. Over those inter-
vening centuries, references to vampires increased in frequency from
Bulgaria and Macedonia to Serbia and Bosnia, but there is no record
of the word outside Slavic regions until 1679, and it is found then only
in a discussion of the Greek Orthodox Church by an English author
named Paul Rycaut.[8] In Bulgaro-Macedonian reports, vampires become more and more folkloric in their nature, and the characteristics
attributed to these quasi-demons begin to increase in their resemblance to those associated with the familiar folkloric vampire of later
centuries. Furthermore, while references to the vampire before the
fourteenth century are found only in Christian polemic, the context
becomes more secular in succeeding centuries. Vampires are mentioned, for example, in pseudo-Christian magical "prayers" of the
early seventeenth century, by which time vampires are quite clearly
considered demonic and supernatural—there is no suggestion that
vampires are natural living beings.

As the vampire changes from an anathematized individual to a folkloric entity with no objective correlative in the actual world, he also
comes to epitomize all that is considered unnaturally dangerous or
anathematic. During this period of folklorization, the vampire acquires
the now essential attributes of being a nocturnal animated corpse who
is known only by the evident effects of his actions: inexplicably sick or
dead livestock, breakage and loss of household property, intractable or
painful disease, and so forth. The vampire's nocturnal aspect excuses his
invisibility: in Bulgarian folklore, for example, the period between the
first hours after midnight until dawn (usually designated by cockcrow,
reminding us of the vampire's agrarian background) is referred to as *lošo
vreme,* "the evil time." In the Balkan village of earlier centuries—and to
some extent even now—there is a strong taboo against going out of the
house during this darkest time, which of course is also the time when
the entire village is supposed to be asleep. As a being that comes out of
the grave during this period, the vampire not only violates a taboo,
which renders him liable for retribution communal or divine, but also
becomes responsible for destructive actions for which there are no eye-
witnesses.[9] This anonymity means that an invisible cause—that is, the
vampire—can be provisionally assigned to a visible effect, and further
assignment of the cause to a specific (dead) individual can proceed in

good time. The vampire can be instantiated when a suitable candidate can be found.

In the village setting, the usefulness of an unseen, but clearly guilty, vampire should be obvious: in a society lacking an extensive tort code and where neighbors must often depend on each other's help for provisioning in the face of unpredictable natural occurrences, there is very good reason to avoid direct accusation of other (living) members of the community when guilt is not unambiguous. In the absence of any officially sanctioned group—such as heretics—on whom it is possible to heap blame with impunity, the now purely folkloric vampire seems to fill that slot quite adequately. Furthermore, the presumed devilish unnaturalness of the vampire means that virtually any activity can be ascribed to him, and any collective reaction can consequently be justified. Collective attacks on a deceased and buried member of the community, in the form of exhuming a corpse and performing some act of ritual mutilation, are well documented, though certainly not to the same extent that the executions of supposed witches were recorded in the West.

By the middle of the seventeenth century, the types of accusations against vampires found in various Balkan writings are essentially the same as those cited in reports of vampire "epidemics" brought into the southern regions of the Habsburg Empire in the beginning of the eighteenth century. There is, perhaps, one notable difference: the notion still popular in the West that vampires beget other vampires (e.g., by biting) is not attested in Bulgarian folklore. Rather, this feature seems to have achieved a special importance when the vampire "crossed over" from the land of Orthodoxy into the land of Counter-Reformation Roman Catholicism and Protestantism. In Slavic folklore, the vampire may have some connection with personified disease, a link that goes back even to the eleventh century, but the idea that a vampire is caused by another vampire seems to occur only rather late and only in a region relatively close to the border with Hungary.[10]

The history of this notion of the contagious vampire is unclear, but if we trace the sources of the belief in Western literary works, it would seem that the idea emerged alongside an increasing Enlightenment tendency to discover rational causes behind all kinds of phenomena, including epidemic diseases and so-called supernatural events. In addition to the vampire's contagiousness, of critical importance for Westerners contemplating the vampire was the notion that the corpse did not decompose, and this, were it true in the least, would require a good deal of explanation. One passage that was influential in forming the Western conception of the vampire is from the anonymously authored *Travels of 3 English Gentlemen from Venice to Hamburg, Being the Grand Tour of Germany in the Year 1734* (not actually published until 1810, nine years before John Polidori's *The Vampyre*).

> And, though they have been much longer dead than many other bodies, which are putrefied, not the least mark of corruption is visible upon them. Those who are destroyed by them, after their death, become Vampyres; so that, to prevent so spreading an evil, it is found requisite to drive a stake through the dead body, from whence, on this occasion, the blood flows as if the person was alive.[11]

Here we have a brief report, in English, of the vampire epidemics that occurred in the 1730s in northwestern Serbia (present-day Slovenia), which caused such a stir in the West (primarily Austria) that journalists and physicians felt obliged to investigate and report on them. These well-known cases of vampire hysteria are widely discussed elsewhere,[12] and there is no need to recount them in great detail here. However, it is worth observing that these historical events have attracted much more attention from Western vampire writers and scholars than has earlier testimony about the vampire in the Balkans, in part because the Slavic documentation has not been very accessible. As a consequence, even fairly recent serious books on the subject, when discussing possible "origins" of the vampire myth, tend to look back in time no further than the eighteenth century, while even well-known linguists have consciously ignored etymological evidence from the eleventh century because it did not conform to modern beliefs about vampires.

I believe this general inability to see the political and religious underpinnings of vampire narratives, especially in the folklore, is closely linked to the vampire's invisibility or ability to shift his shape. The unambiguousness of the vampire's monstrosity is what confers on villagers armed with antivampire paraphernalia the right to go out in the middle of the night and, against the vocal urgings of the parish priest and certainly against common sense, exhume and then "murder" a corpse. The presumption of guilt, applied to an immobile—and thus, in all likelihood, innocent—corpse, is required to unify the aggressive actions of the villagers in a forever-secret bond—any doubt, any sense that the sleeping body might itself have been a victim of unjust cruelty would tend to subvert the execution of this collective violence and thereby block the functioning of the scapegoat mechanism. From the time of the vampire's very origins, the attitude of the local Christian populace was that the inherent guilt justifying the vampire's abjection—guilt of paganism, of heresy, and later of suicide and anathema—was absolute, a condition of its very nature, and needed no further discussion. The evident inability of the community to see the other side of the coin, to imagine, for example, that condemnation or excommunication of a fellow villager might have proceeded too quickly or without due process, has been an integral part of the vampire story from the beginning.

This same obscuration seems to be at work in the contemporary tendency to regard the vampire as purely demonic and, in turn, to assert that folkloric vampire narratives derive from, for example, some general ignorance on the part of poor illiterate East European peasants who simply had no other way of explaining why corpses dug up from shallow graves by hungry wolves showed signs of lividity.[13] In other words, the general refusal of Western scholars to try to understand the ritual nexus of vampire belief—a basis that is actually clear even in Bram Stoker's *Dracula,* where the plot is full of apotropaics and taboos and gestures for blocking or dispatching a vampire—represents the same complacency that characterizes the scapegoat mechanism.

In actuality, *Dracula* is clear about the vampire in other ways that seem to have been obscured over time by this same mechanism. The novel's subtext can be read as the historical translation of vampire beliefs from Eastern Europe (according to Stoker, Transylvania, which lies within modern-day Hungary and Romania) to Western Europe (specifically, England). Count Dracula's purpose in changing his place of residence is to move from the mountain village where his castle is located to an urban center: "I long to go through the crowded streets of your mighty London, to be in the midst of the whirl and rush of humanity, to share its life, its change, its death, and all that makes it what it is."[14] This fictional translocation mimics precisely the historical transfer of the vampire's epicenter from the agrarian Orthodox Balkan village to the urban complexes of Enlightenment Austria, Hungary, France, Germany, and, of course, England. This is not to say that the folkloric vampire ceased to exist in his homeland as the idea of the vampire was picked up by Western European societies with otherwise little or no general interest either in Orthodoxy or South Slavic culture. Indeed, more or less uncorrupted vampire lore persists even to this day in small Turkish family communities called *maxalas* in Bulgaria and Macedonia.[15] But in Eastern Europe, the vampire as a folkloric entity never held the enormous mass appeal that is responsible for the continuous retellings, in many different forms, of *Dracula* and other literary vampire narratives in the West. It is almost as if the change of context enabled the vampire to survive and grow stronger, by providing him with a new, metaphoric function, while further obscuring the folklore's roots in collective violence and social inequity. Another way of putting this is that in Bulgaria and other South Slavic countries, the vampire is thought of as only one member of a whole system of lower mythological "demons" and spirits that were not entirely expunged by Orthodoxy, and therefore the vampire is never particularly exotic. In Western European culture, where there was a more comprehensive and effective attempt to push all traces of pre-Christian religion underground—except, perhaps, at certain bounded times (e.g., Halloween)—the vampire's incursion provoked a true fascination with the return of the abject or the repressed.

THE VAMPIRE COMES TO EUROPE

The most succinct chronology for the introduction of vampire beliefs into Western Europe is in Katharina Wilson's review of various hypotheses about the migration of the word *vampire*. Thus, the Slavic folkloric vampire came into the consciousness of the Germans in 1721, the French in 1737, and the Austrians in 1725. The belletristic use of the term, although it is encountered in Germany as early as 1748 and treated more fully by Goethe in 1797, only became broad following the 1820 translation, into French, of Polidori's *The Vampyre* (which became popular in part because it was originally published under Lord Byron's name). If we look more closely at the migration of the vampire concept from Slavic into Germanic and Romanic lands and languages, it appears that mention of the vampire in the West before the epidemic years (1725–32) is sporadic and not particularly detailed, while from 1725 forward—especially after 1732, when there occurred in Serbia something of a famous hysteria surrounding the late, yet animate, Arnold Paul (Paole)—there is a pattern of reportage that seeks first to detail this curious lore and then to debunk it.

The Hungarian historian Gábor Klaniczay has noted the coincidence of the rise of vampire scandals and the height of witch persecution in the Habsburg Empire at the beginning of the eighteenth century. Witch hysteria came to Hungary relatively late, the first waves occurring in the 1720s, a century after reaching their peak in Germany, France, England, and Spain.[16] Fourteen witches were burned following a trial in Szeged in 1728, and over the next forty years, 450 witches were tried in Hungary. Despite the increasing persecution of witches, Empress Maria Theresa adopted several measures to outlaw any form of witch hunting. Although her legislation was modeled on similar moves to block witch hunts in France (1682) and Germany (1728), it was actually the attention brought by a case of vampirism in Hermersdorf, Moravia, in 1755 that first provoked the empress to issue a decree forbidding "posthumous magic" and, a year later, the Imperial and Royal Law Designed to Uproot Superstition and to Promote the Rational Judgment of Crimes Involving Magic and Sorcery. Aside from the gender of the vampire, the case itself was not unusual, as far as eighteenth-century vampire tales go.

> [T]he corpse of Rosina Polakin, deceased a few months previously, was exhumed by municipal decision, because people were complaining that she was a vampire and had attacked them at night. Her body was found to be in good condition (as befits vampires), without any signs of decomposition, and with blood still present in the veins. According to local custom, the poor family of the deceased was forced to drag the corpse, by means of a hook attached to a rope, through an opening made in the wall of the graveyard, to be beheaded and burnt outside.[17]

As can be inferred from the details of this story and from the title of Maria Theresa's imperial law, the Enlightenment attitude toward accusations of witchcraft and sorcery—and, by extension, vampirism—was one of intolerance. Such beliefs, in the Habsburg view, were clearly rooted in the superstitious past and were hopelessly irrational. In advance of issuing her decree, Maria Theresa sent her court physician, an erudite scholar named Gerard van Swieten, to Hermersdorf to determine what should be her appropriate response to the tale of Polakin. Upon his return, this Dutch physician recommended utter elimination of any form of criminal justice that was grounded in such "superstition."[18]

Earlier investigators from the West (the French Jesuit Dom Calmet in 1746, the Austrian physician Flückinger in 1732, and several other scholars during that significant decade) were concerned to describe for their audiences, whether common, ecclesiastical, or royal, a supernatural curiosity from neighboring Turkish-held Slavic regions.[19] These reporters were generally quick to raise serious doubts as to the possibility of animated corpses, a folkloric notion that until then had no clear precedent in Roman Catholic and Protestant countries. In East and South Slavic regions, any question of the actuality of the vampire was moot, since the folkloric vampire represented above all a mode of village justice in ambiguous cases where having an unknown agent was intolerable. The identity of the vampire was always either inferred from the visible residue of his activity or determined by a designated expert[20] (to which I shall return in the next chapter), and the closure to any vampire "attack" lay in the possibility of punishing a corpse. Thus, the events for which the vampire was held responsible were real, as was the possibility—sometimes carried out, more often merely discussed—of taking a violent, ritualized, restraining action against a corpse. Since the vampire was already dead, furthermore, there was no need to worry about the legality or outcome of any proceedings against him.

The functional aspect of the vampire within an extralegal system of blame and punishment and its homology with that of the Western witch were apparently not recognized by those who were intent on looking at the phenomenon from a purely rationalistic point of view. It was incumbent on the rationalist scientists, coming away from centuries of horrifically unjust persecution and torture of so-called witches, to refute any argument by any authorities that vampires could exist by any supernatural causes. Therefore, accounts of vampire events are often filled with "eyewitness" details about the corpse's state of decomposition (or lack thereof): it was precisely to these pathophysiological phenomena that the medical establishment of the time responded with speculation about their physical or medical causes. It was also at this point that the vampire accounts in areas close to Hungary and Austria began to involve trials[21] that challenged the validity of claims based on magical or supernatural events.

We have no proof that a contagious etiology of the vampire, which is clearly present in Flückinger's 1732 account of Serbian vampire epidemics,[22] originates only within this context. But the premise that a vampire victim in turn becomes a vampire does not seem to occur in vampire folklore in the Balkans, where there is no possibility of interference on the part of Western investigators. In predominantly Slavic Orthodox settings, the way in which a vampire may come into being is always an unnatural or violent death, the deceased's moral choices while alive, or some accidental interference in the funerary process (with the presumed disturbing consequences of any of these endings for the soul on its path to the otherworld). The meaning of the vampire in its native cultural context is inextricably linked to the stable arrangement of categories defining the natural order and the boundaries between it and the afterlife (the otherworld, in Slavic terms), only the disruption of which results in a vampire. Within such a system, there would be no purpose in devising further, epidemic reasons for the presence of vampires.

Such a purpose might be sought, however, in a culture where the logics of cause and effect, accusation and due process, were considered the most potent antidotes to hysterical accusations. Epidemics of vampires, perceived from abroad as mass delusions, might certainly occur when the underlying belief system, in which a vampire may only be instantiated according to one of the three causes cited earlier, is unrecognized, on the one hand, and distorted by a need to shift blame, on the other. Thus, analogously, during the Inquisition, those confronted with accusations of witchcraft could sometimes get off the hook by naming those who supposedly indoctrinated them or else caused others to become witches by casting spells. This multiplicative effect not only provided grist for the Inquisitors' legal mill but also led to localized chain reactions that could be characterized as epidemics.

It is the contact of Eastern European vampire beliefs with Western witchcraft beliefs, I propose, that geminates the notion that vampires, like witches or sorcerers, can themselves bring other vampires into existence. As vampire folklore became known in Western Europe, an analogy from witchcraft trials spread into vampire folklore in the form of an Inquisition-like chain of incrimination: vampires were caused by other vampires. Compounding this view was a sort of medical materialism that tended to interpret outbreaks of vampire reports as a sort of epidemic. As rationalist explanations of the phenomena behind the received vampire tales became increasingly necessary to prevent the recrudescence, in Western Europe, of social inequities based on unprovable accusations of supernaturalism, the vampire subtly and invisibly changed from a demonic being in an agrarian folklore system into something that was now (for lack of a better word) a metaphor.

6

SEERS AND SLAYERS

In chapter 4, I pointed out that the vampire's appearance can range from invisible to amorphous to ordinary. In some regions, the shape of the vampire is simply one or the other of these. In others, however, these forms in fact correspond to vicissitudes of maturity as the vampire "survives" his time as a revenant without being dispatched. Minimally, this period lasts forty days, but it is often a year. As Evgenija Miceva points out, in Bulgarian folklore there seems to be a pattern whereby the more defined (and humanlike) the vampire's features become, the more dangerous he is and the more destructive and violent are his actions.[1] What these three phases of "vampirization" or "fleshing out" have in common is that there is no time at which the vampire can be distinctly recognized as a demon or monster by an ordinary conscious individual.

When the vampire is in his invisible state, he is capable of visiting his widow in her dreams and having sexual relations with her, which almost invariably leads to pregnancy (it is usually the otherwise inexplicable pregnancy that retrospectively tips the village off to the presence of the vampire). Vampires at the other end of the evolutionary spectrum can impregnate as well: when they acquire a mimetic human shape (albeit without a skeleton!), they are thought to move to another village, where they may take up with another woman and even raise a family.[2]

It is only during the middle, amorphous stage that vampires do not appear to have intimate encounters with humans. The puffed-up skins filled with black blood or a bloody jelly known as *pixtija* are only seen at a distance, tumbling across the hillside in the twilight or moon-light—they are not seen during the day. Vampires fear the light, and during the day, they are supposed to be back in their graves.

Although it is never stated explicitly in the individual narratives, it is clearly the third sort of vampire, the one that closely resembles the living human, that is most insidious and poses the greatest threat to the village, at least during the time before he has moved to another village. Such a translocation, by the way, indicates the completion of the scape-goat cycle. In the Old Testament tradition (Leviticus 16:8), the goat in-tended for Azazel is taken out of the village into the desert, the de-monic, undifferentiated world, carrying with it whatever uncleanness it has been saddled with. The transfer of the expiatory sacrificial victim, the scapegoat, to the desert is equivalent to sending it back in time, that is, into the demonic and animistic world that predated Judaic monotheism. Recall that in the Leviticus story, there are two goats: one is sacrificed for the community of Israelites; the other is sent to Azazel, a pre-Judaic deity. Uncleanness and defilement are thus appropriate for the unclean world. Once again the scapegoat is linked to the tension between monotheism and paganism (with its demand for expiatory sacrifice). What is critical in this lesson is that the goat leave the com-munity. Violence and destruction are not mandatory, so long as the un-cleanness is removed from the community permanently.

This is also true of the vampire: once he has moved to another vil-lage, he is no longer a problem, unless, of course, he for some reason returns. He takes his marked status with him. His self-imposed exile or gullible expulsion constitutes a kind of expiation or redemption: his re-turn to human form elsewhere is no longer of concern; the local anxi-eties have been quelled.[3] Whether or not the vampire is still anathema becomes moot, and no further action is required—not even alarming the neighboring village to the intrusion of a vampire in their midst.

Although it is primarily when the vampire becomes truly mimetic of the human that the skills of someone who can recognize him for what he is are necessary, vampires of the first two types also need to be destroyed or, at the very least, prevented from wreaking further havoc. A vampire can be recognized in one of two ways: either ritually or by means of a seer, someone with second sight who can identify these otherwise invisible or indistinguishable beings.

Recognition of a vampire by ritual means is possible when there is little ambiguity about who the local vampire might be. In villages of no more than a few thousand people, under normal environmental circumstances unnatural deaths are rare. By unnatural is meant here any death that results in some interference with the performance of canonical burial rites. Therefore, any evidence of a vampire attack occurring within, say, forty days of an unnatural death will point unequivocally to that recently deceased person as the aggressive vampire. Everyone in the village would be aware that the local priest had declined to say the usual mass for the dead (as in the case of suicides), and thus recognition of the vampire would be universal, requiring no special skill.

Vampires can also arise from natural deaths, however. In such cases, it is the funerary process that is somehow disturbed. By far the most common cause of a vampire in contemporary folklore is the random ritual infelicity of a cat or animal jumping over the corpse while it is lying in state, usually in the very house where the person has died. In such cases, the association is between evidence of a vampire attack and a recent death that was otherwise natural, except for the postmortem intrusion into the sacred space around the deceased's body. The apparent coincidence of a quite recent death and posthumous evidence is also enough to peg someone as a vampire even if he seemingly died of natural causes. In both of these cases, the identification of the vampire is easy and nearly unanimous. Although perhaps no one actually saw the cat jump over the body (perhaps whoever was supposed to stay awake to guard the body fell asleep or left the room during the night), a presumption can be made that this nevertheless must have happened if, in the following days, a vampire attack occurred, especially in or near the same house.

When the identification of the vampire is unambiguous, the villagers can take preemptive action without further consideration. For example, vigilante groups of (usually) men,[4] having identified the guilty vampire, may plan to assemble late at night, during *lošo vreme* (the evil time), and proceed to his grave, there to perform whatever dreadful actions are necessary to prevent his return. The local priest is usually left out of these posses, in part because it would put him in the difficult social position of having to express Christian abhorrence at the defilement of the dead, on the one hand, and of condoning evil, on the other. Theologically, the priest must always come down on the side of permitting the destruction of the vampire rather than reversing the possible injustice of not performing a rite over the dead—unless certain "neutralizing" actions by the community have been performed.[5] After all, if a person becomes a vampire by dying under circumstances that prevent him from being properly buried, then giving him a proper burial should in theory be all that is required to block the vampire's vengeful aggression. But this is never done. The ecclesiastical reason is clear: in the case of a suicide, for example, going against the canon and performing a proper mass would be tantamount to removing the taboo against suicide. From the Orthodox theological perspective, permitting ritual mutilation of a corpse apparently constitutes the lesser of two evils.

In any case, it should be noted that taking the correct destructive or apotropaic actions against known vampires is always effective. This is because such actions are usually not taken until after the crisis has peaked or the evident mischief (sometimes as harmless as rattling on the roof) has ceased. Consequently, the cause-and-effect relation between group ritual violence—even directed against a harmless corpse—and the desired outcome (elimination of any further threat) is reaffirmed almost every time and thus perpetuates the need for carrying out such actions whenever possible. The ritual aspect of the violent response, by the way, serves not only to guarantee the efficacy of the actions taken[6] but also to channel the aggressions of the villagers as they are discharged.

Historically, the actions taken against vampires by a community, whether in the form of a vigilante group or embodied in an individual, such as a *glog* or *vampirdžia,* are less reliably documented in Bulgaria and Macedonia than in Serbia, where the influence of the more elaborate Western legal code is in evidence. The testimony about village violence in the regions south of the Danube is almost completely anecdotal, while further to the north there are transcripts of trials and legislative documents, such as one going back to the thirteenth century, under Dušan's canon, forbidding the practice of removing the heart of a buried corpse.[7] Certainly by the time of the vampire epidemics in early eighteenth-century Serbia, a tradition of documenting procedural prosecution not of vampires but their accusers and tormentors is well established. This can only be due to the closer proximity of the Serbian state to Austria and Hungary, where there was a parallel push to bring any sort of witch hysteria to an end.

Hysteria, at least of the sort that characterized some of the extended witch hunts in Western Europe, is not a common feature of village actions against vampires in Orthodox Europe. Of course, this is in part because the vampire is always a corpse, and corpses tend not to assemble, nor do their numbers swell outside catastrophic circumstances. Consequently, there is no association between vampires and conspiracy as there is with witches, who were considered politically insidious and were thought to gather at sabbats to carry out nefarious intentions. But perhaps a more significant reason that vampire attacks in the Balkans were less likely to produce a hysterical reaction is that there existed well-known prescriptions for coping with vampire attacks, and in the event that the villagers deemed themselves incompetent to identify and slay the unruly vampire, it was often possible to find a designated individual to handle the case.

As with the vampire, the markings, the capabilities, and even the names of these vampire hunters or slayers may vary from region to region, but the tradition of delegating to someone deemed to have special powers the authority to counteract a demonic or supernatural threat is ancient and in all likelihood linked to a shamanic healing function. Éva Pócs points out that in the shamanic religions of pre-Christian Hungary, for example, the *táltos* had the power to heal those who have been sickened by witchcraft, because he had the ability to enter into and return from the world of the dead.[8] This ability to cross between existential regions is of course not something that is given to everyone, and one might argue that the vampire also possesses this ability, but the vampire's return is considered evil, because, unlike the shaman's, it is contaminated and not motivated by purified human intention. The possibility of a link between the vampire seer and early European shamanism is significantly more tenuous than that between witch seers and shamanism, which has been asserted convincingly by

Carlo Ginzburg[9] as well as Pócs and Klaniczay. There do, however, seem to be some clues in the folklore that would suggest that such an assertion is not far-fetched, but written testimony concerning vampire slayers is evident only fairly late. In more contemporary folklore, these hunters and slayers are well known, but naturally the focus of most vampire tales is on the vampire rather than the slayer.

EARLY SLAYERS

The systematic collection of folklore in rural Bulgaria did not begin until the overthrow of the "Ottoman yoke."[10] However, as a sign of the growing nationalism that had spurred Bulgaria and other Balkan nations to finally evict their Turkish overlords in the last decades of the nineteenth century, ethnographers and folklorists from the Slavic regions of the Balkans began to investigate in earnest the customs and tales of Bulgarians, Moldovans, Ukrainians, Macedonians, and other groups living in or near the Bulgaro-Macedonian region of the Balkans. Elicited reports of customs and beliefs were collected in the field, then written up and submitted for consideration to such encyclopedic publications as the *Sbornik za bâlgarski narodni umotvorenija* (*SbNU*), a regularly published collection of folklore and customs. There are several references to vampire slayers in *SbNU,* dating back to 1891.

In the earliest *SbNU* report of a vampire slayer,[11] from the Demir-Haskov region, the vampire, called in this case a *vrkolak,* appears as a shadow (*sjanka*). The vampire slayer is referred to as either a *sâbotnik* (see discussion in chap. 4) or a *vâperar.* The *vrkolak* in this region was said to come into existence from the blood of someone killed with a gun or a knife: the blood that poured out from the violent wound could become a vampire after fourteen days had passed. The shadow is quite explicitly considered a double, that is, an invisible simulacrum that can only be seen by the *vâperar,* who is called on to kill the vampire. In this report, the existence of the shadow/vampire was evidenced by an epidemic among livestock.

Like the *vâperar,* the *sâbotnik* may also be called on to kill the *vrkolak,* using, according to the report, a knife or a gun. The specification that the vampire slayer[12] use the same tools to return the violence as that which ultimately brought the vampire into existence is intriguing:

not only do we see the vampire as a double who has been engendered (or contaminated) by violence, but the vampire's mortal enemy—who has the capacity to become a vampire—is here also his "reverse" double, who ritually reverses the vampire's coming into existence by reenacting the violent scene that promoted a victim to a villain. There is a kind of antisymmetrical connection that persists throughout the folklore in the relationship between the vampire and the slayer, and this quite Slavic theme of doubles and reversals,[13] while certainly encountered frequently enough in various notions of ritual magic, appears even in the later, popular literary conception of the vampire as having no reflection (the mirror image is his enemy).[14]

In the same report from Demir-Haskov, we are told that there are also *sâbotnik* dogs, who can detect vampires and drive them away. The dog, too, is considered a double or alter ego, who is capable of destroying the vampire with its bite. The most common and most ancient[15] cause of vampire death, as we have seen, is piercing the skin with a sharp pointed object, which allows the blood to pour out freely. Here, the dog's fangs puncture the vampire's skin and cause his immediate death.

A similar report occurs in *SbNU* two years later,[16] from Veles, where the vampire slayer is called now a *vampirdžia,* who also can kill the vampire with a gun. *Vampirdžii* are described in an 1895 report from Bitola, Macedonia, as "people determined from birth to hunt vampires."[17] Here, the vampire slayer is something of a Pied Piper, charming the music-loving vampire with drums[18] or pipes. The *vampirdžia* is thought to be able to see the vampire and kill him on Saturday evening, having led him to the graveyard, where he is scalded or burned. The *vampirdžia's* ability to detect the vampire is not entirely unaided. He carries in his mouth a "poison herb," which allows him to see things his companions cannot. Anyone traveling with the *vampirdžia,* however, sees only the black blood that remains when the vampire is killed. It is tempting to associate the herbs with some sort of shamanic soma, and we shall see that in Hungarian folklore about witch seers, hallucinogenic plants were also thought to play a role in amplifying the seer's abilities. But the references to these poisonous or hallucinogenic herbs in the Bulgarian lore are both few and late, so for now the connection between the vampire slayer and the shamanic healer remains speculative.

Like a shaman or at least a healer, the vampire slayer at the end of the nineteenth century was something of a professional, in some cases even mercenary. In Târnovo, for example, Turkish *vampirdžii* were called from Tsaregrad as specialists to cope with local vampires.[19] The fact that vampire slayers in the nineteenth century had a special, widely recognized status in village society and were considered professionals and allowed to collect money or other gifts for their services suggests that the tradition of hiring slayers already had deep historical roots. During the late eighteenth and early nineteenth centuries, "professional" *sâbotnici* or *vampirdžii,* using their magical powers, were able to earn a great deal of money thanks to very widespread fear of vampires, which apparently became especially acute during the darkest periods in winter and after midnight.[20]

Even earlier, in 1575, at the request of some Greeks, Turks were called in to incinerate the body of a Greek man who had remained whole but without skin for two years after his death.[21] While there is no indication in this very early report that the Turks who incinerated the nondecaying corpse had special gifts or sight, it is nevertheless documentation of a case where a special, separate class of people was called on to process the dangerous dead of another group. What marks the Turks as viable candidates for this task, we may surmise, is precisely that they were not of the Orthodox faith and therefore not in danger of being contaminated by contact with the unholy.

The earliest folkloric vampires were invariably excommunicates, considered godless and thus outside the natural order. In a report from 1557, it was claimed that excommunicates did not decay, "because the Devil entered them at night."[22] Rather than call on Turks to handle the case in this report, however, everyone from the village assisted in the destruction of a presumed vampire by bringing two pieces of wood each to the pyre on which the exhumed corpse was to be incinerated, while the priests stood before them and performed the called-for rites. The mandatory participation by everyone in the destruction of the excommunicated corpse serves to absolve any individual from guilt by effectively distributing it throughout the entire community. Reflexes of such beliefs may be seen in the contemporary practice of throwing a handful of dirt into the grave at someone's burial and in the use of firing squads (where the multiplicity of marksmen absolves any one of them from being the prisoner's executioner).

In these early cases of the ritual destruction of a vampire, a folkloric pattern seems to have already stabilized: (1) evidence of some inexplicable catastrophe or other phenomenon becomes linked to a demonic force that needs to be removed; (2) the demonic intention is to punish or wreak vengeance and becomes incarnate in a deceased excommunicate or accursed individual,[23] who is reanimated by the collective imagination (perhaps because the community in some sense feels responsible for expelling the individual, who may then desire retribution);[24] (3) the task of identifying and dealing with the evildoer falls either to marked individuals or nonbelievers (*vampirdžia, sâbotnici,* Turks) or to the excommunicating community as a whole; (4) ritual destruction of the corpse is carried out in such a way that no ordinary member of the community may be held responsible. This pattern changes over time and eventually extends to involve vigilante groups and even ordinary individuals, but the early notion that the unholy vampire can only be destroyed by designated individuals who either have special powers—or objects representing those powers (e.g., icons or crosses)—or who are otherwise not at spiritual risk from effectively condemning the dead twice is a fundamental theme in vampire lore right up to the current century.

The special powers available to a vampire slayer derive, in general, from violation of some taboo connected with bounding sacred times or from genetic affiliation with a vampire. Saturday, especially the Saturday before Easter, is a dangerous time to be born: if the native does not become a vampire, (s)he may become a *sâbotnik.* This would suggest that, at a minimum, roughly one in seven people is capable of seeing vampires, but of course no one's really counting: all that is necessary is that there be a good deal of flexibility in designating certain individuals vampire slayers when it is necessary, just as there should be flexibility in identifying (i.e., instantiating) vampires when that becomes necessary.

The Unclean Days are a time when not only vampires but vampire slayers can be conceived or born: according to Bulgarians living in Moldova and southwestern Russia, people born between Christmas and New Years can see not only vampires but all "unclean spirits" (*nečistye duxi*).[25] As I noted in chapter 3, the midwinter Unclean Days are laden with taboos, especially concerning household activity and marital intimacy, and Christian rites are usually not performed during this dangerous time. The fact that both vampires and slayers are associated with this twelve-day period underscores their deep, reciprocal relationship to each other. The vampire slayer is cut from the same cloth, is the product of the same social or religious violations, as the vampire. Whereas testimony from the sixteenth century tells us that vampires were those deceased who had been formally excommunicated or were otherwise accursed, in later centuries there is a generalization and extension of the conditions by which almost any corpse may become a vampire, the mere misfortune of having been conceived at the wrong time being sufficient.

This relaxation of the conditions for vampirization naturally broadens the category "vampire" substantially. But more important, it also signals an increasing folklorization of the vampire, a detachment of the demonic from the beliefs or actions of an individual, as the memory of heresy and paganism recedes further into history and as excommunication from the Orthodox church becomes both less frequent and less important socially. The tension between Christianity and whatever is left of an earlier, autochthonous religion is now maintained purely symbolically: recall that a regional nickname for the Unclean Days is "Pagan Days." The individual's deeds or affiliations with persecuted or marginalized groups are no longer critical to the production of a vampire. Rather, both the vampire and the vampire slayer now represent a specific social tension that has its history in the ancient conflict between agrarian Slavic religions and Eastern Christianity.[26] As increasingly folkloric and decreasingly religious symbols, these two actors serve also to reinforce or reify the polarization between Christian and non-Christian beliefs about the cause of evil and misfortune in daily life—a polarization that was amplified by several historical processes, such as increasing urbanization and, of course, the influence of the Islamic administrators on Bulgarian social and religious life.

MORE RECENT SLAYERS
Bulgarian and Serbian Evidence

Although the category "vampire" became more inclusive and hence somewhat diluted in its application as Balkan Orthodoxy had less and less to worry about from pagans and heretics and more to worry about from Ottoman Muslim overlords, the folkloric matchup between the vampire and his slayer persisted well into the twentieth century. In fact, one consequence of the changing contour of the vampire's etiology was that it became harder and harder for members of the community to discern who, among the local recently deceased, had become a vampire. The once unequivocal link of a vampire to anathematic status had weakened so much that by the early twentieth century, a vampire could come into being simply by having a cat jump over a corpse lying in state. This produced a side effect of making the distinction between the ordinary and extraordinary (dangerous) deceased more problematic and resulted in a concomitant extension of the category "vampire slayer" to accommodate the increasing fuzziness of the category "vampire."

By the end of the nineteenth century, there is rich testimony about the activities of *vampirdžii* and the like across the entire Bulgaro-Macedonian region. Xristo Gandev notes that toward the end of the Bulgarian Early Revival (1860), there are tales of vampire slayers to be found in "Prilep, Kjustendil, Lom, Pleven, Provadija, Varna, Sliven, Kotel, Karnobat, Panagiuriste, and Karlovo."[27] Clearly, by this time, the vampire slayer had become a significant personage in Balkan vampire folklore.

In the twentieth century, the forces of urbanization[28] and secularization began to erode the folkloric base of the vampire, and this erosion accelerated after World War II, in part due to the imposition of Soviet-style communism, with its antagonism toward religious expression. By the mid-twentieth century, authentic vampire lore in the Bulgarian (and Yugoslavian) village context appeared to be dying off. More and more narratives recorded in the later decades of the century are of the "fabulate" type, in which the teller speaks of vampire or vampire-killing activity as hearsay rather than personal encounter (the latter being characteristic of the "memorate" narrative). Virtually all of the informants of contemporary ethnographers that admit to having knowledge of vampires are semiliterate farmworkers in their late seventies or eighties.

The common regional nomenclature for vampire slayers has been maintained, but the slayer's connection to the vampire is not always strong. For example, in one narrative collected by Miceva in the Mixajlovgrad region in 1982, the informant states, somewhat proudly: "I am a *sâbotnik*, but I've never seen a *plâtenik*. But I *have* seen a *samodiva* [an evil female spirit in South Slavic folklore]."[29] Here is evidence that the

Fig. 5. Bulgaria, 1994. From the Perry-Castañeda map collection, http://www.lib.utexas.edu/maps/europe/bulgaria.jpg. (Courtesy of the University of Texas Libraries, The University of Texas at Austin.)

folklore about the class of vampire slayers is still productive, and although the speaker does not state how she knows she is a *sâbotnik,* it is likely that she simply met the condition of having been born on a Saturday. Furthermore, the speaker's regretful denial of ever having seen a vampire and her admission of having encountered a *samodiva* may constitute more than mere theatrical embellishment to please the inquiring ethnographer. There is here a belief both in the reality of the *sâbotnik* (at least to the extent that someone born on Saturday is automatically such a thing, by definition) and in the *sâbotnik's* ability to detect demonic beings. The speaker's added clarification also presupposes belief in vampires and *samodivi* and belief that both can be detected by the right people.

Also interesting in this short conversation is the open admission by the speaker that she is a *sâbotnik*. Ordinarily, no one would admit to being a vampire of any sort (since to do so would be to acknowledge one's marginal or negative social status, as well as to confess that one was in fact dead),[30] but while the vampire slayer is marked by a connection to the demonic, this special status is not something that must be hidden.[31] On the contrary, it is clearly something of a heroic role to be a vampire slayer or someone with the capacity to identify vampires and other evil beings.

It would appear, from a survey of the contemporary folkloric data, that the use of guns by *vampirdžii* and *sâbotnici* to kill vampires was more prominent in earlier centuries. This may reflect the fact that during the uprisings against the Turks in the 1870s, firearms were available to Balkan revolutionaries as well as to their Turkish opponents; guns therefore might slip more easily from daily life into the folklore. Later, following a return to a less turbulent agrarian national life and restrictions on ownership of guns, they play a less visible role in folk culture. At any rate, it does seem to be the case that the methods used by vampire slayers in the latter half of the twentieth century are more ritualistic in nature. The use of a gun does not disappear altogether, however: in the town of Smoljan, in the Rhodopes, a band of vigilantes decided to kill a *drakus* (the common name for a vampire in the mountainous region of Bulgaria close to the Greek border) with a gun that was shot from the left hand. The *drakus,* whose form was that of a sack of blood, burst open, and black blood poured out.[32] In this same region of Bulgaria, where the landscape is dotted with small Turkish family communities known as *maxalas,* it was claimed that Turkish devils known as *džini* (commonly known in the West by the name *genie*) could be killed by a silver bullet.

DOG AND GLOG

Because he is able to detect a vampire that otherwise is unseen or goes unnoticed, the vampire slayer is the vampire's natural enemy. I have already hinted that this function, of seeing and eliminating demonic forces, is a religious one: the task of purifying the community by identifying the spiritual cause of a calamity or disease and driving it out is performed by the heroes of many religions, Christianity among them. Since the earliest vampires were linked, in the minds of Orthodox Christianizers in the Balkans, with pre-Christian beliefs, we might expect to find evidence that the vampire's folkloric enemies emerge from that same crucible.

Of course, the vampire's truly greatest enemy is Christianity itself, which vehemently condemned, in the image of the vampire, the pagan's literalization of the Eucharist and Resurrection as blood drinking and reanimation or reincarnation, respectively. But at the community level, the tension between the personages embodying evil or anxiety and those embodying good or wholeness must be resolved internally. The vampire and the vampire slayer are similarly marked as "non-Christian"; they are in a sense related to each other and in all likelihood reenact a mythological struggle that pre-dates Christianity. In other words, where Christianity finds the vampire, it also finds his slayer. At the purest theological level, Christianity abhors annihilation even for the sake of expiation, Jesus having served as the ultimate scapegoat.[33] It therefore can condone neither vengeful violence nor deliberate contact with the unholy or defiled.

The fact that dogs born on Saturday are considered to possess the same antivampiric efficacy as a *sâbotnik* is revealing. Other animals are not thought to possess this ability—only dogs. The dog, however, is a domesticated descendant of another animal also often thought to be an enemy of the vampire, the wolf. Wolves are mentioned quite frequently in folklore about vampires, and a Serbian word designating the folkloric equivalent of the *vampir* is *vukodlak* or *vulkodlak* (among other spellings in transliteration), which is a compound derived from an Old Slavic phrase meaning "wolf pelt." The wolf as the vampire's enemy does not have to have any special markings as the domesticated dog does. We may thus conjecture that the wolf is totemic, whereas the dog is an intrinsic part of the human community and must be specially marked in order to serve as a vampire slayer.

The link asserted earlier connecting the vampire to the slayer is supported by the dual role of the dog and the wolf as both were-animals and enemies of the vampire. Dogs that function as vampire slayers may be considered *sâbotnici* but never *vampirdžii.* They are never, that is, considered the offspring of the union between a woman and a vampire, which must always be hominid. If vampire-seeking dogs are not *sâbotnici,* they then have other notable characteristics: they may, for example, have four eyes or pronounced eyebrows,[34] or they are mentioned as being large or black. Sometimes, dogs play the role of a familiar or assistant to the *vampirdžia,* helping him see or even kill the vampire. One curious way that a dog can quell the activity of a vampire is to be buried with him, as a sort of sacrifice. In a tale collected in 1995, two vampires buried outside a church in the Sakar-Harmanli region continued to surface from their graves, despite repeated attempts by the parishioners to bury them once and for all. The earth had rejected them, according to the informant. But when a dog was buried with the vampires (there is no mention of how a dead dog was obtained), the earth no longer rejected them, and the village had no more trouble from the ambulatory dead.[35]

Man's best friend, however, may also become his supernatural enemy. A vampire can take the form of a dog, especially in the more urbanized settings where wolves are infrequently, if ever, encountered. Vampire dogs tend to be harmless, especially in tales from the later twentieth century. They tend to be small, perhaps sheepherding or stray. In one amusing anecdote, one night a homeless dog jumped up on a woman wearing a red dress and bit off a piece of the fabric. Startled, the woman ran home, but her husband was not there. When he finally returned, she told him what had happened, but he just smiled, revealing strands of red thread between his teeth. Either because she realized her husband was a vampire or perhaps just because she wanted revenge for his lack of sympathy, she killed him by setting up a booby trap with a pitchfork.[36]

Such a tale clearly must have been told with tongue in cheek, suggesting that folkloric vampires today, even in the village setting, have lost much of their ability to frighten. But the story demonstrates the vampire's shape-shifting ability.[37] Regardless of their metamorphosis, vampires in animal form seem bound by the taboos and physical constraints that affect them otherwise. As dogs, for example, they are only out at night, and the vampire's noted fear of water[38] extends even to their canine form. In *Pazardžik,*[39] an informant reported that her sister had seen a dog by the old graveyard after dark. In a contemporary vampire movie, that fact alone would signal the sister's imminent demise. But in this case, the dog stopped in its tracks, unable to jump over a gully where there was running water. The vampire's oft-cited cowardliness is actually a result of his being hemmed in by taboos.

The dog's braver cousin, the wolf, also plays a dual role as both a morph of the vampire and the vampire's mortal enemy. The wolf, of course, is at the center of a great deal of European folklore, religion, and mythology (assuming one knows where to draw the lines between those rubrics). The role of dogs in contemporary vampire folklore represents a diluted form of earlier beliefs about wolves. The dilution is a consequence of domestication, urbanization, and the concomitant reduction in the European wolf population, but more important, it is the result of the elimination of any sort of totemic function for the wolf. That wolf cults and their associated rituals form the basis of beliefs about wolves and vampires is attested by the link between calendar rituals and taboos involving both vampires and wolves.

Tempting as it may be at this point to gather up the diaphanous threads tying wolf folklore in the Balkans to documented wolf cults among the Bulgarians' ancient neighbors (including Romans, Greeks, Scythians, and Thracians)[40] or even to follow the path leading from the *vukodlak* to an ancient Slavic deity connected with both the underworld and wild animals (i.e., Veles), it is enough for my purposes here to note that the wolf's presence in folklore is linked to that of the vampire through the attribute "pagan." If Slavic or other cults that honored the wolf were viewed by the Orthodox Christian through the same lens as the one applied to the early vampires, then we can see how the wolf may at once be a hypostasis of and an enemy of the vampire.

Belief in the northwestern *vukodlak* is attested as early as the eleventh century.[41] In fact, the "werewolf" had apparently already been folklorized at that stage, one commonly held view now being that the antecedent of the *vukodlak* was perhaps an initiate in some kind of *männerbund* (man federation) where the wolf pelt was the costume of either the initiates or full warriors.[42] In any case, in that same century, the term *vampir* designated a live member of some still-visible group or cult; it was not yet folkloric. Since it is stated in both the later folkloric reports and the scholarly literature that in many areas *vukodlak* eventually became just another name for a vampire, the attributes of the Slavic werewolf were probably transferred to the *vampir* rather than the other way around.⁴³

In chapter 4, I discussed in some detail the period known as the "Unclean Days" (Bulg. *Mrâsnite dni*), a prolonged calendrical ritual following the winter solstice, where taboos abounded to enforce avoidance of contact with evil spirits (i.e., pre-Christian demons or divinities), who are said to surface during this dark time. The period is also known popularly as the "Pagan Days" or the "Vampire Days." It either coincides with or, more often, is preceded by another ritual period, dedicated to wolves, known as the "Wolf Holidays" or simply the "Wolf Days" (Bulg. *Vâlčite praznici*). This period, too, is bound by several taboos, intended to prevent reincarnation or to block attacks on livestock, especially sheep.⁴⁴ Like *vampirdžii* born or conceived during the Unclean Days, a lame wolf encountered during the Wolf Days was thought to be a person possessing inherent magical powers and the ability to guide all wolves. In Dobrudja, meanwhile, a *vrk* is a dead person who was buried in clothes that were made during the Wolf Days.

Many wolf taboos concern eating meat. An extension of this taboo outside the calendrical period of the Wolf Days is the prohibition against a pregnant mother tasting the meat of any animal bitten by a wolf. A violation of this proscription means that her child will come back from the dead. Even the name of the wolf has power: on the one hand, it must not be uttered during the Wolf Days, yet the wolf is mentioned in many pseudo-Christian blessings, especially of sick or weak children. Magical charms akin to rabbits' feet were once made from dead wolves.

A special type of vampire slayer whose characteristics and name suggest a connection with pre-Christian cults is the *glog*. The *glog* is very much like the *vampirdžia,* similarly being the child of a vampire. But where the *vampirdžia* may use such ordinary weapons as guns to kill a vampire, the *glog* uses tools—such as carved stakes—made from black hawthorn. His name, *glog,* is the Bulgarian name for a type of black hawthorn that grows in central Bulgaria (*Crataegus pentagina*).

The berry-producing hawthorn plant itself is considered by some to have magical or medicinal properties, and we may suppose that some aspect of the plant's mystical efficaciousness is embedded in the folkloric references to the plant as capable of preventing vampire attacks, much like garlic, which of course is also used to hem in vampires. In fact, in some areas, wreaths woven of hawthorn and garlic are used to prevent vampires from entering a house. Hawthorn is used apotropaically against epidemic diseases, such as plague and cholera, as well as against epilepsy. Amulets or crosses of hawthorn worn around the neck block the influence of the evil eye. Despite the widespread folk medicinal uses of this species of hawthorn, however, there is little information about any ritual use of the plant outside the vampire context. Its symbolic use seems to be greater than its actual medicinal purpose, since there is nothing particularly extraordinary about the hawthorn— it is not exactly rare, it has no noted hallucinogenic properties, and its physiological benefits are as modest as those of garlic. But we must be careful not to apply the point of view of contemporary Western science to folk medicines or other symbolically used plants, which often possessed value beyond the purely physiological for reasons that are no longer clear.

Presumably the same or a closely related species of hawthorn was the plant used by ancient Thracians as a prophylactic against plague.[45] An "old saying" recounted by an elderly woman from Mixajlovgrad links the hawthorn to a good harvest from the vineyard. At an earlier stage in the Balkans, the plant embodied or was used by the forces of good and of healing: there do not seem to be any references to the plant as evil or harmful. In the folklore about the vampire, it is the plant's thorny nature that is thought to be responsible for its efficacy. The vampire is often thought of as being full of blood, and sharp objects that can pierce the skin are used to destroy it. Thus, the thorns of the *glog* plant can prick the bloated vampire and destroy him. But thorns are also used in other ways, which suggests that the focus on the thorns themselves is a folk explanation for the power of hawthorn against vampires.

Vampires are thought to be afraid of thorns in the same way they are afraid of running water. Thorny branches, placed around the grave or even on the deceased body, have an effect on the vampire as powerful as kryptonite on Superman: the vampire is effectively transfixed, immobilized. Thorns are put in fireplaces, windows, doors, and even keyholes to prevent entrance of a vampire. Sometimes the thorns are set on fire, even inside the oven, especially at New Years. While ordinarily *glog* is used for these purposes, in Slivengrad another species is used, *Ruscus aculeatus,* which is known locally as *vampirski bodil,* or "vampire's thorn." Thorn branches even serve as surface graves for those not entitled to proper burial: in Sakar Harmanli, for example, children who die unbaptized are thrown into piles of thorns. These children, which in other areas are called *navi,* here are interestingly referred to as *evreiče,* meaning something like "little Jews." Since these now dangerous little souls had not yet been initiated into Christianity, they are linked to the Jews, who cannot enter paradise because they are not baptized. In cases where a priest is unable to say a proper burial mass, thorns are placed in the grave until he can.

Curiously, even when the local vampire slayer is known by a name other than *glog,* hawthorn is the preferred substance for destroying vampires. In Provadja at the end of the nineteenth century, Bulgaro-Turkish vampire-pursuing "magicians" known as *džadžii* would dig up the corpse of the suspected vampire, pierce it in the chest with a hawthorn stake, and then burn hawthorn bushes above him.[46] Hawthorn itself is so strongly connected with the vampire that it is nicknamed *vapirse.*[47]

From the foregoing, we see that there is a chain of relationships linking vampires to slayers and linking both, in turn, to dogs and wolves and to a special species of black hawthorn called, in Bulgarian, *glog,* which is also the name of a particular type of slayer, who in all likelihood got his nickname from the use of *glog*—either its thorns or its branches—to destroy vampires. While hawthorn is certainly not the only substance thought to have magical efficacy against the vampire—iron, for example, is often cited as well—its wide distribution throughout vampire folklore for several centuries tells us that the plant must have had properties thought to assist the vampire seer in the encounter with the dead. Further, since there is some evidence that even the smoke of burning hawthorn had powerful properties, it is difficult not to consider that this particular genus or species once played a role in the rituals of shamanic healers.[48] Direct proof of such an assertion is lacking. In the following chapter, however, we will encounter some parallels to the axis I have just drawn, parallels that may throw some light on whether or not the Slavic vampire slayer is at all connected to a shamanic precursor.

7

SEEING THE DEAD

A large variety of regional names used in the Balkans for semi-supernatural individuals might be covered by the popular American term *vampire slayer*—though it needs to be restated that no nickname equivalent to *slayer* ever shows up in the Slavic folklore for the *sâbotnik, glog, vampirdžia,* and so on. Yet despite their number, all the regional names tend to fall into one of only two basic groups. The *sâbotnik* type is the more extensible class, applying, as we have seen, even to dogs. These vampire seer-slayers meet a very simple condition for their existence—namely, being born on a certain day (Saturday) or during a certain period (usually the Unclean Days, from Christmas to January 6). The second type is marked by being "genetically" linked to a vampire, the offspring of an unnatural union between a vampire and a human mother. While, technically, women born during taboo times can become *sâbotnici,* mention of a female *glog* or *vampirdžia* is difficult to come by. Aside from these differences of special origin or marking, these individuals otherwise seem to function identically: they are all able to detect vampires, whereas other members of the community cannot, and they are granted by villagers an effective license to destroy any vampires they do uncover. Most often, this requires that they identify as vampires those who have been buried, since the slayer's method will usually involve ritual actions at the grave site. However, there are occasional tales in which slayers use guns or knives or other puncturing objects to dispatch those insidious, ambulatory vampires that have "taken on flesh" (*plâtenici*).

If we look at this classification scheme from a slightly different angle, what appears to constitute two different groups distinguished by etiology resolves into only one, for both types of slayer have in common the fact that they are connected intimately to their enemy, the vampire. The *sâbotnik* type is someone who was born during a proscribed period, and in some regions those born during the Unclean Days or on other sacred or marked days may also become vampires after death. (True, people born on Saturday do not automatically or even usually become vampires, as they do *sâbotnici,* but in all likelihood the designation of Saturday—the Jewish Sabbath—as a quasi-unholy day represents a generalization from more definite calendrical periods during which evil influences were thought to be more powerful.) The *glog* and the *vampirdžia,* meanwhile, are by definition half-vampire.

Thus, both the vampire and the vampire slayer of any type either derive from the same pre-Christian belief system or at least were perceived, in the view of Orthodoxy, as being of the same essentially un-Christian stock. The fundamental difference between them lies not so much in their historical origins as in their respective inclinations to do good or evil within the folkloric system that has evolved. Those opposed capacities of course galvanize along the poles of life and death: the vampire is directly connected to the world of the dead, while the vampire slayer, though he may have the ability to enter that world, is a living being (ordinarily human) able to return. Whereas the vampire represents the extraordinary capacity of the dead to enter and influence (negatively) the world of the living, if only temporarily, the vampire slayer possesses the inverse power, namely, the ability to enter the world of the dead, also temporarily. This capacity for *ekstasis* is evidenced both by his ability to see the vampire and by his ability to take on an animal shape. For both the vampire and the vampire slayer, then, the membrane separating the living from the dead is permeable.

The reciprocity between the vampire and his slayer is based on their mutual ability to enter the world of the other. The vampire, too, is an ecstatic, insofar as leaving the grave is equivalent to departing the buried corpse.[1] The enmity between the vampire and the slayer reflects the polarity of values assigned to the directions of their (spiritual) movements: for the dead to cross into the world of the living is dangerous, unnatural, monstrous, and, in broadest terms, destructive and life- or energy-draining. What is destroyed by this creature, according to the folklore, are conditions for wholeness and fertility: livestock is weakened, people become sick or die unnaturally, food is spoiled, and things break. The sole purpose of the slayer in this context is simply to oppose or negate the negative, draining force—to destroy the destroyer and reverse the processes of barrenness, decay, weakness, and disease. The vampire slayer battles for fertility in its most general sense, restoring the natural healthy order that has been upset by a demonic attack on the conditions necessary for collective survival.

The opposition between the vampire slayer and the vampire, however, is not at all like the tension between, say, police authorities and criminals, nor does this folkloric antagonism reduce neatly to any sort of simple mythological battle between good and evil. Indeed, a sense of violent, combative struggle is entirely absent from at least the Bulgaro-Macedonian folklore that has been recorded in the last century or two. Quite to the contrary, there is a feeling of ritualized finality, in which the vampire slayer never encounters real resistance, never has to track down his elusive prey, but instead must simply identify his enemy among the recently deceased—the obvious vampire—and perform the necessary and proper gestures to destroy him once and for all. The vampire slayer never loses; his actions are never thwarted. The focus of these narratives, in other words, is never on the drama of the encounter between the slayer and the vampire but always on the certainty of the result—namely, the elimination of the threat to the village's sense of well-being. In this way, the interaction between the vampire and the slayer is analogous to that between a sacrificial victim (or scapegoat) and the sacrificer.

Recall that the vampire is frequently portrayed as being stupid, gullible, and docile, as well as fearful, if not ashamed.[2] While the vampire is certainly feared for his destructive nocturnal attacks on people and animals and things, the notion that he can be easily vanquished, once identified (correctly identifying the source of the problem is the truly hard part), is most reassuring to the community. The vampire slayer's perceptiveness alone reveals the true powerlessness of this attack from the dead, since his ability to see the vampire is really all that is required; the ritual destruction of a corpse (in reality or in folkloric narrative) and the consequent removal of the vampire's implicit curse are more or less faits accomplis.

It is here, in the vampire's passivity before the fertility-restoring actions of the *sâbotnik* or *glog,* that vampire lore seems to diverge decisively from a pattern of folklore in surrounding regions about heroic, gifted, but also marked, individuals who in some ecstatic mode, usually at night, do battle against forces that threaten regional fertility (usually witches or sorcerers, to whom vampires are often related). Carlo Ginzburg has revealed in some detail a system of folklore in Central Europe regarding such battles for fertility, suggesting that the existence of such highly similar beliefs across a large expanse of space and time may indicate a substratum of shamanism that entered Europe through contacts with the Scythians, Thracians, and Celts.[3] While it is not my purpose to restate Ginzburg's arguments or even his data, the historical and cultural complexity of the area stretching from the Balkan Peninsula to the northern Adriatic and into the West Slavic regions, across Transylvania and into the Carpathians, is such that it is almost impossible to avoid remarking on some of the parallels between Bulgaro-Macedonian vampire slayers, such as *glogove* or *sâbotnici,* and the folkloric/ecstatic witch seers of Hungary, Romania, Yugoslavia, and northeastern Italy.

If we inspect all the Balkan vampire slayers with an eye toward connecting this class of folkloric being to similar figures in the regions surrounding present-day Macedonia and Bulgaria, the features that they share emerge to form a link that is unlikely to be accidental. Ginzburg, speaking of the Hungarian *táltos,* the *benandanti* of Friuli, the *kresniki* of Serbia, and the werewolves of the Baltic region, notices that these figures are, exactly like the Bulgarian *sâbotnik, glog,* or *vampirdžia,* (1) marked by a precise ecstatic vocation announced from birth by peculiarities, physical or otherwise, and (2) designated "specialists" who have a symbolic relationship with the realm of the dead.[4] In addition to the Hungarian and Serbian parallels, the Romanians have *strigoi,* while the Greeks have *kallikantzaroi* (the Bulgarian equivalent of which is termed *karakondžoli,* who are typologically closer to the vampire than to the *vampirdžii*). A brief discussion of the characteristics of a few of these neighboring ecstatic types should be sufficient to highlight their similarities to and differences from the Bulgarian vampire slayers.

BENANDANTI

From 1575 to the second half of the seventeenth century, reports emerged concerning certain individuals from eastern Alpine Italy who asserted their power to protect the agrarian community from the harmful activities of witches. Under questioning, these *benandanti* admitted to Inquisitors that their souls were able to leave their bodies while asleep and then travel through the air, sometimes riding on a cat, until they came to those places where a society of (female) witches had gathered for their orgiastic and demonic sabbats. These witches, according to Ginzburg, were in all likelihood followers of the goddess Diana,[5] which for our purposes is significant because they are thus linked closely with paganism and heresy, at least in the minds of the Inquisitors.

Of particular interest is testimony from 1390 by a certain Pierina who confessed that she had paid homage to a local manifestation of Diana named Oriente. Oriente was claimed to have the power of restoring life to sacrificed oxen by gathering the bones and tying them inside the animal's skin, although the revived animal was never again useful for working.[6] While this belief in the power to reanimate the dead may not be directly connected to the Bulgarian belief in the vampire, it certainly seems to be a survival of a pagan belief in reincarnation of the physical body through sacrificial ritual, and the image of the reanimated skin of a sacrificial animal is reminiscent of many descriptions of the amorphic type of vampire as being like a leather bag filled with blood. The vampire, however, is often explicitly thought to exist without bones, even when he has taken on the form of a human. The danger of the vampire is that he is reanimated without ritual or without blessing.

A person could not simply become a *benandante*—he or she had to be born one. The identity was revealed—immediately to the parents, eventually to the community, and ultimately to the native, at a certain age—by the presence of a portion of the amnion around the infant's skull at birth. The caul, a relatively uncommon congenital marker, was a sure sign of special powers in many areas of Europe, but in this Alpine region it meant specifically that if the child was a boy, he would grow up to fight witches (i.e., the followers of Diana), while if a girl, she would be able to see the dead. The parents were obliged to have the caul baptized along with the child, and they either preserved it or made the child carry it on their person, in recognition of the special role of the *benandante*. The caul, by the way, played a similar role in marking vampires in West Slavic folklore, which again points to a mutual transferability of characteristics between vampires and slayers. As a physical marker of social difference, it was in some sense the source of special powers, often having to do with the ability to see things that others cannot. In the case of the Polish *upior* or Kashubian *òpji* (vampire), the caul was to be ceremonially incinerated and later fed to the unknowing child on reaching puberty, to prevent him or her from becoming a vampire after death. Similarly, the *benandanti* were obliged to go on their witch-battling missions as long as the caul was in existence: the only way a *benandante* could avoid participating in such ecstatic battles was to somehow lose the consecrated membrane, which could never be destroyed or discarded intentionally[7]—the loss had to occur without the involvement of individual will. The caul thus functioned as something of a badge, outwardly revealing extraordinary powers; it was the visible sign of a special social status that would otherwise remain unknowable by the rest of the community.[8] The community, in turn, through ritual reinforcement or taboo surrounding the disposal of the membrane, exhibited a strong interest in having such a visible sign of the capacity for ecstasy. After all, for *benandanti,* it provided an implicit permission to identify insidious evil and destroy it—a sort of license to kill.

Benandanti supposedly went on their ecstatic voyages four times a year, during the so-called Ember Days. These correspond to the transitional periods between the four seasons in the temperate climate of Europe (the English term *Ember Days* being derived from Latin *quatuor tempora*) and have special significance in primarily agricultural societies. One such period, as we have seen, conventionally begins after Christmas (i.e., the winter solstice) and lasts for up to twelve days. During these times, the soul of the *benandante* would exit from the body after it had gone into a cataleptic state—a process suggestive of the journeys to the otherworld, the world of the dead, taken by shamans.

The battles between these good healers—fighters for fertility and enemies of the accursed—and the followers of Diana were fought with symbolic weapons. The witches brandished sorghum stalks. The *benandanti* used fennel branches. The use of botanical weapons perhaps provides a clue to the significance of black hawthorn (*glog*) for subduing the vampire, where the ritual (magical) meaning of the weapon is clearly more important than its capacity for inflicting physical harm.

There was a certain danger for the *benandanti:* during the time their souls were off fighting witches, their bodies had to remain completely immobile. Otherwise, there was the risk that the souls might not find their way back into the body, in which case the temporary death of the *benandante* would become permanent. We encounter similar prohibitions in the funeral rituals of the Balkan Slavs, where disturbing the space around the body in the dangerous and fragile period between death and burial is considered a leading cause of vampirism. The semipermeability of the transitional membrane between the worlds of the living and the dead is not guaranteed but is maintained by taboo. The danger for the ecstatic *benandante* is that he will actually die if that space is violated, since the channel back into the world of the living will have been obscured, whereas for the deceased of the Slavs, the dangerous consequence of interrupting that space is the soul's inability to enter the world of the dead normally—that is, permanently. These unfortunates are construed as the "unquiet dead" or vampires or other restless demons with human form. It is likely that the category of the restless or unquiet dead in Slavic belief is an older mythological category than the vampire, since related beliefs about the unfortunate consequences of premature death or improper burial are found in many Slavic (and even non-Slavic) areas where vampires are either nonexistent or insignificant.

The role of the *benandanti* in fighting off evil threats to the fertility of the community by entering into the world of the dead (represented either by the witches at their sabbats or by literal perception of the throngs of the dead) is clearly very close to that of the *glog* or the *sâbotnik,* who protects the village from the draining effects of the vampire. However, two fundamental differences between *benandanti* and Balkan vampire slayers undercut any assertion that these two folkloric groups are completely homologous, either functionally or historically.

First, the *benandanti* engage in their ecstatic battles only at four specific times of year (the Ember Days, which belong to the Catholic, but not the Orthodox, liturgical calendar),[9] while folklore about vampire slayers imposes no such calendrical constraint (since the threat posed by the vampire occurs randomly). The vampire slayer, furthermore, does not abandon a sleeping body in order to do battle. Second, the *benandanti's* opponents are primarily females in groups, while the vampire slayer's enemy is usually an individual deceased male. There may be several reasons for these nuanced distinctions, including differences in religious context (Western European Catholicism versus Eastern European Orthodoxy) and concomitant differences in the underlying ethnicity and syncretic layers behind the folklore. However, we may suppose that the first difference noted between *benandanti* and vampires is really a consequence of the second: since the nature of the threat posed by the vampire is not something that can be dealt with at specific times of year, it thus cannot be linked specifically to notions about agricultural fertility and periodic propitiatory ritual. Instead, the vampire represents a kind of unpredictable destructive aggression, like pernicious disease, and must be dealt with in an expiatory fashion, as the need arises—namely, whenever there is visible evidence of a vampire's attack. However, as we shall see from a brief examination of the *táltos* and the *kresnik,* the demarcations between healers and slayers and between propitiation and expiation are not entirely sharp across the regions of Central and Eastern Europe.

THE *TÁLTOS*

The Hungarian folkloric figure known as the *táltos,* a professional seer like the *vampirdžia,* is able to see witches (rather than vampires) and to discern the location of hidden treasure. The marker for this personage is likewise the caul or, in some areas, a double set of teeth. Éva Pócs, who perceives in the *táltos* and other shamanic shapeshifters a system of ecstatic doubles or alter egos, imaginatively interprets the meaning of the caul as the emblem of a second body, the vessel of ecstatic power. The distribution of the caul versus double sets of teeth (or the presence of teeth at birth) corresponds to folkloric differences between the Slavs, on the one hand, and Lapps, Finns, Hungarians, and Turks, on the other.[10]

Like the *benandanti* during the Inquisition, the *táltos* is mentioned by various accused during the Hungarian witch trials in the late sixteenth century, who claimed, for example, that the *táltos* was good rather than evil, able to see all the witches in town and able to heal people cursed or harmed by witches. Although their ecstatic ability was conferred automatically by their markings at birth, their ability to see the dead was sometimes enhanced or induced by "herbal grasses from snowy mountains."[11] As mentioned in chapter 6, similar hallucinogenic herbs promoted the visions of the *vampirdžia*.

The magical caul of the *táltos* was kept on his person, and its inadvertent destruction or loss would mean the loss of the power to peer into the land of the dead. In the nineteenth century, it was reported that a caul that had been sewn into the lining of the coat of a *táltos* had been destroyed when the coat was accidentally incinerated. As a result, the *táltos* immediately lost the ability to detect treasure.

The *táltos* would use a magical drum or sieve as ecstatic devices to assist him in perceiving witches. The drum most likely serves the same function as the drum used by Siberian shamans, and perhaps the ecstatic music helps to explain the vampire's susceptibility to music. A sieve (Bulg. *sito*), meanwhile, is often cited as an apotropaic object to be hung on doors or gates in Bulgaria to frighten away vampires. Once again, the antipathy between the healing European shaman and the vampire becomes apparent.

Klaniczay makes the interesting observation that the violent hostility of Christianity toward pagan beliefs in Hungary (and presumably elsewhere in Europe) between the sixteenth and seventeenth centuries led to a fusion of witchcraft and shamanistic beliefs. As the residues of these beliefs were almost totally obliterated, the ecstasies attributed to the *táltos,* for example, took on a "secret, lonely, night-time character," as opposed to the quite public ceremonies of Siberian shamans—even under the suspicious eye of the Soviets.[12]

The benevolent *táltos* figure (Pócs prefers the term "semi-*táltos*") is promoted more as a seer than a battler or a killer. In the Hungarian lore, the healing aspect is stressed over retributive violence, especially in regard to reversing the curses cast by witches. Here again, the differences in the nature of the healers' enemies account for the differences in their methods. The witches in Hungary are linked to female fairies, whose behavior was considered perhaps not so malefic as that of the devotees of Diana engaged in Alpine sabbats, and they are certainly not as dreadful as the unquiet dead who come out of their graves and thus threaten not merely fertility or well-being but the entire natural relationship between life and death.

KRESNIKI

The *kresnik,* or *krsnik,* is a transitional figure between the *benandante* and both the *vampir* and the *vampirdžia,* insofar as his domain is roughly from Slovenia to Serbia (i.e., between Italy and Macedonia-Bulgaria) and inasmuch as he is a deceased person who is able to emerge from his grave to drive away evil spirits or who may himself be an evil being. Once again, the folklore insists that the moral dispositions of both vampires and vampire slayers are unstable and even occasionally interchangeable: slayers may have many of the same markings and attributes (including behavior) as vampires. One way to explain this is by reference to the vampire's original status as a pagan. On the one hand, there seems to have been a class of shamanic or quasi-shamanic individuals who were thought to be able to enter an ecstatic state in order to somehow enter into the world of the dead and there acquire powers to destroy evil influences in the actual world. On the other hand, despite the healing or "white magic" abilities of these healers, they nevertheless represented a worldview that was intolerable to Christians. Hence, at the local level, such extraordinary individuals may have been believed to be fighting to ensure fertility or promote well-being, while from the church's point of view, they were almost as evil as the demonic forces they were said to be battling.

The markers of the *kresnik* are that he was born with a caul or has died in an unbaptized state (*krs-* is the Serbian root for "cross"; *krštenje* means, among other things, "baptism"), perhaps as a result of being born during the Wolf Days. On the Croatian peninsula of Istria, *kresniki* were thought to brandish sticks in battle against witches (*strigoi*) in the air near crossroads. We may connect this weapon to the sorghum and fennel stalks used by the *benandanti* and their opponents and perhaps also to the hawthorn stakes so often used to destroy vampires. The animals available to the *kresnik* for shape-shifting were dogs and horses;

kresniki were also sometimes giants.[13] Another enemy of the *kresnik* in various regions of Istria was called the *kudlak,* which is undoubtedly a simplified variant of the Serbian werewolf-vampire, the *vukodlak/vrkolak.* The battles between the *kresniki* and *kudlaki* were also fought at specific calendrical times, namely, during the Ember Days. (While the predominant religion of Serbia is Orthodoxy, that of Croatia is Roman Catholicism. The link between the activities of the *kresnik* and the Ember Days suggests that this folkloric detail was attached to the Serbian variant of the *kresnik* via Croatia and Slovenia, perhaps ultimately from northeastern Italy.)

The *kresnik* is thus both vampirelike (being unbaptized, a reanimated corpse) and slayerlike (fighting werewolf-vampires with weapons). But he is also *benandante*-like, the main difference being that the *kresnik* fights *kudlaki* rather than witches and changes into a different type of animal in the ecstatic state. Klaniczay is of the opinion that the folkloric battles between *kresniki* and *vukodlaki* reflect prehistorical clashes between "sorcerers" of different classes.[14] Whatever the case, ecstatic encounters with the dead are still at the center of all these types *(benandanti, kresniki,* various vampire slayers), and the ability of one type to share characteristics with or even become equated with another is an indication that in the popular mind, not only did these figures have a great deal in common, but the dualistic categories of good and evil that were superimposed onto the folklore by various forms of Christianity did not effectively account for the more useful agrarian categories of fertility and barrenness that are more closely associated with these ecstatics.

Quite similar beliefs and practices surround a broadly dispersed group of folkloric figures in southern and central parts of Europe who all functioned on the positive side of the village social ledger yet nevertheless were themselves associated, in the Christianizing mind, with their very enemies—witches, sorcerers, vampires. This can be taken as evidence of a historical connection between the antecedents of these characters, perhaps tied, as Ginzburg and Klaniczay suppose,[15] to early shamanistic religious beliefs in parts of pre-Christian Europe. Heretofore, a connection between Slavic werewolves (which eventually merged typologically with Serbian-Macedonian-Bulgarian vampires) and both the Hungarian *táltos* and the Italian *benandanti* has been proposed and investigated, but the suggestion of an additional link reaching from this constellation down to the Balkan vampire slayers, the *glog, sâbotnik,* and *vampirdžia,* has so far not been made. Ginzburg is tentatively of the opinion that the Bulgarian folklore may "add a relevant nuance to the European quasi-shamanistic layer,"[16] but a great deal of work remains to establish the pathways of contact and syncretism that would also explain the substantial differences between the Western European witch seers and the Eastern European vampire hunters (if such a broad geographic and cultural boundary may be temporarily drawn).

Although in some sense all of these seer-slayers have symbolic contact with the dead or the realm of the dead, the fact that the vampire slayer is engaged with an actual corpse is not an insignificant variation. The vampire, for all the varieties of etiology and characteristics and activity, is still in all cases an individual whose exclusion from the community goes far beyond mere marginalization. The vampire is an evil culprit only ex post facto: he is known by his deeds, and the effect-and-cause relationship between any evidence of an attack and a putative vampire may be certified by an outside professional whose conferred ability to detect and destroy vampires absolves his employers from any subsequent charge of injustice.

The injustice, of course, lies in blaming an innocent person for a crime he or she cannot possibly have committed. In the case of witches, their crimes were implicit in their supposed heretical and orgiastic behavior at sabbats, and the true injustice of the accusations against them, such as occurred during the Inquisition, was ultimately obscured by the confirmation to be found in the fate of the witches themselves. Whereas eventually the *benandanti* (among others) complied when asked to identify insidious witches, a confession by an accused witch (generally under torture) unequivocally validated the claims of the accuser. Barring such a confession, the accused witch's failure to pass a life-or-death test of guilt naturally could also absolve the accusers of any injustice, since succumbing to lethal torture was not in itself exculpatory evidence of witchcraft or a pact with the Devil.

South of the Danube, the dynamic of accusation and punishment of vampires was markedly different. Heresy in the Balkans had long passed as a motive for persecution and a cause of epidemic misfortune, the heretical Bogomils having been driven underground and perhaps into Europe some time in the fourteenth century.[17] Certainly, some residue of Orthodox hostility to paganism and heresy remained long after the Byzantine polemics against them had quieted. But without specific living targets of persecution (such as remained in Catholic Europe) and with the superimposition of a foreign, Islamic authority, the mechanisms of accusation and scapegoating necessarily shifted.

Witch trials of the sort that occurred during the Inquisition and in Hungary could only come about in a society where there was a pre-existing code of evidentiary procedure that could be applied to legal cases brought against living individuals. Among the consequences of the European Enlightenment was the emergence of the precept of separation of church and state, which came about partly as a reaction to the perversions of justice carried out against witches by courts that were tethered too closely to ecclesiastical powers. No such historical movement developed in southeastern Europe, since the legal precedent of the Inquisition was based on Roman law.[18]

The possible reasons that witch trials did not occur in Bulgaria and Macedonia, at least not with the same frequency or intensity as in the West, are far too complex to discuss here, but the fact of the matter is that until the early eighteenth century (i.e., toward the early stages of the Enlightenment), the vampire was essentially a Slavic and Balkan phenomenon, confined to the domain of Orthodoxy. Functionally, vampires shared many characteristics with witches and sorcerers: they were all despised, abject figures, marginalized or persecuted, at the low end of the totem pole and therefore subject to distortions and abuses of power and liable to be held responsible without due process for any number of phenomena, ranging from the unpleasant to the catastrophic. But the attacks on heresy gathered a kind of momentum under Western European law that they never did in the Eastern European countries, perhaps because the domination of the Balkans by the Ottoman Empire had quelled any impulse toward scientific rationalism while it paradoxically suppressed the deeply embedded religious intolerance that ultimately led to the Inquisition.

From a purely ethical vantage, there is something to be said in support of a folkloric system that focuses collective blame not on innocent, living individuals but, rather, on those whose lives are already over and whose bodies therefore can be presumed to be insentient. However gruesome the rituals prescribed for disposing of a vampire—and the techniques certainly compare with the methods of torture of witches[19]—it was of course always understood that a corpse imagined as ambulatory would nevertheless feel no pain when impaled or incinerated or hobbled. The guilt of the vampire required no real evidence, since the causes of vampirism were in any case held to be outside the control of the village, a matter of either a debauched or wayward life or else an improper death or burial. What was important was not to prove that a particular vampire committed a particular social injury; rather, it was necessary merely to demonstrate that there was indeed a vampire afoot. Identification of the vampire was thus not unlike selecting a black sheep from a flock for ritual slaughter. The marking alone was enough to determine the victim.

A vampire, though, was generally not visible to ordinary people, at least not according to the preponderance of Balkan folkloric accounts. The task of the special seer in Western Europe was to identify actual defendants in a court proceeding (whether sham or not). In the region of the vampire, however, the seer selected a vampire much like a dowser finds water, and his mystical pointer was by definition infallible. How could it be otherwise? How could a village in search of a vampire to destroy argue with the professional seer that had been consulted to do nothing more than choose—not really identify—a deceased victim for ritual immolation? By definition, when alive, the vampire would have been either someone no one cared much about (an alcoholic, a suicide, a heretic) or, in those cases where the vampire had come into existence as a result of some inadvertent violence or ritual funereal infelicity, someone whose unfortunately unquiet soul needed to be liberated (by mimetic violence) from the demonic and abject corpse and set back on the natural path to the otherworld. The choice made by the vampire slayer was therefore unquestionable. There was really no point in arguing with him, since there would never be anything resembling due process, and besides, the individual identified was dead.

We may imagine that the vampire slayer, having become aware of his special powers in early adolescence (if not earlier), would know all the possible ways a person could become a vampire and the ways in which a vampire could be destroyed. But more important, the slayer would have learned how to be sensitive to the unstated will of the community and would be able to "read" the community's wishes in selecting the most likely candidate vampire. In other words, like any other gossip or scandal in a small community, people would have already known who the vampire was. They just needed a slayer to point the accusing finger and perhaps even perform the ritual violence that they could not bring themselves to do.

8

THE RATIONAL SLAYER

The violent and unjust excesses of the Inquisition in Western Europe and of a later, but parallel, series of witch trials in Hungary in the second half of the seventeenth century led, ultimately, to many philosophical, theological, and legal inquiries attempting to explain the phenomena of witchcraft. Growing intolerance for the rather lopsided system of accusation and persecution evolved into a concerted and widespread attack on religious zealotry in mainstream European society. However, the attempt to eliminate zealous witch persecutors naturally also resulted in the elimination of visible witches once and for all. The "scientific" explanations of witchcraft and sorcery (and vampirism) succeeded in pulling the rug out from under the Inquisitors by denying the reality of the very object of their accusations. Thus, rationalism was a more effective tool for eradicating witches than were the witch trials themselves, since the residual pagan beliefs that were held by the worshipers of Diana, for example, were shown to be simply irrational and thus not of any further consequence. Vampires likewise represented an impossibility, since from the new, Cartesian perspective, a being could not logically be dead and alive at the same time.

I propose that the new inquirers—such as Gerard van Swieten—who were charged by the leading political figures of Enlightenment Europe with proving the irrationality of pagan beliefs were in fact completing the task set by the Inquisition. They accomplished this not by bringing heretics to trial and executing them (which had the unintended effect of reifying the subversive power of the persecuted groups) but by effectively debunking heretical and pagan beliefs as superstition. Those who held on to such beliefs were no longer to be persecuted by the now magnanimous state; rather, they were to be pitied.[1] In their reports, the investigators into witchcraft and vampirism attempted to show the absurdity of any beliefs that were not in accord with what could be proved by the emerging scientific method, on the one hand, or confirmed by Judeo-Christian scripture on the other. While this shift in attitude resulted in a drastic decrease in persecution of those individuals formerly at risk of being labeled witches, it also trivialized their actual beliefs and practices by considering them misguided and irrelevant rather than politically dangerous. The Catholic Church was rapidly losing political power to the secular state.

As I noted in chapter 5, this rationalizing impulse led to the incursion of vampire beliefs into Western Europe from the Balkans. Beginning around the end of the seventeenth century, at the boundary between the territories of the Ottoman and Habsburg empires, local vampire beliefs were suddenly amplified by the same sort of epidemic hysteria that rose up around witchcraft beliefs in the West. Stories about vampires quickly became newsworthy and intriguing to the literate classes. Because Slavic vampire tales had until then been little known outside lands controlled by the Ottoman Porte, they represented a new threat, a new form of strange magic and supernaturalism from the Orient that needed to be dealt with in the same way as witchcraft: they needed to be explained away, lest a whole new project of inquisitional proportions arise.

In the eventual translation of the vampire from the Eastern into the Western European worldview, certain things were lost. First, the Slavic/Orthodox conceptions of the otherworld and the natural path of the soul after death were never taken into consideration in the reports of vampire activity brought back from Serbia. In fact, there was little attempt on the part of the investigators to understand the cultural context of the folklore; rather, they simply tried to somehow explain the reported phenomena as though the narratives referred to real events. Second, in the east-west boundary regions, vampires were seen as being conspiratorial, like witches, although this attribute is never found elsewhere in South Slavic folklore. It was difficult for the new rationalists, now peering more deeply into the strange Orient of the Ottoman Balkans, to understand in the vampire a mechanism for handling village accusation and justice under certain well-defined circumstances. Instead, they could only perceive the vampire as a strange variant of the witch, who, as an actual living being, was susceptible to the full force of a complex prosecutorial system inherited from Roman law.

Still, the rationalists' purpose was to completely destroy the imaginary and the folkloric and to replace them with the materialistic and scientific, partly as a reaction against the sort of violent, elaborate fantasies that had tormented the Inquisitors as much as their victims and led to cycles of extreme persecution and excessive punishment. Once science had explained away the vampire as unreal, it was no longer possible for this sort of folklore to have any autonomy among the folk—especially in those areas where the vampire was not native. No longer would the imaginings of illiterate farmers or herders in the mountain villages command the attention that was now properly devoted to the project of science and technology. In the West, vampire folklore could therefore never take root, but following the reports that began to flow into Austria and beyond, the vampire soon became an object of fascination to artists and writers, who saw in these tales new metaphoric opportunities for expressing symbolic aspects of social power relationships. The Western authors, however, were unaware that the version of the vampire they had inherited from the journalists had been contaminated by projected notions about witches and, thanks to medical materialism, epidemic disease. Perhaps the one person most responsible for the link between the vampire and epidemic disease was the Dutch physician Gerard van Swieten.

THE LOWLANDS SLAYER

Van Swieten was first and foremost a physician, eventually named chief physician at the Court of Vienna by Maria Theresa (r. 1740–

Fig. 6. Gerard van Swieten. (Courtesy of the National Library of Medicine, Bethesda, MD.)

80), who came to trust him more than she trusted any of her other advisors. In his early years, he had been one of the most gifted pupils of the renowned Dutch medical scientist Herman Boerhaave, and he already possessed a significant reputation as a physician in his home city of Leiden when his erudition and relationships to many eminent scientists came to the attention of the Austrian empress. Frank Brechka considers Van Swieten worthy of biography not because he was "a founder, maker or incarnation of the age" but, rather, because he was "so intimately involved in the typical problems and attitudes of the time." In the domain of medical science, Van Swieten became certainly the most important and visible representative of the Enlightenment in Austria. But beyond that and more important for our purposes, he served, as noted by Brechka, as an "intermediary between the Lowlands and Vienna, between the advanced culture of western Europe and the backward condition of Austria."[2]

Among its other holdings, the Habsburg Empire controlled most of the area to the north of the Ottoman-controlled Slavic countries on the other side of the Danube, having finally pushed back the Turks from Hungary in the late seventeenth century.[3] In the middle of the eighteenth century, Austria was facing a crisis in the form of military challenges from two technologically advanced modern European powers to the west and north, France and Prussia. Frederick the Great had invaded Silesia in the north, and the newly enthroned empress quickly understood both the nature of the threat posed by European modernity and the need to reform the underdeveloped regions of the Habsburg dominion and bring it into contention with other emerging Enlightenment centers. For political reasons having to do primarily with serious tensions, at that time, between Roman Catholics and Protestants, the empress sought out advisors for her reforms who were, like her and like Austria itself, Roman Catholic. The Dutch, meanwhile, were widely admired for their scholarship and progressiveness, qualities that were not in abundance in Vienna.

Since the Lowlands, or southern Netherlands, belonged to Austria in 1714, Van Swieten was already a de facto citizen of the Habsburg Empire. Furthermore, though a devout Roman Catholic, he was reportedly anti-Jesuit and tended to hold a number of heterodox secular opinions, in part the result of his broad exposure to the scientific thought of the day. He had, for example, encountered through his brief education at the University of Louvain the views of the seventeenth-century Belgian Jansenist Zeger Bernhard van Espen,[4] who had penned several anti-Jesuit treatises against religious fanaticism and veneration of saints, as well as essays asserting "the true foundation, origin, and nature of the two powers, God and Caesar."[5] Later, at the University of Leiden, having abandoned the study of law at Louvain, Van Swieten became immersed in the wake of the late seventeenth-century controversy over Cartesianism and mechanistic philosophy. Leiden, where

Descartes himself had lived for many years, was a focal point of discourse surrounding skeptical philosophy and natural science and had been the site of a great deal of interest in practical medicine (including anatomical dissection) and scientific experiment. It was at Leiden, under the influence of Boerhaave, the most brilliant and influential physician of Europe, that Van Swieten acquired his philosophy of and approach to medicine and science and naturally became a major proponent of Enlightenment values.

By virtue of his citizenship as well as his scientific knowledge and religious views, then, Gerard van Swieten was the perfect choice for Maria Theresa to employ in reforming Austro-Hungary's position in regard to science and medicine. Van Swieten had acquired his medical education just as the science of medicine was undergoing great change in the West, and experimental results were beginning to undercut the predominant but archaic theories of Galen. Van Swieten's mentor had called for physicians to be thoroughly versed in all branches of science, including chemistry, pharmacy, and botany. Understanding of anatomy and of the circulatory system was a mandatory precursor to understanding theoretical and therapeutic medicine.[6] Van Swieten adhered to these recommendations tenaciously.

After receiving his medical degree, Van Swieten spent the years from 1725 to 1745 practicing in Leiden and working as a scholar of medicine and its history. Perhaps because he held Catholic religious beliefs (while the Netherlands was a Protestant country), but more likely thanks to the professional jealousy of his less erudite colleagues, he was never allowed to teach at the University of Leiden, though he did conduct private lessons. He attended virtually all lectures of Boerhaave for twenty years, and from his verbatim notes, he compiled a collection of Boerhaave's aphorisms, which he ultimately published with his own commentaries in five volumes (1769). In this work, he discussed contemporary theories of disease and therapy, especially in regard to the causes and treatment of fevers. However, since the germ theory had not yet been advanced, his conclusions about the physical causation of corporeal diseases remained vague and incomplete, and his popular books were eventually rejected as being incorrect and out of date. Still, his reputation as an encyclopedist of medical knowledge preceded him to Vienna.

In late 1744, Maria's sister, Marianne, the Austrian archduchess, became very sick with a septic high fever following the stillborn delivery of a girl, who would have been princess. Count Kaunitz, who was aware of Van Swieten's reputation (although the physician's chapter on diagnosing and treating fever had not yet been published), summoned him to Brussels to care for the archduchess. Van Swieten arrived on November 11 but was too late to save Marianne. This was not merely a personal loss for the empress; Marianne had been married to Charles of Lorraine, and her death weakened the political connection between the Houses of Habsburg and Lorraine. Although Van Swieten could not save Maria's only sister, he cared for her to the utmost, which ingratiated him to Maria Theresa enormously. After Van Swieten had returned to Leiden, the Austrian empress entered into a very warm correspondence with him, in which she expressed both her grief and her gratitude. On the basis of the trust built up during this correspondence, Van Swieten eventually moved to Vienna to become the court physician.

Van Swieten's primary role in the now formal coalition between Austria and Hungary (the Hungarian and Austrian provinces had been declared inseparable in the Pragmatic Sanction of 1723)[7] was, in a sense, to bring the Enlightenment to the Habsburg domain. Hungary in particular had suffered from almost two centuries of defensive wars, and Maria Theresa well understood the need to improve culture, education, and science across the board. The task, as Brechka puts it, was to do away with faculties that taught useless knowledge and resisted new ideas, with apothecaries that dispensed incorrect drugs and threatened the lives of citizens, with papal agents who interfered with necessary change. A self-sufficient, unified, and effective state could afford neither divisiveness nor stupidity. Moreover, the new knowledge of the West would have to be admitted.[8]

Van Swieten used his scholastic training and gift for classification and organization and his capacity as both chief physician (*protomedicus*) and court librarian (*bibliothecarius*) to help modernize the University of Vienna. He also eventually became the president of Maria Theresa's Chastity Commission (*Keuscheitskommission*), which had been created in 1753 to save the public (Catholic) morals and, more important, to limit exposure of the literate populace to any dangerous ideas that might potentially subvert the goal of bringing Austria into the enlightened West. Curiously, while Van Swieten had been hired to look forward and help create a progressive society, he nevertheless found himself in the position of having to ban certain books. He even maintained a list, the *Supplementum librorum prohibitorum,* apparently annotated in a script that only he could decipher.

It might seem a contradiction that the same person who sought to expose to the light of reason the fallacies and illogic of vampire beliefs should also uphold the mandate to suppress books of "false science." Among the books he condemned were works suggesting that there was a scientific basis for palmistry and astrology.[9] Alchemy, too, was regarded as charlatanism. While, from today's perspective, we might view censorship itself as opposite to the aims of Enlightenment politics, it was actually Maria Theresa who created the Chastity Commission, out of fear that she would not be able to prevent contamination of the new, emerging knowledge by the old. This fear must have arisen in part as a result of the rapid resettlement that occurred following the decline of Turkish occupation of Hungary, whereby Bohemian Slavs from the north, Serbs from the south, and Germans from the west began to move into the Hungarian plains.[10] Mobile ethnic groups tend to bring with them their religious beliefs. Meanwhile, witch accusations had become epidemic in the 1720s in southern Hungary (Szeged). Clearly Maria Theresa was concerned lest some of these beliefs reemerge and interfere with the task of advancing science and education.

The concern was pragmatic: theoretical sciences developed during the Renaissance were now being harnessed to practical and utilitarian aims. Science, as such, was to be utilized for the material betterment of humankind, in the form of better technology and better medicine. Superstitious belief was no longer a matter of religious heresy but, rather, was evidence that believers in such things could not successfully participate in the movement toward social enlightenment. Indeed, Central European anti-Semitism is evident even in the opinions of Van Swieten, who claimed that "the superstitions of the Jews prevented them from becoming *useful members of society.*" (italics added)[11]

What is important to see in the co-occurrence of the attempt to create a progressive and enlightened state with the establishment of the Chastity Commission or the preservation of anti-Semitic beliefs is that the very blind spot that formed the logic of the Inquisition had not really been eliminated by Enlightenment politics. Rather, as the old beliefs were equated with ignorance, pity was shown to those who had been labeled sorcerers, witches, and the like—the empress herself pardoned a Bohemian peasant who had been sentenced to death for sorcery—and this pity effectively became a new mode of marginalization. Social usefulness became the greater measure of worth, and as Austria and Hungary attempted to align themselves with the more urbane cultures of the north and west, agrarian beliefs naturally confounded usefulness in the sense of scientific progress.

In regard to this book's theme, a shift occurred around the mid-eighteenth century that not only redefined the vampire as a symbolic (eventually literary) creature rather than a folkloric one but also established the role of the vampire slayer as a rationalist, whose tools against the vampire were no longer physically destructive and no longer belonged to the same ritual system but instead relied on learning and scientific knowledge to destroy the demons of the unconscious past. The victory of the new rationalism became self-evident, and any resistance to it constituted nothing more serious than a form of pitiable self-delusion. Paradoxically, in the attempt to destroy the social injustices that were being perpetuated on the purveyors of false religion and, therefore, false reason, alternative beliefs were ignominiously swept away by the growth of the new state.

In order to understand the logic that was being mobilized to squelch, once and for all, belief in vampires and witches, it is worth taking a look in some detail at the arguments that Van Swieten raised in his report from 1755. We shall see there that Van Swieten himself made no important distinction between witchcraft and vampires, at least with regard to their treatment after death. Curiously, despite his grand attempt to rationalize folk beliefs, he could not seem to avoid bringing religious ideas about the sacred and evil into his reasoning.

GERARD VAN SWIETEN AND HIS CONSIDERATION OF THE CLAIM OF POSTHUMOUS MAGIC

In 1755, Maria Theresa dispatched Van Swieten to Hermersdorf, Moravia, to investigate the postmortem treatment of a certain "Rosina Polackin" (Van Swieten's spelling).[12] His primary obligation was to defuse any possibility of a renewed epidemic of vampirism such as had occurred twenty years prior. He would accomplish this by writing up for the empress a report in which he explained, according to the medical and biophysical understanding of the day, the phenomena usually associated with vampires, especially regarding the physical state of their exhumed corpses. This report would then serve as guidance and rationale for imperial policy with respect to such beliefs and provide Maria Theresa with the scientific authority to intervene in any future cases where a deceased body was mutilated as a result of belief in vampires.

Van Swieten's ostensible goal, then, was not so much to destroy vampires as to undercut the motive for retributive violence done to the body or the grave of the deceased. In that respect, we cannot legitimately call Van Swieten a vampire slayer. He directed his antagonism, at least in his treatise, not at those who were considered vampires (who were, after all, from a medical point of view, quite dead) but, rather, at the survivors whose beliefs led to sacrilegious defilement and propagated irrational ideas about the processes of death and decomposition. But with the issuance of Van Swieten's report, which proposed the clear superiority of a materialist explanation for supernatural events, any remaining folkloric or mythological function of belief in the animated dead crumbled immediately into dust. Perhaps equally important is the fact that the so-called demonic ceased to exist, having been replaced for the time being by a more abstract, Christian view of evil, which the Catholic Van Swieten offered as a real force but one subservient to God. With the death of the demonic in Western Europe, vampires and witches ceased to have any real interest that was not either nostalgic or romantic.

Van Swieten's *Consideration of the Claim of Posthumous Magic* first sets up the problem of supernatural occurrences within a Christian frame. He personifies abstract evil as an "Evil Spirit" (*lo Spirito maligno*) or "the Demon" (*il Demonio*), but never refers to it—as others had done so often during the Reformation and Counter-Reformation—as "Satan." Perhaps bowing to Maria Theresa's distaste for Protestants, Van Swieten finds it important to cite right away the philosophical problem of whether there can be supernatural causes behind phenomena that are not otherwise easily understood.

> When people observe extraordinary effects whose causes are unknown, they always attribute them to some higher powers. The history of every

century demonstrates this. Now it is a certainty known from the Holy Scriptures, whether through the holy angels, His prophets, apostles or other holy men, that by His omnipotence God created such marvelous effects. Ecclesiastical history can convince those who are more incredulous that on account of the beautiful principle of Christianity such marvelous effects did not ever cease. Scholarly persons and honest Protestants have not been able to deny that the Holy Apostle of the Indians has proved his mission by such clear miracles. It is equally true that the Evil Spirit must have permission from God to produce effects that surpass natural causes. That which occurred when our Savior was tempted in the desert suffices to prove this.

No Christian can deny that there are persons possessed by the Evil Spirit, and that consequently this malignant spirit can act upon human bodies. It is likewise true that the Demon disturbs men with noises and frightening visions. The Protestants themselves confess that the idolaters of the abominable Indians prove the malice of the Master, whom they serve; but as soon as they have destroyed the bonds of their slavery to the Demon through the holy sacrament of the baptism, and become members of the Church, the diabolic illusions come to an end; this has served to convert many people.[13]

Here, Van Swieten is quite careful to establish that there exist both true miracles, which are authored by God alone, and supernatural illusions that are produced through the agency of a deceptive, "diabolic" force. Enticement by illusions is tantamount to possession. But these two similar phenomena can ultimately be distinguished through a kind of exorcistic gnosis; that is, the grace that accompanies baptism apparently has the power to banish possessing demonic forces. Dr. Van Swieten opposes both miracles and demonic illusions against a third class of appearances, those things that appear to be miraculous or supernatural because a reasonable physical explanation is not available. If, by the way, we examine Van Swieten's remarks from the point of view of the history of medicine, clearly the dominant rational belief in mid-eighteenth-century Vienna was that physical maladies had definite physiological—and therefore treatable—etiologies (even though not all of them may yet have been understood), while psychiatric diseases were still bound to demonic influence. In one sense, Van Swieten is fobbing off onto the church the intractability of psychiatric disorders, but there is a hint, in his text, that he is aware that these diseases, too, are medical in nature and subject to treatment. Perhaps it is no accident that psychiatry becomes a separate discipline in Vienna a hundred years after Van Swieten (d. 1772).

Van Swieten later points out how in the absence of scientific explanation, technological and perceptual curiosities can be exploited by those seeking to gain personal power. He assumes that "posthumous magic"—namely, the inexplicable failure of the body to decompose completely after burial—is one such type of exploitative wizardry, whereby people may be convinced of a supernatural cause when none really exists. He attributes the origin of the belief in vampires to the "Schismatic Greeks," which is correct to the extent that the belief arises in the context of conversion of the Balkan peoples to Byzantine (Greek) Orthodoxy, though he is naturally unaware that the word *vampir* is Slavic. He bases this conclusion on the writing of the French botanist Joseph Pitton de Tournefort, who had traveled to the Levant and described vampire beliefs he encountered during his travels.

> Gunpowder, electrical phenomena, or optical illusions have the ability to astonish all that do not know about them; and charlatans use this to make the credulous public believe they are most powerful wizards. Therefore it is again certain that marvels diminish when measured by science. The posthumous magic treated here provides new proof, because all those tales come from countries where ignorance reigns; and it is very likely that the Schismatic Greeks are the main progenitors. Tournefort, a scholar and evidently a doctor, and the greatest botanist of his century, was sent by Louis XIV into Asia, primarily to examine some plants in Greece that had been imperfectly described by ancient Greek medicine. There he was able to see at very close range a corpse that had been accused of demonic magic, and also how all means were used to impede the Demon, so that more would not use dead bodies in order to torment the living.[14]

Curiously, Van Swieten seems to take the various reports of vampirism (and antivampire behavior) at face value, even though his entire physician's argument that such things are nonsense derives both from a devotion to autopsy (whose Greek-derived name literally means "seeing with one's own eyes") and from the logical arrangement of demonstrated facts. It is as if he is in such a hurry to provide a scientific explanation for the phenomena on which he is reporting that he ignores the question of whether these things really happened in the first place and, if they did, the question of whether the testimony surrounding them might exhibit any discrepancy that would suggest something other than peasant ignorance at work.

Van Swieten takes Tournefort's mention of vampires in Hungary (not Greece) as primary data and as the first mention of vampires that he is aware of. By the time of Tournefort's journey in the late seventeenth century, the epidemic aspect of the vampire was already present. Van Swieten includes the actual passage from the third letter of Tournefort's *Travels,* but he annotates it thus:

> This story can reveal what ought to be thought about that which happened in 1732, in a small town in Hungary, in a region named in Latin *Oppictum Heidonum,* situated between the Thiess [*Tisza*] and Transylvania. Posthumous magic predominated in this letter about the little town. The dead men, who were completely godless, were called "vampires," and they were believed to suck the blood of persons and even beasts, and when they had eaten the meat of such beings, they joined the dead men and changed into vampires; and in this way one who had been a passive vampire during life then became an active vampire after death, unless one consumed the earth of the vampire's sepulcher or rubbed it with its blood.
>
> I have not told this story without reason. I also believe that the official record was sent to the Imperial Council of War in Vienna at the beginning of 1732. The ceremony that was practiced was dictated by a *haiduk,* that is, by the local judge, a man quite expert in vampirism. A sharp stake is passed through the chest of the hunted vampire; then the head is cut off; everything is incinerated and the ashes are thrown into the grave.
>
> Vampirism spreads quickly and is as contagious as mange. Some credence is given to the notion that a cadaverous vampire in a very short time can infect every other body buried in the same cemetery if the first one is not destroyed immediately.[15]

The fact that an "official record" of vampire events in rural eastern Hungary was submitted to Vienna is proof enough for Van Swieten, especially since the ritual for disposing of a vampire had been "dictated by a *haiduk, . . .* a man quite expert in vampirism."[16] Since the *haiduk*'s report describes actions that are cited in much vampire folklore in the Balkans and surrounding areas, there is certainly no reason to mistrust it, except for the fact that the actions prescribed are somewhat excessive: first the stake is driven in, then the head is lopped off, and then the whole dead thing is burned and the ashes are thrown back into the grave. Van Swieten does not question whether this report from Hungary might in fact include an expedient and exaggerated synthesis of several different practices known folklorically to the townsfolk (including the local judge). Rather, the official's presumed expertise in such matters passes as sufficient evidence that vampires in this Hungarian town were rekilled by every possible means. It is advantageous for Van Swieten to accept this distant testimony literally, since the excessive violence done to the dead serves his purpose and justifies authoritarian intervention in such extreme practices.

Despite the case Van Swieten is attempting to build—namely, that the existence of supernatural vampires cannot be proved by the visual evidence available at exhumation and, therefore, that there is no reason to exhume and immolate suspicious corpses—he cannot avoid repeating that the dead men in this case were "completely godless." Van Swieten's skepticism is still informed by religion-centered moral judgments, according to which some impiety may be, if not an excuse, at least a legitimate explanation for the reactions of the townspeople. Vampires or no, it is understandable—if we may read between Van Swieten's interpretive lines—that people would consider godless people to be somehow connected to evil and would thus be inclined to take violent action to stop its spread.

As I pointed out earlier, the idea that vampires are like disease (in this case, they are likened to mange) is a belief that attaches itself to vampire notions late and generally outside the Balkans proper. Here, if we are to believe Tournefort, the notion is encountered in Hungary, where vampire beliefs had come into contact with Western European witchcraft beliefs. But Van Swieten amplifies the urgency of dealing with this epidemic aspect: Tournefort's letter does suggest that bloodsucking or eating flesh of humans and vampires turns those (living) victims into vampires, but Van Swieten links this capability to the rapid spread of vampirism among the dead within a cemetery. This notion, as we shall presently see, possesses immediacy for Van Swieten because of his personal experience in Moravia. On the one hand, Van Swieten is quite certain that epidemic vampirism is a false belief needing to be demystified, yet on the other, the flat assertion that vampirism "spreads quickly and is as contagious as mange" contradicts the intention to show that vampirism does not exist. We must suspect that Van Swieten thus accepts that popular notions about vampires constitute an authentic, but misguided, version of some physiological facts that he can refute beyond doubt with counterevidence from his own experience as a scientist as well as from other reports.

It is true that our vampires of 1755 had not yet become bloodsuckers, but they were all predisposed to becoming such. Because the executioner, a person no doubt quite truthful concerning the matters of his trade, asserted that in cutting up the cadavers that had been condemned to the fire, some blood flowed out with vehemence and in abundance. This in spite of the fact that it is generally agreed that after death there usually remains no more than a spoonful. This affects the story a great deal. The extraordinary facts that are believed to have been observed can be brought down to these two points:

1. that cadavers of posthumous magic, or vampires, do not decompose, but instead remain whole and pliable;
2. that these vampires bother the living with apparitions, noises, suffocation, etc.

I will succinctly consider whether these two points are possible.

A corpse is ordinarily inclined to rot, during which process virtually all parts of the body are dissipated, except the bones . . . Proof of this is that when a coffin was opened fifteen years after a woman had died, and it had not been struck with anything, the corpse seemed to remain whole. The lines of the face and clothes etc. were still discernible. But when the casket was moved even quite deftly, everything immediately turned into shapeless powder, and only the bones remained.

Since the dead must make a place for the burial of their successors, there is a fixed term of fifteen years in many countries after which gravediggers may move the corpse. I have assisted many times at such tomb openings, and with a little bribe of food I was at least able to get the gravediggers to open some of the caskets very carefully. From that experience I remain convinced that after we die we are not the pasture of worms, at least not always, because if that were true, this powder would not retain facial details. When the contents of the grave are removed, sometimes whole corpses are encountered rather than putrefied ones, but they are quite desiccated nevertheless, and of a brownish hue, and the flesh is very toasted without the cadavers being in an embalmed state. The gravediggers assured me that it was common for about one out of every thirty corpses to be desiccated without putrefaction. I therefore concluded that a corpse can remain incorrupt for several years, without there being some supernatural cause.[17]

Van Swieten evidently considers vampire beliefs—and perhaps all folkloric beliefs—to be superstitions based in ignorance: he reduces the evidence from vampire reports down to two basic assertions: that vampires do not decompose in the grave and, therefore, that they are capable of walking around and interfering with the society of the living. By demonstrating that the first assertion is illusory—in fact, under certain quite demonstrable and natural conditions, corpses decay only very slowly and may even retain some detail in their features, so long as the coffin is not jarred—it becomes easy to assert the impossibility of the second. The belief that the corpse can be ambulatory is contingent on the lifelike appearance of the desiccated corpse.

In contrast to this sort of explanation, it is worth noting that in most South Slavic folklore about vampires, the condition of the corpse is not of particular interest. The identity of the vampire only needs to be confirmed either by ritual means or with the help of some sort of vampire seer. The villagers may or may not go so far as to dig up the corpse and perform some vampire-destroying ritual, but if they were to take action, it would be extremely rare for anyone to go to the extremes cited by the *haiduk* (since carrying out the ritual violence in one form or another is all that is important). In other words, in the Orthodox context, physical evidence of vampirism after the fact is irrelevant, since the vampire is originally identified (i.e., instantiated) to explain certain local phenomena. Imagine if this were not the case: for example, if a particular deceased person were labeled a vampire for any of the reasons discussed in earlier chapters and then the corpse was dug up in order to be transfixed, what would happen if it were then discovered that the body had indeed decomposed naturally? Would this result somehow disprove the accusation of vampirism?

In Moravia, Silesia, and other areas around and within Austro-Hungary, vampire beliefs had migrated from regions across the Danube, and thus came to survive outside the context of Orthodox Christianity and its views of the afterlife. (Indeed, in Orthodox belief, failure of the body to decompose may be a sign of saintliness, not evil.) Within their new Protestant cultural context, the emphasis of vampire narratives shifted away from the problem of burial infelicity and toward descriptions of the more literal encounter with the decomposing body. The vampire now posed a different sort of philosophical problem, having to do with the dangerous kind of directed magical power (notice how Van Swieten and Tournefort refer to "posthumous magic") that had been the subject of accusations against witches and sorcerers. The question of the reality of this supernatural power to reanimate the inanimate was still on the minds of the post-Reformation politicians: in Central Europe, the vampire represented an instrument of this power, capable of infecting (in the same way witches were capable of "spoiling") various village resources (especially human).

In his *Consideration,* Van Swieten brings other evidence that corpses do not decompose at the same rate: he points to a case in Devonshire, England, in 1751, where a man buried in a family grave site eighty years earlier was exhumed, revealing the "body of a completely intact man." Since the local parish registry confirmed that no one had been buried in that crypt after 1669, Van Swieten amusedly points out, "[H]ere is an English vampire who over the course of eighty years stayed tranquilly in his tomb without disturbing anyone." Having brought forth secondary evidence disproving the contention that vampire corpses unnaturally refuse to decompose, Van Swieten then reports his personal experience—namely, the case that brought him to Moravia.

> We see at last the facts alleged as evidence of vampirism. Rosina Polackin, who died on December 22, 1754, was disinterred on January 19, 1755, and declared a vampire worthy of cremation, because she had not yet decomposed. The anatomists can keep corpses in the open air during winter for up to six weeks, even two months without putrefaction. It should also be noted that this particular winter was severe beyond the norm. In all the other corpses, decomposition had already consumed the greater part of the body. It sufficed that if not everything had putrefied, the body was suddenly to be worthy of the fire! What igno-

rance! In the writings of the Consistory the sure signs or countersigns on the corpses of vampires are described, but these are not specific to any part. Two bumbling surgeons, who had never seen a desiccated corpse and did not know the details of the structure of the human body as they themselves confessed to the Commissary, testified that they recommended a sentence of burning. It is quite true that the Commissary of Olmutz had not always brought surgeons to examine the facts, they had only sent a spiritual Commissary, who quite unwillingly made judgments about cases of vampirism; since it had resulted from a previous act, that in the year 1723 they burned the body of a man thirteen days after his death, and in the sentence alleged that the reason was that his grandmother had not lived in good repute in the community. In 1724 they burned the corpse of a man eighteen days after death, because he was a relative of the person mentioned previously. It was enough to be related to a supposed vampire, and the trial became good and final. Thus, they burned the body of a man two days after his death for this very reason, without other testimony, that the corpse retained a good complexion after death, and the joints were still flexible.[18]

A good deal of impatience is evident in this section of Van Swieten's treatise. He seems barely able to conceal his contempt for so-called surgeons whose ignorance of postmortem processes allows them to side with the authorities recommending cremation of an exhumed corpse. He is even more annoyed at the reasoning behind the desecration of a man's corpse only eighteen days after his death. The last straw for Van Swieten is the illogic of a case on April 23, 1723, where the Consistory of Olmutz caused nine corpses to be burned, since it was believed they had been infected by a vampire buried before them in the same cemetery. Such a violent fate, however, did not await those who had been buried before the supposed vampire. On the contrary, they received mercy, even though, later, "Commissaries Wabst and Gesser showed that in these unsuspicious corpses are still found parts not yet corrupt and in one, even a little blood."[19] Van Swieten insists (rightly) that these two conditions are not necessarily compatible: if lack of decomposition and the presence of venous blood are sure signs of vampirism, then they cannot be conveniently ignored in the case where vampirism is instead determined by some presumed sequence of infection.

Van Swieten thus insists that there should be an internal logic to folkloric beliefs, which, of course, there frequently is not. In fact, we might claim that lack of coherent logic becomes the primary accusation of this Enlightenment physician, as if rational thought and reality were inextricably linked. Like dreams, folkloric narratives frequently embody apparent contradictions, yet Van Swieten uses this fact as confirmation that the narratives cannot possibly describe real events. The superordination of the empirically real to the imaginal is so critical to Van Swieten that he cannot see any social value in systems where contradictions and anomalies are not resolved.

Van Swieten's motive, we must not forget, is to promote the cessation of mistreatment of both the dead and the living as a result of these irrational folk beliefs. This apparently noble purpose, however, is linked to an intolerance for ambiguity and anomaly and thus ends up destroying one of the very mechanisms available for expressing conflicts that cannot be expressed in more Cartesian terms.

Van Swieten exhibits a clear compassion for those who are persecuted for their misguided superstitious beliefs. In one passage, for example, he shows that a peasant woman's herbal folk remedies and claims to magic were in fact harmless, amounting to nothing more than common chicanery. But her eventual exhumation and incineration, in Van Swieten's view, are excessive and completely unwarranted—a sentence, he claims, that could have only been harsher if she had been alive. His report, meanwhile, confirms for us that witches and vampires were interchangeable, since poor Mrs. Sallingherin is accused not of being a vampire but of having been a witch during life.

> A certain Sallingherin, also known as Wenzel-Richelin, had been buried for eighteen months. It was claimed she was a witch, and was the cause of many evils. But where is the proof of such witchcraft? This woman dispensed remedies, and her son discovered all her mysterious tricks. There were eyes of lobsters dissolved in water; some grasses and roots without a shadow of superstition. In order to embellish her cures and lend credence to their mystery, to make someone ill she would send four escutcheons grouped in one of their cases and then she would send the remedy. It was claimed that the disease was bewitchment. The Commissary has looked into this case and found that it was a serious but natural disease called *Colica pictonum,* which makes those who become ill attracted to their members. We are cur-

rently employed to heal similar diseases at the City Hospital. Other magicians have foretold the day when a disease would be cured. Here is all the evidence of witchcraft: these practices should not have been considered efficacious during the life of that woman. Since she attended the Sacrament, she died in the bosom of the Church and was buried with a sacred ceremony. And eighteen months after her death she became a witch suited for incineration.

Upon foundations of this sort have arisen this entire history, sacrileges were committed, the asylum of the tomb was violated. The reputation of the ancestors and their families remained blackened, who might expect the same fate if such abusive ways were not eliminated. The dead bodies of innocent lads were placed in the hands of the executioner; men whose way of life was above reproach underwent the disgrace of being disinterred in the cemetery, after a supposed witch had been buried. They are declared to be witches, their bodies are consigned to the executioner to reduce them to ashes, but they receive this sentence which could only have been harsher if they had been alive; and they burned their bodies with infamy, serving as notice of an example to their accomplices.[20]

Van Swieten's anger, which is barely restrained by the end of his treatise, seems justified: "This transfixes me and so much anger rouses me that I must come to a conclusion in order to not go beyond my limits."[21]

It may be difficult for us to imagine the frustration Van Swieten experienced when asked to explain the goings on in Moravia. He was, after all, a reasonable man who was devoted to the power of science to explain much that had previously been in the domain of religious belief and faith. It was that devotion that earned him the trust of Maria Theresa, who needed men like him to bolster her attempts to turn Austria and Hungary into more modern European states. From the foregoing examination of his *Consideration,* we see also that his sense of compassion had been piqued by the mistreatment—at the hands of officious, but ignorant, civil authorities—of people who were persecuted even after death. Clearly, it made no sense to Van Swieten to punish the dead, for the corpse was in fact nothing more than decayed matter, regardless of its possibly lifelike appearance, and was therefore incapable of any sort of reanimation. But his compassion for the victimized and his ostensibly noble motive ought not obscure the fact that in dismissing belief in vampires as absurd, he also destroyed the ground on which this imported agrarian folklore was based. By subjecting folklore—even if it happened to fit uncomfortably in the post-Reformation Habsburg Empire—to the intense light of rationalism, he was pushing those beliefs further into the shadows. More than anyone else, Van Swieten helped to destroy the folkloric vampire in Western Europe.

There were certainly several others from the late seventeenth to the mid-eighteenth century who participated in the rationalist movement to explain the stories of the walking dead that had entered into Western European consciousness from the Balkans as political contact increased with the countries occupied by the Ottoman Turks. About twenty years prior to Van Swieten, for example, an Austrian regimental field surgeon named Johannes Flückinger was sent by Emperor Charles VI to Medvegia (Serbia), to report on vampire activity there. His minor report *Visum et repertum* became a source of popular knowledge about vampire beliefs and customs.[22] Yet despite these broad attempts to repress the irrational by means of explanation rather than violence, there was something in the stories of vampires that was, as we know, irrepressible, and the vampire was destined to rise again—this time, however, as a literary figure, much harder to kill than before.

9

FROM VIENNA TO LONDON

Gunpowder, electrical phenomena, or optical illusions have the ability to astonish all that do not know about them; and charlatans use this to make the credulous public believe they are most powerful wizards.

Dr. Gerard van Swieten,
Consideration of the Claim of Posthumous Magic

Let me tell you, my friend, that there are things done today in electrical science which would have been deemed unholy by the very man who discovered electricity, who would themselves not so long before been burned as wizards.

—*Dr. Abraham van Helsing,*
Bram Stoker, Dracula

The history of the vampire in Western Europe after 1732 has been well documented. In fact, for many modern inquirers into this subject, it is as if the term *vampire* had no true significance before the Protestant and Roman Catholic world adapted Balkan folklore to its own purposes and preconceptions. But with the vampire's migration north and west, a strange thing happened. The vampire as a member of the village community was eventually replaced by the vampire as someone who was not at all a member of the peasantry but, rather, a bloodsucker, a greedy self-serving and infectious dead man who easily came to symbolize a kind of social parasite among the nobility. Furthermore, in English literature in particular, the image of the vampire became firmly connected to the ancient and mysterious East. By virtue of his age and stature, this English vampire was familiar with mysteries that had been lost, according to the Romantic view, in the urbanism of contemporary England. The disease that somehow comes from contact with Turkish, Arab, or Muslim culture, which seemingly had absorbed the ancient mystical knowledge of Egypt and Mesopotamia (as well as the historical context in which Jesus, too, was able to rise from the dead),[1] threatens to obliterate the decorum of British society, even as it opens up the possibility of eternal life. This new meaning of the vampire cleaves this creature neatly from its earlier function in Balkan folklore. The vampire has become a monster in the modern rational world.

Despite their professed homage to secondary folkloric sources, such as Tournefort and Calmet,[2] the English Romantics distilled the image of the vampire into a form that would have been unrecognizable to his Balkan progenitors. No longer anathema (because anathema is a religious status, and religious belief has been stripped from the new vampire narrative), no longer agrarian, no longer abject, no longer hemmed in by calendrical or ritual taboo, the figure of the new European vampire is both sophisticated and alienated. Whereas the vampire's external form in later Balkan folklore can range from amorphous to nondescript (humanoid) to invisible (the latter form being encountered more frequently in Islamic communities), his features in the burgeoning Western literary tradition gradually coalesce into a type whose appearance is more finely detailed and human yet intentionally monstrous. Deviations from this monstrosity do occur, such as with the exotic female vampire Carmilla created by Sheridan LeFanu, but these alternative images self-consciously amplify the erotic aspect of the Romantic archetype. It is here in vampire fiction, rather than in the earlier folkloric reports, that the vampire acquires both class markers (e.g., a noble title or a privileged heritage)[3] and features commonly associated with werewolves and witches. The elaboration of the vein-penetrating fangs, for example, is a late development, derived from the image of the canine teeth of wolves (and maybe vampire bats, a New World phenomenon).

In other words, under literary transformation, the vampire acquires a face, a personality. The vampire's personality is further developed in extended fiction, such as James Malcolm Rymer's *Varney the Vampyre* (1847), but is only brought to its fullness in Bram Stoker's character of Count Dracula of Transylvania.[4]

This dramatic personality is critical to literary narratives in which the vampire, of whatever sex, is an actor with a will, rather than merely a destructive automaton and passive target of ritual violence. In a sense, the specific will behind the vampire's aggression makes him more like us: except for his aging features and his preference for coffins, the literary vampire, Dracula in particular, does not really appear to be dead.[5] As the portrayal of the new vampire becomes more refined, the vampire becomes more criminal, more violent, and, ultimately, more unambiguously responsible for specific evil deeds. Whereas in folklore, an unseen vampire could be held responsible for such slight infractions as making noise on the roof, turning over pitchers of water, and perhaps making the livestock tired or even ill, these quaint and even amusing qualities eventually became of little interest to Western writers after the vampire acquired a metaphoric value. The vampire became a specifically antihuman threat, and his actions were no longer merely disruptive; they were something to be feared.

Gábor Klaniczay has pointed out that the emergence of the vampire motif in Hungary, which was the nexus of contact between Western witch hysteria and Balkan vampire hysteria, occurred as a direct consequence of the abeyance of the witch trials that took place in Hungary on the model of the Inquisition.[6] The broader historical context, as I discussed in chapter 8, was the expansion of Enlightenment attitudes toward both religion and all forms of magic and the so-called supernatural. The attack on magic and the supernatural came not only from rationalists and scientists but also from religious figures, such as Dom Calmet.[7] Under the guise of promoting humanist views of tolerance, forbearance, and justice so that the poor peasants who believed in such things would no longer be subjected to legal action or torture, hunting of witches and exhumation of vampires were expressly forbidden. Furthermore, vampires as a class were finally exterminated by means of logic and scientific proof rather than hawthorn stakes and icons. This accomplished in one stroke what the church had previously been unable or unwilling to do—namely, the utter destruction of the last vestiges of a pre-Christian belief system. While it was difficult to demonstrate that witches could not have supernatural powers (especially since the Inquisitors and their henchmen had done such a good job of proving that witches could), it was far easier to demonstrate logically that the dead could not rise from their graves, torment the living, and then return to their graves—at least not without mussing up the soil.

Since the vampire, which replaced the European witch as the bringer of evil, could be shown not to have any objective reality, no folk demonology remained that could subvert the scientism of the Enlightenment. To the extent it was known, the Slavic mythological and cultural context was discarded as insignificant, and so the vampire no longer had any relationship to a folkloric system in which the associated ritual functions had any structural value. After stripping the vampire of all but the surface trappings that were found in the tales bandied about during the early eighteenth-century epidemics, the vampire was ready to be used exclusively as metaphor.

The predominant metaphor of the new European vampire, as has been pointed out by many scholars of this period, pertained to the growing economic disparity between social classes. Whereas the vampire in Eastern Europe had been a local villager marked as an outsider on the basis of behavior (including such antisocial gestures as suicide) or accidental features, the new vampire took on the demeanor and characteristics of the nobility. This new type was seen to be sucking the energy from the working and peasant classes in order to feed the growing demands of the emerging mechanized (capitalist) economy. While it has been observed that this gentrified vampire was first elaborated by Polidori and other Romantics, the change parallels a shift in accusations of the upper classes that had in fact occurred in both the Western European and Hungarian witch trials two centuries earlier.[8]

Among the most well-known cases of such accusations is that of the infamous Elizabeth Báthory, the Hungarian "blood countess" who was accused (and convicted) of hiring her maidservants to kill local village girls by draining their blood. Elizabeth would then supposedly drink or even bathe in the collected blood as a way to avoid aging. Klaniczay explains that the charges against Elizabeth, which were brought by her sons-in-law (who stood to inherit her estates), were based on a preexisting stereotype of the aristocratic witch, exclusively female, who did not practice witchcraft herself, but hired professionals (popular wise women, magical specialists) to provide her with effective magical tools to assist her if she wanted to cast spells personally or to harm her enemies in other ways.

Klaniczay continues:

Although these servants were declared guilty and punished, the responsibility was shared by the cruel lady-witch who embodied the dimension of moral evil. She plotted the whole enterprise and it allegedly served her pleasures, her perversities, or her personal vengeance.[9]

My reason for making this brief digression about the trial of Elizabeth Báthory (1609–11) is not simply to underscore the fact that the transfer of witch accusations to the upper classes preceded by over two hundred years the assignment of upper-class markers to literary vampires. Of more significance to my theme is that the presumption of Elizabeth's guilt has persisted up to the present day without any of the several authors on the subject ever bothering to question whether or not her trial and the accusations against her were factual or, instead, merely of the formulaic type that also characterized the patterned witch accusations of the Inquisition.[10] As awareness of the countess's infamous trial spread into Western Europe, it was apparently not accompanied by any understanding of either the Hungarian pattern of accusations or the laws of inheritance that provided the context for the trial, with its fantastic charges. Aside from any questions of cui bono, also ignored for four centuries are the personal motives of those servants who testified against their mistress and thereby sealed her fate—namely, imprisonment for life within the turret of her own castle.

This demonstrates how a failure to consider prevailing cultural context and folkloric motifs, especially in the area of the scapegoat phenomenon, actually maintains the collective blind spot that is obligatory in the justification of group (vigilante) violence. This failure, while perhaps not conscious or intentional, is in fact part of the mechanism of translating a scapegoat drama from one culture to another. Put another way, the unconsciousness of those who would, on the one hand, blindly accept as fact trial data presented during a time of group hysteria while, on the other hand, ignoring contextual nuances (e.g., a stereotypical pattern of witchcraft accusations) is the pathway by which the scapegoating psychology is transferred and allowed to persist.

I am claiming, on this basis, that the incomplete translation of the system of vampire accusations and remedies without regard for their original (Slavic/Balkan/Orthodox) social context led to the same sort of result. The guilt of the vampire quickly became an unassailable and intrinsic characteristic of this now literary demon. Once it had been demonstrated scientifically that the dead cannot in fact arise, any social benefit that might be derived from the collective act of executing an insentient corpse imagined as alive—rather than an actual, living individual—was completely obliterated.

Gone henceforth was also any ambiguity or question about the vampire's role in society when he was alive, about the validity or harmlessness of excommunicative accusations, or even about the presumed innocence of those who are doing the marginalizing or persecuting. The dualism that once characterized the heresy that so deeply threatened the medieval church and eventually led to the emergence of the folkloric vampire ironically reemerged in the establishment of the vampire as a clear-cut symbol of utter evil. Almost by definition, those who would fight against the vampire would be on the side of good and righteousness.[11]

As an unambiguous symbol of immorality or evil, vampirism may now be linked to any lopsided, inequitable social process that can be characterized by aggrandizement, that is, by the uncompensated transfer of resources (including energy, whether physical or metaphysical) from one person or group (the victim) to another. If Marx can so easily associate the vampire with capitalism and thereby assign implicit nobility to the operations of the proletariat as oppressed victim, could we not, with equal compassion for the downtrodden, view the absorption of folk religion by the new state religion of rationalism as equally vampiric? Does not the anti-imaginal methodology of the Reformation[12] and its subtle sublimation in the Enlightenment ultimately destroy vampire folklore—indeed, folklore in general—by sucking out its essence, invalidating the beliefs used by the agrarian populace to order their natural world?

Marx's equation between the vampire and capitalism is of course a political, not an economic, one, and as such, it is intentionally divisive. What Marx perhaps failed to see in his equation was that by accepting the single meaning of the vampire as evil, he himself had succumbed to a certain social blindness. By painting the proletariat as victim, he subverts it, robbing it of its imaginal energy and therefore of its potential. This act itself is vampiric, because, again, the question of the vampire's negative nature is left unquestioned, and therefore so is the implied positive evaluation of the vampire's enemy. The vampire slayer, who, in this metaphorical case, is any enemy of capitalistic economic structures, implicitly becomes a hero, merely by the syllogism of the equation that the enemy of one's enemy is a friend.

It is perhaps here, in Marx's well-known equation (rather than in Romantic or Gothic literature), that the possibility of a heroic slayer who represents the forces of unquestionable good is first defined with reference to the absolute and unquestionable evil of the metaphoric vampire. In any case, by the time Bram Stoker takes up the myth, he is already relying on a common understanding of the vampire as a member of a privileged class that no longer has any economic function in the modern world but that is desperate to cling to existence by corrupt means. If there is any public sympathy for the vampire, it is hardly tied to a guilty suspicion that he may have been exiled or executed unjustly. Rather, his pitiful alienation is his own doing, the outcome of class narcissism inflated by a life of nonexistent accomplishment, and his loneliness is pathetic. His immense need to attack contemporary vitality derives from his refusal to abandon his commitment to a power hierarchy rooted in the past. As Senf puts it, "later writers [including Stoker] will use the vampire to reveal the power that negative social values from the past often have over the present."[13]

As we shall presently see, the sympathy that Mina Harker shows toward the hunted Count Dracula, who is about to be mercilessly executed at the hands of a genteel lynch mob without ever having been brought to a fair trial, has absolutely nothing to do with any sense of injustice. She does not in the least rue the fact that the forms of social justice that were established as a corrective response to the outrageous witch trials seem not to have been put into practice in an ostensibly civil society. Rather, her sympathy—pity, actually—is based on her belief that Dracula's evil, extended life is so miserable, so abject and alienated from righteousness, that his demise will bring him a certain peace.

> Just think what will be his joy when he, too, is destroyed in his worser part that his better part may have spiritual immortality. You must be pitiful to him, too, though it may not hold your hands from his destruction. (367)[14]

This condescending attitude naturally restates the condescension of the church with respect to pagans and heretics. Indeed, during the persecutions of the sixteenth century, none other than Martin Luther pointed out the risk of damnation for those witches who were not brought to justice before death.

> But whilst they go about to bewitch God, they bewitch themselves: for if they continue in this wicked opinion which they conceive of God, they shall die in their idolatry and be damned.[15]

Sympathy for those whose evil ways have blocked them from salvation is only available from individuals who, for whatever reason, imagine themselves to have clearer access to paradise. While there is nothing in Stoker's novel to suggest that any of the vigilantes who are pursuing Dracula may count themselves among the spiritually elect—we do not see them praying deeply or doing good works, for example—their assumption of self-worthiness is based on a perception of themselves in relation to that which they have labeled evil. Mina, because she feels herself to have been contaminated by her (intimate) contact with Dracula, sees herself as a sinner who may also need spiritual support at the moment of her own death if she is not to be damned. But the self-righteousness of the actions by Mina, Dr. John Seward, Arthur Holmwood, and the others, who are certainly among the more secular characters of English literature, is actually an acquired attitude. Their right to feel morally superior to the evil Count Dracula is conferred by Dr. Abraham van Helsing.

Van Helsing constructs for his British disciples a persuasive revelation of the count's vampire nature, which otherwise would have gone unnoticed or been interpreted differently. An omniscient interpreter of Dracula's mysterious actions and movements, Van Helsing becomes the first professional vampire slayer in English vampire literature and the model for all that follow. As vampires generally have received more attention than slayers, both in the popular mind and in criticism, so the figure of Dracula has tended to overshadow that of Van Helsing. Since, throughout this study, I have intended to explicate the changing role of the vampire slayer in justifying the killing of the dead, perhaps it is time to bring the lens a little closer to the good doctor.

THE PROFESSOR FROM THE NETHERLANDS

In chapter 9 of *Dracula,* Dr. John Seward first considers calling on his old friend and colleague Abraham van Helsing for a possible consult regarding Lucy Westenra's anemic ennui when he concludes that her condition is of a functional, rather than organic, nature. This request for assistance from the Dutch physician is somewhat strange, insofar as Seward receives notice of Lucy's malaise from Arthur Holmwood, Lucy's suitor, on August 31, only a day after Lucy has written to her friend Mina that she "[has] an appetite like a cormorant, [is] full of life, and sleep[s] well." Seward has his doubts about her claims, however, and writes in his journal (September 2), "[T]here must be a cause somewhere, I have come to the conclusion that it must be something mental." Seward's befuddlement before a seemingly ordinary constellation of symptoms (difficult breathing, "lethargic sleep," bad dreams) would seem to reflect a natural uncertainty about the diagnostic methods of the relatively new science of psychiatry. However, Seward is certainly rather quick to call in a specialist from Amsterdam, and the specialist from Amsterdam is rather quick to agree: on September 2, Van Helsing commits to coming to London to help his friend, if only to repay the debt of his life, which Seward once saved by sucking gangrenous poison from a wound Van Helsing sustained.

The vagueness of Lucy's symptoms and the lack of scientific discipline on Seward's part[16] set the tone for subsequent encounters with disease and death that occur only after Dracula's (and Van Helsing's) arrival in England. (Why, the engaged reader might ask upon reaching chapter 9, does Dr. Seward not first prescribe some medicine, if only placebo, for the hysterical Lucy[17] or ask some more local physicians in for a second opinion?) Lucy's debilitating maladies, both physical and psychological, present a clinical picture that is not unlike the sorts of encounters with inexplicable conditions that would provoke the summons of a *vampirdžia* to a Bulgarian village.[18] A disease or catastrophe that, should it go undiagnosed, would disrupt the local order provokes a mistrust in the usual social analyses or remedies, and this in turn demands that an external savior be appointed. (However, a medical condition whose cause might lead to great embarrassment might also demand the hiring of someone from outside, to misdirect the attentions of the suspicious.)

Whatever Dr. Seward's reasons for giving up on Lucy's diagnosis so quickly, he clearly trusts only a single person in all the world to be discreet enough to put an adequate interpretive frame around the situation. (Other interpretations, given her symptomatology, might include any of several uninvestigated diagnoses, including complications of pregnancy.)[19] To treat Lucy immediately, Seward summons to the diagnosis a person who in many respects resembles Gerard van Swieten.[20] Like Van Swieten, Van Helsing possesses broad erudition; he "knows as much about obscure diseases as anyone in the world" (*Dracula,* 147), which ought to recall for us the fact that Van Swieten was a medical encyclopedist and had published a compendium of commentaries regarding diagnosis and treatment of obscure "fevers." Seward admires Van Helsing for being, on the one hand, a man of science like himself yet, on the other, open-minded, that is, open to nonrationalist explanations of certain otherwise inexplicable phenomena.

> He is a seemingly arbitrary man, this is because he knows what he is talking about better than any one else. He is a philosopher and a meta-physician, and one of the most advanced scientists of his day, and he has, I believe, an absolutely open mind. This, with an iron nerve, a temper of the ice-brook, and indomitable resolution, self-command, and toleration exalted from virtues to blessings, and the kindliest and truest heart that beats, these form his equipment for the noble work that he is doing for mankind, work both in theory and practice, for his views are as wide as his all-embracing sympathy.

Seward's extreme regard for Van Helsing borders on sycophancy, but his description foretells us that "the professor" is indeed no ordinary man—on the contrary, he has the right stuff to be a match for the extraordinarily powerful Dracula. That right stuff embodies something of a contradiction: as one of the most advanced scientists of his day, Van Helsing would naturally believe in the rigor of the scientific method, yet as a philosopher and metaphysician, he is keenly aware that the universe is bigger and more complex than the seen world. A hundred and forty years after the publication of Van Swieten's *Consideration of the Claim of Posthumous Magic,* with its imperative to employ purely physical terms for explaining all the medical and pathological phenomena pertaining to vampires (except, of course, phenomena that were brought on by God or Satan), medical rationalism had been tempered by two modern movements that were gaining acceptance in Stoker's England: psychoanalysis and theosophy.

Concerning the latter, some have claimed that Stoker was loosely affiliated with the most prominent spiritualist society in London, the Order of the Golden Dawn, but as Elizabeth Miller points out, there is no evidence that he was ever a member of this organization.[21] Consequently, it is impossible to claim that the organization and its precepts served as a model for particular ideas in his novel. Still, the fearless vampire killers who travel together to Transylvania do so as a band of blood-initiated urban adventurers who share a single common, untested, yet apparently unassailable, belief—namely, that Count Dracula is a monstrous, supernatural vampire who deserves to be hunted down and destroyed. This belief is carefully and coyly inculcated in the others by Van Helsing, as a tenet in a system of faith in the underlying reality of Transylvanian folklore and the possibility of return from the dead and animal metamorphosis. Because of Van Helsing's intimidating portfolio of professional credentials ("M.D., D.Ph., D. Lit., ETC., ETC." [148]) and achievements strongly vouched for by the esteemed head of an insane asylum, he is not automatically dismissed as a kook. The clear contradiction of his medical (and legal) training and his denial of the finality of the body's death (along with his acceptance of possible danger of contagion from Dracula and his undead minions) goes unchallenged by several sophisticated, law-abiding residents of England in the industrial age. How can that be?

Van Helsing's power to persuade Dr. Seward, Arthur Holmwood, the American Quincey Morris, and even the hyperrational Mina Harker to accept his improbable analysis of the situation—that there are such things as vampires and that Dracula is chief among them—

derives certainly from Seward's high opinion of Van Helsing.[22] But perhaps a stronger reason for Van Helsing's immediate believability is his very foreignness, which Stoker exaggerates by providing the professor with a strange English idiolect. Lucy's relatively rapid decease, which curiously occurs around the same time as her mother's fatal infarction, is hard to account for in the absence of a medical explanation. Such explanations, however, might not have been all that difficult to find: Herbert Mayo's 1851 article on the causes of vampirism (cited in n. 17 in this chapter) at least acknowledges well-known alternative explanations, such as hysteria, somnambulism, and the "death trance," any of which might have been considered by a scientist of Seward's reputation. In the terms of the novel, more plausible explanations are never sought; rather, a system of folk belief is superimposed on the local scientistic system by a chosen "expert" who, like Van Swieten, had knowledge both of modern medicine and of folk medicinal customs.

Dracula, of course, is also foreign, and he represents a set of customs and beliefs that were entirely unfamiliar to the English, whose cultural contact with the Ottoman-dominated Balkan countries before the late nineteenth century had been virtually nonexistent.[23] Unlike most movie versions of *Dracula,* the novel contains no unambiguous social contact between the count and any of his future hunters. On the contrary, the novel's first mention of his name in England is Mina's journal entry of September 24, when she (mis)quotes and comments on a statement from the diary of her husband, Jonathan: "The fearful Count was coming to London . . . 'If it should be, and he came to London, with its teeming millions.'" The contrast between sparse and rural Transylvania and dense and urban London is clear and highlights the fact that the threat posed by Dracula actually lies in his plaguelike aspect.[24] A bacterium or virus invading a dense population (especially an insular one) that possesses no natural immunity poses a potentially serious threat unless a viable immune response can be provoked. Dracula is thus a disease, and the medical analogy demands that teeming London be provided with frontline immunization. In the absence of natural defenses, this immunity can only be conferred by a vaccine—which (to extend this epidemiological analogy perhaps well past its acceptable limits) must resemble the disease. Van Helsing is thus chosen to cope with Dracula primarily on the basis of two of the former's personal attributes: his unnaturally inclusive mind and his foreignness, which somehow included knowledge of the folkways of Eastern Europe. In a way, it is the latter that allows him to possess the former: his personal experience with vampires or, at least, with vampire beliefs extends his medical knowledge into the metaphysical.

Van Helsing, like Van Swieten and, in fact, like all vampire hunters before him, has been called in primarily to explain. In Stoker's late nineteenth-century world, where spiritualism was clashing head-on with faith in industrial technology for the privilege of making life better or at least more interesting, the limits of scientific knowledge were becoming clearer. Contemporary medicine was inept at describing much human behavior, especially the pathological, and could not account any better than religion could for such sensations as what Freud called in 1918 "the uncanny."[25] Psychoanalysis, a term coined by Freud a year before the publication of *Dracula,* was to become the inheritor of the data unearthed by nineteenth-century European investigators whose primary intellectual concern was the reconstruction of origins and earlier, often idealized, forms of culture. Both Darwin and Sir James Frazer[26] pointed to the value of (hypothesized) protoforms—be they biological or cultural—to explain atavistic forms and processes in the present. Van Helsing naturally represents this same sort of figure, a person intellectually committed to rationalism and the scientific method yet dependent, in his descriptions, on the inclusion of "the primitive" to account for all phenomena that lay outside the domain of the rationally explicable. (We shall see in chapter 10 how Giles from *Buffy the Vampire Slayer* also depends on the primitive—in the form of mystical texts—to understand the modern.)

Like Freud, both Seward and Van Helsing are devotees of the neurologist Charcot, whose ideas concerning trauma-related hysteria eventually led Freud to his theory of neurosis. But Charcot himself was a figure who stood at the center of a widening circle of miscomprehension and misdiagnosis as modern medicine became increasingly unable to explain a range of psychosomatic states (especially hysteria). According to Richard Webster, there was "a vast labyrinth of medical error which had been created over hundreds of years, and which Charcot himself had brought to an unprecedented level of complexity." Webster explains:

In conditions where hundreds of subtle neurological disorders and other medical conditions remained wholly or largely unrecognised, the failure to make accurate medical diagnoses had led, almost inevitably, to the massive inflation of a pseudo-diagnosis—"hysteria."

What made the resulting labyrinth of medical error all but inescapable was that practically every other physician had become lost within it. Over and over again, highly trained medical practitioners, confronted by some of the more subtle symptoms of . . . common or uncommon conditions, would resolve their diagnostic uncertainty by enlarging the category of hysteria yet further. As a result medical misconceptions which sprang from one misdiagnosis would almost inevitably receive support, and apparent confirmation, from misdiagnoses made by other physicians.[27]

It is within this "vast labyrinth of medical error" that Seward so quickly declines to diagnose Lucy and instead calls on Van Helsing. It is clearly not Van Helsing's familiarity with Charcot or other contemporary medical theorists that Seward is seeking; for that, he could have consulted any of his London colleagues. Rather, it is Van Helsing's ability to cite both spiritualistic thinking and primitive folklore as excuses for his own inability to explain Lucy's condition and behavior. The encounter between Van Helsing and Seward in chapter 14 of Stoker's novel is revealing.

"Do you not think that there are things which you cannot understand, and yet which are, that some people see things that others cannot? But there are things old and new which must not be contemplated by men's eyes, because they know, or think they know, some things which other men have told them. Ah, it is the fault of our science that it wants to explain all, and if it explain not, then it says there is nothing to explain. But yet we see around us every day the growth of new beliefs, which think themselves new, and which are yet but the old, which pretend to be young, like the fine ladies at the opera. I suppose now you do not believe in corporeal transference. No? Nor in materialization. No? Nor in astral bodies. No? Nor in the reading of thought. No? Nor in hypnotism . . ."

"Yes," I said. "Charcot has proved that pretty well."

It is only hypnotism that Seward concedes here has some reality, yet he does not argue with Van Helsing's sly attempt to toss Charcot's theories into the same pot as those of Madame Blavatskaja as a way of validating the latter. But at this point, thanks to Seward's obsequiousness and perhaps his own inferiority complex, the mystification of Lucy's condition is complete. Van Helsing's reasonable-sounding, but circular, justification for accepting the limits of science (the same argument provided by Van Swieten in his *Consideration*) and therefore also for accepting the reality of paranormal phenomena and experiences of the uncanny provides the frame around a confusing situation in which Van Helsing will create and then play the role of explicator.

Trust in Van Helsing is then quickly transferred, like a bite from a vampire, from Seward to Arthur, then to Lucy and from Lucy to Mina, and then to Jonathan and ultimately Quincey. Van Helsing's deft assumption of the role of vampire seer is allowed to proceed because everyone implicitly trusts Dr. Seward, who, for apparently Oedipal reasons, seems incapable of challenging the mystical nonsense (then quite current in London society) being proposed quite calmly by Van Helsing. Later, in chapter 14 of *Dracula,* once Jonathan Harker's private fantasies are divulged by the intrusive Mina as confirmation of the emerging vampire hypothesis, neither the vigilantes nor the reader are capable any longer of considering any other hypothesis, and all subsequent testimony and circumstantial evidence is now fit into Van Helsing's well-built frame.[28] Van Helsing's scientific knowledge is never actually called on, save for the administration of narcotics and the hooking up of transfusion equipment whenever he sees fit. Nevertheless, Van Helsing is perceived as a Gothic mentor, and from this perception derives the unanimity that is required for the vampire seer to have his power.

For all of Van Helsing's knowledge of the strange ways and supernatural figures of Transylvania, and despite his mastery of "the ghastly paraphernalia" (157) of medicine (and, by extension, vampire slaying), he is missing an essential attribute of both the witch seer and the vampire slayer: he has not personally entered into the world of the dead, he is not in any way specially marked, nor does he personally possess any mystical insight into the demonic—he only possesses "rational" knowledge, irrational as it may appear from the point of view of medical science. His knowledge of folklore and ritual is as a scholar, not as an insider. As a result, he is incomplete as a vampire slayer; he cannot "see"

Dracula's will (as the madman Renfield can) and thus cannot easily track him—at least not alone.

Van Helsing is the grand interpreter, for his ignorant friends, of all the events surrounding the undead Dracula, and he claims to possess an incredible and unique command of the apotropaic charms and techniques necessary for counteracting Dracula's aggression. He knows the proper rituals for circumscribing vampires in their graves and knows what forms of violence will suffice to destroy the vampire forever. But when Dracula begins to move away from the vigilantes in response to his persecution, the task of tracking the crafty vampire's moves exceeds Van Helsing's competence, because to do so demands extrasensory perception. Van Helsing acknowledges that his scientific knowledge may be of limited use, when he asks, according to Mina's September 30 journal entry, "How shall we find his where, and having found it, how can we destroy?"

MINA THE VAMPIRE SLAYER

Mina's incredibly important role as a seer—a psychic able to observe, through her "dreams," the secret movements of Dracula— is usually ignored or downplayed in cinematic versions of the story and given short shrift in most literary discussions. The novel's main battle is usually construed primarily as a phallic one, a struggle of wills and intellect between a supernatural and lecherous vampire, on the one hand, and an erudite lecherous scientist and his posse of blood brothers on the other. Yet nothing else in the novel is so clearly reminiscent of *benandanti* or other types of shamanistic seer as Mina's special sight, which is acquired through intimate contact with Dracula. Unlike Lucy, who cannot be saved from vampirization following her several encounters with Dracula (because the protective measures prescribed by Van Helsing were ignored), Mina is aware not only that she may be in danger of becoming a vampire but also that she can use this special knowledge— equivalent to entering the otherworld—to help destroy her adversary.

Her special sight, she comes to believe, is actually bestowed by Dracula himself, as a kind of gift for his bride.[29] Not in her own diary but, rather, as reported speech in Seward's long journal entry of October 3 (*Dracula,* chap. 21), Mina recounts a conversation with Count Dracula that occurred in her sleep (after taking, naturally, a "sleeping draught"). Acknowledging that while she was waiting for the effects of the soporific to kick in, she was beset by "myriads of horrible fancies . . . connected with death, and vampires; with blood, and pain, and trouble," Mina describes a rather cruel figure of Dracula, about to drink her blood for the third time since September 30.

> Then he spoke to me mockingly, "And so you, like the others, would play your brains against mine. You would help these men to hunt me and frustrate me in my designs. You know now, and they know in part already, and will know in full before long, what it is to cross my path. They should have kept their energies for use closer to home."

What links Mina to Dracula's undead world, however, is not Dracula's consumption of Mina's blood but, rather, her (forced) drinking of his blood.

> "You have aided in thwarting me; now you shall come to my call. When my brain says 'Come!' to you, you shall cross land or sea to do my bidding; and to that end this!" With that he pulled open his shirt, and with his long sharp nails opened a vein in his breast. When the blood began to spurt out, he took my hands in one of his, holding them tight, and with the other seized my neck and pressed my mouth to the wound, so that I must either suffocate or swallow some of the— Oh my God! my God! what have I done? (344)

Mina's connection to Dracula is at his invitation: he intends to use her as a psychic maidservant if not wife, to do his bidding and, presumably, to telegraph to him through her consciousness the vengeful intentions of her cohorts. But Mina, being a modern woman, turns this psychic connection into a two-way channel: her intimate contact with the dead, symbolized by a kind of oral-erotic communion, gives her the ability to sense Dracula's presence and his intentions. Rather than magical rituals or even mind-altering drugs, hypnosis becomes the preferred method of gaining access to Mina's shamanic powers.

It is from this point on that Mina is given full access also to the plotting of the brotherhood.

> When the question began to be discussed as to what should be our next step, the very first thing we decided was that Mina should be in

full confidence; that nothing of any sort—no matter how painful—
should be kept from her. (346)

Once Mina demonstrates her mystical acquaintance with Dracula, in
other words, she is invited into the men's club with full membership
rights. If there is an unstated condition, it is that Van Helsing have un-
fettered access to her unconscious. Her ritual initiation is carried out
by Van Helsing when he touches her forehead with a eucharistic wafer,
which has the effect of branding her or, rather, baptizing her into the
moral world of the men. This baptismal insignia is a token of membership, but it is also an external marker acknowledging her sinful
(pagan?) contact with the irrational world of Transylvania and the undead. It also seems to provide her with a kind of compassion for Dracula (with whom, after all, she has been intimate), insofar as she intuits
that, like herself, he is indeed a kind of victim.

Mina's unexpected compassion is a result of her identification with
the pursued monster. Leonard Wolf strangely interprets the logic of
Mina's compassion as being "dictated from afar by Dracula" (*Dracula*,
367 n. 17). Quite clearly, the plea for compassion is an acknowledgment
that she is now somehow like Dracula and thus potentially subject to
the same violent destruction. Yet her compassionate position is self-
righteous in nature. Like Inquisitors who saved their accused heretics
from the torment of eternal damnation by immolating them all for
righteousness' sake, Mina urges violence but insists that it be carried out
with a morally impeccable purpose. Her compassion has the effect of el-
evating her position above even Van Helsing, for not only is she the
chronicler of the tale of Dracula's death, but she also now dictates the
group's moral purpose, whereas Van Helsing's purpose is more myopic.
Between the two of them, Mina Harker and Abraham Van Helsing,
there is one complete vampire slayer, a union of rational intellect and
the spiritual power derived from "feminine intuition." In a way, this
replicates the tension discussed earlier between scientism and spiritualism, which were pervasive in Europe toward the end of the nineteenth
century. Whereas early on, before Mina has access to Dracula's "unconscious," Van Helsing himself manifested this split, now the tension has
been resolved by splitting into masculine and feminine components.

Mina's inner awareness is linked to her dream life, and she harnesses this access to become a sort of ad hoc oracular priestess. Following a restless night, Mina demands that her husband bring the professor to her in order to hypnotize her.

> She said to me hurriedly, "Go, call the Professor. I want to see him at once."
>
> "Why?" I asked.
>
> "I have an idea. I suppose it must have come in the night, and matured without my knowing it. He must hypnotize me before the dawn, and then I shall be able to speak. Go quick, dearest, the time is getting close." (369)

Mina suddenly becomes aware that she has a gift, a special connection, that will enable her to divulge to her friends the modes of Dracula's travel. Under Van Helsing's rather facile hypnosis, Mina enters a séance-like trance, in which she can be questioned regarding what she sees. That she has entered the world of the dead is clear from the following remarkably imaginative passage:

> "Where are you?" The answer came in a neutral way.
>
> "I do not know. Sleep has no place it can call its own." For several minutes there was silence. Mina sat rigid, and the Professor stood staring at her fixedly. The rest of us hardly dared to breathe. The room was growing lighter. Without taking his eyes from Mina's face, Dr. Van Helsing motioned me to pull up the blind. I did so, and the day seemed just upon us. A red streak shot up, and a rosy light seemed to diffuse itself through the room. On the instant the Professor spoke again.
>
> "Where are you now?" The answer came dreamily, but with intention. It were as though she were interpreting something. I have heard her use the same tone when reading her shorthand notes.
>
> "I do not know. It is all strange to me!"
>
> "What do you see?"
>
> "I can see nothing. It is all dark."
>
> "What do you hear?" I could detect the strain in the Professor's patient voice.
>
> "The lapping of water. It is gurgling by, and little waves leap. I can hear them on the outside."
>
> "Then you are on a ship?" We all looked at each other, trying to glean something each from the other. We were afraid to think. The answer came quick—

"Oh, yes!"

"What else do you hear?"

"The sound of men stamping overhead as they run about. There is the creaking of a chain, and the loud tinkle as the check of the capstan falls into the ratchet."

"What are you doing?"

"I am still, oh so still. It is like death!" The voice faded away into a deep breath as of one sleeping, and the open eyes closed again.

Stoker's evident interest in hypnotism as a technique for gaining access to hidden regions of the mind is prefigured in the conversation between Van Helsing and Seward regarding corporeal transference, materialization, astral bodies, and hypnotism, the validity of which was proved by Charcot. Of the several techniques cited for entering the spirit world, the more modern one of hypnosis has the advantage of being a "scientifically proven" psychotherapeutic technique, yet it serves the purpose of restoring a shamanic channel, by which it is possible to return from the world of the dead with messages and observations.

Ultimately, Van Helsing requires a feminine medium to gain access to Dracula's whereabouts, which suggests that Van Helsing's powers have a limitation that he has been at pains to conceal since his first arrival in London. As the crew tracks Dracula, his coordinates are verified by no other source than Mina's hypnotic reports. Indeed, Van Helsing becomes so addicted to her special insight that he in fact abuses this power, which begins to fade the longer the time passes since her contamination and, as Wolf points out, the closer she gets to the evasive Dracula. Notwithstanding Van Helsing's recognition of his own dwindling masculine powers and of the increasing vagueness of Mina's reported fantasies, he has no trouble demanding from his disciples extreme forms of sacrifice. Everything he demands of them is couched in the language of crisis, which of course amplifies their dependence on him to save not only them, but, alas, humanity. Naturally, this has the effect of dissuading them from challenging his authority or the correctness of his vision.[30]

> I asked him again if it were really necessary that they should pursue the Count, for oh! I dread Jonathan leaving me, and I know that he would surely go if the others went. He answered in growing passion, at first

quietly. As he went on, however, he grew more angry and more force-
ful, till in the end we could not but see wherein was at least some of that
personal dominance which made him so long a master amongst men.

"Yes, it is necessary, necessary, necessary! For your sake in the first,
and then for the sake of humanity."

While Dracula is on board the ship heading for Varna, Mina's hypnotic reports grow tiresome, since, evidently, nothing can be detected
but the lapping of the waves against the ship. Eventually, once he is off
the ship, she provides an accurate report of his coordinates, which becomes the basis of the group's final descent on him, but she becomes
less reliable as a medium, as if her ability to see Dracula were somehow
exhaustible. As she becomes more easily hypnotized by Van Helsing,
the less interesting or useful become her reports of Dracula—a certain
perfunctoriness creeps into the mystical communion, which Mina realizes as she begins to become aware again of her personal interests.

Eventually, of course, Dracula is found, thanks to the psychically
embedded reporting by Mina. The ultimate violence is performed in a
nonchalant way by the antiritualistic American Quincey (who is then
violently wounded and dies—in Balkan lore, a circumstance likely to
turn him into a vampire). Dracula could never have been made so vulnerable without betrayal by one who had sympathetic access to his
most intimate intentions. While Van Helsing provides the frame
around Dracula that leads to his persecution and execution, it is the
susceptible Mina who is able to reveal at every step his movements, setting the stage for his destruction. Mina allows herself to be taken
wholly into the fantastic world of demons in modern times that is constructed by Abraham Van Helsing; she does so in part because of her
desire for revenge, in part out of rage, which can be focused entirely on
Dracula as its cause. Thus, my earlier statement that Van Helsing is the
first "professional" vampire slayer in English literature is perhaps only
half right. To correct it, I would have to acknowledge that this function
is really fulfilled by the union of the intellect of Van Helsing and the
special perception of Wilhelmina Harker, a modern woman who had
contact with the world of the dead.

10

THE SLAYER GENERATION

From the earliest shamanic seers, through the folkloric period, right up to Bram Stoker's *Dracula,* the person assigned the task of identifying the otherwise unknowable source of disease or evil was given a high degree of authority. Thanks to a unique and valuable skill acquired either through traditional knowledge or else simply by virtue of some special marking that separates him from ordinary folk, the seer-healer has complete jurisdiction over the identification and ultimate punishment of the evildoer and thus the curing of the social ill. This naturally represents a kind of abdication on the part of the community, which either does not have the will or else has no other mechanism or resources for selecting one of its own as the unseen cause of destruction, death, or mayhem. Once Van Helsing is invited into England to help the friends of Lucy determine the nature and cause of her vague illness, there is no doubting his opinion that her condition is the work of a Transylvanian vampire. Once the secret brotherhood is given over to this explanation, there is no need to seek any other, which is precisely the point: consideration of other verdicts would risk introducing more disorder, either by disclosing dangerously insidious and hidden motives or by acknowledging the truly transcendent nature of misfortune. Relativism, nuance, and even justice are unwanted in the presence of a crisis that may implicate the community itself.

As I have noted, the vampire represents a localized solution to the problem of injustice, a solution that was not available in that part of the world that produced the Inquisition: "killing" a corpse in fact harmed no one (although, naturally, it disturbed sensibilities about the sanctity of graves and funeral rites). In the Orthodox context, where the forward progress of the soul on its journey into the otherworld was an important matter, destroying a vampire was a righteous act, not only for the community of survivors but also for the deceased. The act of killing the dead polarized and literally grounded the ambivalent energy of misfortune in a single individual. More important, it also reestablished, as sacrifice always does,[1] the susceptible boundaries between right and wrong, good and evil, power and powerlessness. To the extent that ideas about good and evil are socially transmitted—that is, encoded in the myths, rituals, and laws of a community—they tend to represent the status quo and to help maintain the current distribution of power. Consequently, when that which has been labeled unambiguously evil is finally destroyed, the destroyers are vindicated, and any violence done to social categories is healed.

The lack of any ambiguity about the righteousness of the destroyers of evil is a feature not only of the cinematic *Dracula*, in all its incarnations, but of other so-called horror movies at least through the first half of the twentieth century. The emphasis of such stories was less on the process of identification than on the process of eliminating the threat. At some point, however, especially in the United States and England around World War II, the horror genre took on additional characteristics, which overrode the narrative features of particular subgenres, such as vampires and other unnatural monsters. The emphasis shifted toward what Noel Carroll calls the "complex discovery plot," whose structure has "four essential movements or functions . . . : onset, discovery, confirmation, and confrontation."[2] This structure represents a merger with the detective story, but in this case, the perpetrator of the offense is no ordinary criminal but, rather, a supernatural entity. In one important variation of this plot, the person who first discovers that supernatural forces are afoot is mocked as a fool or worse. While this adds a layer of dramatic tension in which the audience can see something through the eyes of the discoverer that the other characters are blind to, as far as the vampire slayer is concerned, it completely changes his social status. No longer the invited specialist or healer trusted to identify a demonic force, now the person who first notices the vampire or suggests that the cause of some strange eventuality may be supernatural represents a possibly more serious threat to the categories of ordinary reality. When both the foolishness of the seer and the unwillingness of the society to believe in the supernatural are exaggerated, the result is humorous. In *Abbott and Costello Meet Frankenstein* (1948), a famous takeoff on the Universal Pictures monster pictures, Wilbur (Lou Costello) tries desperately to inform Chick (Bud Abbott) as well as other characters that Dracula and the Frankenstein monster are indeed alive and up to no good, but because he is nothing more than a foolish sidekick (and a patsy for a nefarious subplot), he is not believed until the evidence becomes irrefutable.

The theme of the vampire slayer as a fool does not disappear with the exaggeration of Abbott and Costello. Roman Polanski's send-up of East European vampire tales, *The Fearless Vampire Killers* (1967), makes fools of a couple of professional vampire killers, Professor Abronsius[3] and his assistant, Alfred (played by Polanski himself), who seek to destroy Count Krolock, but their bumbling allows the disease of vampirism to spread beyond its previous limits, into Western Europe. Since the film's locale is Transylvania, however, there is no doubt about the reality of vampires; indeed, all the villagers are much more aware of the presence of vampires even than the vampire killers themselves. *The Fearless Vampire Killers*, however, represents the first time that the occupation is explicitly acknowledged in the Western vampire tradition.

The possibility of doubt about the reality of the supernatural seems almost inevitable in a secular society that places such extreme faith in technology. The proposition that there might be inexplicable deadly forces that cannot be repressed by technology—especially the technology available to law enforcement or the military—lies at the base of the terror,[4] since it portends a return to a worldview in which the influence of the demonic must be acknowledged. This leads to something of a contradiction. On the one hand, the folkloric vampire slayer is required in order to reconcile the moral and ethical problems caused by ritual infelicity when the church cannot do so without undercutting its own tenets of faith. In a rational, secular world, on the other hand, to admit the failure of rationalism constitutes a deep threat in and of itself. There is enormous resistance to accepting the involvement of Satan, Lucifer, or any other embodiment of so-called evil as explanation for observed phenomena. Those who would offer these religious explanations must fight an uphill battle for acceptance. As we shall see, this contradiction is ultimately resolved in the mythology of the television series *Buffy the Vampire Slayer* (1997–2003), but before Buffy, there was first Kolchak, then Mulder and Scully.

THE NIGHT STALKER

If Stoker's Count Dracula was in any way based on the real-life character known from nineteenth-century sensationalist media as Jack the Ripper, this view of the vampire as a serial killer was further amplified by the structure of serial television crime dramas.[5] Among the earliest of these was *Kolchak: The Night Stalker* (1974–75), which followed two made-for-television pilot films written by Richard Matheson.[6] In both the pilots (which held the record for a long time for the largest television audience of any made-for-television film) and the series, Darren McGavin played Carl Kolchak, a down-at-the-heels Polish American newspaper reporter. In the first film, *The Night Stalker,* Kolchak has been fired from a major paper on the East Coast and finds himself working for a sensationalist rag in Las Vegas. Thus, from the very beginning, he is marked as an outsider: first, he is not local but, rather, an unwilling transplant from the civilized world to the Babylonian West; and second, his big-city journalistic credentials are tarnished, marginalizing him to work for a nonmainstream paper. Naturally, because of his poor reputation, when he starts to suspect that some local murders of working-class (hence, dispensable) women are the work of a vampire, not only is he not believed, but his tenacious adherence to such an outrageous idea earns him the enmity of the local civil authorities and consequently his editor, Tony Vincenzo (Simon Oakland). (The battle between Vincenzo's incessant desire to legitimate his sensationalist newspaper and his distrust of Kolchak's incessant desire to link newsworthy events to supernatural causes is the backdrop of every subsequent episode in the short-lived television program.)

Fig. 7. Carl Kolchak (Darrin McGavin) tries to stop a vampire in *The Night Stalker*. (© American Broadcasting Companies, Inc.)

Kolchak is more of a seer than a slayer. He has no legitimate authority to arrest, kill, or do anything except try to persuade the local citizens that the strange blood-drinking Romanian (with, alas, a Hungarian name), Janos Skorzeny, is in fact a supernatural vampire. Kolchak, perhaps because of his Slavic ancestry but more likely simply because he is an American reporter in the late twentieth century, is knowledgeable about both the signs of vampirism and the usual techniques for warding off or killing vampires. Whereas in *Dracula* Van Helsing actually informs his otherwise ignorant English cohorts about the existence of vampires, by the 1970s the chore had instead become to argue against the imaginary aspect of vampires with those who know better. Unlike both Balkan folklore and the *Dracula* tradition, where the vampire seer is chosen by some group, in this new version the seer's special vision or insight is suspect from the outset and is in fact rejected in the absence of incontrovertible proof. Social authority—the police force, the city's political administration, even the publisher of the newspaper—represents not only modern rationalism but the supremacy and rigidity of the view shared by the (blind) existing power system, which is devoid of sensitivity and must be subverted by an outsider if the superhuman vampire is to be destroyed and normalcy is to be restored to the community.

The supernatural nature of Skorzeny, however, is not clear-cut, despite Kolchak's dedication to the possibility. Skorzeny, who is actually not clearly seen until the end of the movie, admittedly has enormous, but not necessarily superhuman, strength. His blood-drinking is portrayed more as a pathological addiction than as a supernatural phenomenon: he keeps bottles of blood plasma in his refrigerator, suggesting that he perhaps suffers from some medical or psychological debility.[7] He is clearly a loner, an outsider of the sort that includes sociopathic serial killers, but within the terms of the movie's plot, his supernatural power may be an exaggeration or a misperception: there is no evidence of shape-shifting, and though he is documented to be much older than he looks, his life span—seventy-three years—is hardly impossibly long. Even his confounding ability to dodge bullets may not be extraordinary, insofar as he is fired on at a distance and at night by caricature cops whose marksmanship is questionable. (In the first episode of the *Kolchak* series, "The Ripper"—aired on September 13,

1974, as a condensed and only slightly transposed remake of *The Night Stalker*—the villain, whose character is reminiscent of Jack the Ripper, is likewise reputed to be extremely old and very strong and also is able to elude a barrage of bullets fired by policemen at night. Whether Jack possesses supernatural abilities, however, is again left unanswered, as all of Kolchak's evidence is destroyed in a fire.) Skorzeny's death, which is caused by a makeshift stake wielded by Kolchak, is also ordinary: he does not turn into a pile of ashes or otherwise disappear; he simply dies the bloody death that would be suffered by anyone who had been impaled by a thick wooden stake. Following Skorzeny's death, thanks to the absence of any residue of solid evidence to support his vampire hypothesis, Kolchak is once more booted out of town and instructed by the authorities to keep his mouth shut about his entire claim that Skorzeny was a vampire, in exchange for not being charged with murder.

Regarding *The Night Stalker,* Silver and Ursini assert that the "visuals treat the actual attacks or the coroner's examination as occurrences without need of qualification, as things real because they are on screen," and that "the film's own base reality of image never questions the verisimilitude of vampirism."[8] However, these critics seem taken in by their own predispositions: in fact, the supposedly supernatural on-screen events that fall outside of Kolchak's direct perception are never unambiguous. Furthermore, Silver and Ursini even admit that "the viewer like [Kolchak], can never do more than speculate, not having seen the action."[9]

Kolchak's effort to label Skorzeny a vampire is not only unasked for but meets with strong (and reasonable) resistance, with the result that the vampire hunter never acquires heroic status as the embodiment of the collective will. Still needing to justify his actions, which perhaps ultimately meted out justice but disturbed the social order by unnecessarily proposing a danger from supernatural forces, the exiled Kolchak narrates all of the events pertaining to Skorzeny into a tape recorder after the fact, and it is this confessional record that provides the structure of the movie as well as the ensuing television programs based on the pilot. This structure mimics the first-person narrative of the hard-boiled detective genre, in which the investigator's subjective and cynical recollection of events, in some way opposed to the official or authorized version, is offered as the true story, the one that is free of any political motive to conceal the facts and therefore the one that is most meaningful. This narrative subjectivity in turn implies that the official or rational version of reality is at best incomplete and at worst dangerously corrupt, which increases the indeterminacy surrounding the actuality of vampires or (in the *Kolchak* television series) other monsters. While Kolchak's interpretation of events contradicts the party line, it nevertheless remains unbalanced and unsupported and does nothing to bring Kolchak back into the journalistic mainstream.

The political context in which *The Night Stalker* was produced was one in which the press was seen to have a great deal of power to uncover the truth, which was deemed to be intentionally obscured by vested interests. In 1971, for example, two major papers of record, the *New York Times* and the *Washington Post*, published the so-called Pentagon Papers, which contributed to the uncovering of the Watergate break-in. Indeed, the Watergate scandal was in full swing when *Kolchak* was on the air (1974–75), suggesting a reason for its popularity: the show represented the possibility that the official version of reality was often distorted by individuals with too much at stake to let the truth be known. Here, the vampire seer is both truly subversive, on the one hand, and protective, on the other. The true threat to the public order, vanquished by the self-interested reporter, is not the vampire (or zombie or Indian mystic or werewolf), which can be dealt with appropriately once it is understood that he exists, but, rather, the blindness of authority, which prevents that understanding from occurring. A similar standoff, this time between the forces inside the military-industrial complex and those aware of popular or folkloric evidence that seems to contradict the official explanation of the uncanny, occurs as the weekly backdrop of a television program that was strongly influenced by *Kolchak,* namely, *The X-Files* (1993–2002).

"THE TRUTH IS OUT THERE"

Although the "monster-of-the-week" format that came to characterize the *Kolchak* television series eventually led to the program's cancellation in 1975, it had a major impact on the development, twenty years later, of two very popular programs that dealt with vampires and other manifestations of the demonic: *The X-Files* and, later, *Buffy the*

Vampire Slayer. Chris Carter, the creator of *The X-Files,* has publicly acknowledged his debt to *Kolchak;*[10] in fact, in the third season of *The X-Files,* scriptwriters John Shiban and Frank Spotnitz even went so far as to develop a character named Arthur Dales, the fictional McCarthy-era creator of the X-files division of the U.S. Federal Bureau of Investigation; in the two episodes where Agent Dales appears, he was played by none other than *Kolchak* star Darren McGavin.[11]

The vampire theme is explicit in at least one episode from *The X-Files* ("Bad Blood"), while it is implicit in several others (e.g., "The Host," September 23, 1994; "Shy," November 3, 1995). Like Kolchak and even like Buffy, the principal X-files investigators, Dana Scully and Fox Mulder, are charged with examining many unexplained phenomena besides vampires. Their roles as special FBI agents hunting down possibly supernatural monsters and aliens are, of course, quite parallel to the roles of Mina and Van Helsing in *Dracula.* However, whereas Van Helsing represented the rational scientist and his cohort Mina was the wounded person with a special, intimate, even psychic connection to the object of the hunt, the traditional gender roles are reversed in *The X-Files:* Scully is the rational, sometimes even skeptical, scientist, while Mulder, who believes his sister was abducted by aliens during his boyhood, plays the wounded sensitive, the intrepid believer with strong intuitions about the uncanny. But as in *Dracula,* the roles are complementary, and both are necessary for locating and eliminating any supernatural threat: the rational and analytical side must be tempered by the psychic or feeling side in order to come to terms with the "occult," also known as "the truth." Neither psychological function is sufficient by itself for this work, and whenever one or the other of the pair is absent or nonfunctioning, it hinders the solution of the crime (which, as in *Kolchak,* is never really solved, the evidence usually having been destroyed or the outcome covered up by the authorities). Like *Dracula, The X-Files* is an articulate, but ultimately paranoiac, vision in which some internal anxiety, perhaps deeply incestuous, is projected onto an imaginary threat from outside ("The Truth Is Out There" was one of the show's taglines), which is then reified by invoking arguments from the domains of technical and analytical discourse. But the intuitional component is also required, not only to account for areas where rational argument fails (i.e., phenomena connected to the "other world" or the "twilight zone"), but also to express the erotic, which is intrinsically irrational.

The X-Files, though deriving from *Kolchak* the concept of an investigator encountering inexplicable crimes on a weekly basis, naturally kept pace with the cultural shifts as well as advances in science and technology that had taken place since 1975. In "Shy," for example, the vampire is driven to consume not blood but fat. This represents a highly contemporary and sardonic spin on the ambiguous desirability of the vampire—in this case, an extreme and monstrous method of liposuction in a fat-obsessed society (indeed, the Italian version of the episode was titled *Liposuzione*). Tongue-in-cheek though the episode is, it adheres to several formulaic conventions of vampire fiction, albeit often updated.

The role of the vampire in this episode of *The X-Files* is as something that is both desirable and repulsive, like death itself. In a culture where the solutions to the problem of having to exist within a societally defined and very narrow norm of body weight range from obsessive dieting to fatally compulsive eating disorders, it becomes perversely desirable to have the self-control come from outside the self, in the form of a self-deceptive mirror. The solution to the vampiric crime requires "profiling" the killer on the basis of both scientific and intuitional insights, and there is here, as in virtually every episode of *The X-Files*, a certain frisson between Mulder and Scully as they toy with the eros implicit in swapping traditional gender roles. Scully's saturnine attention to the scientific method or clinical procedure often causes her to fail to ask those questions whose answers will complete the links, while Mulder admits that he sometimes arrives at his special intuitions through identification with the criminal (a common technique of all latter-day "psychological profilers," a relatively new extension of the motif of vampire slayer or witch seer that I have been examining throughout this book).

The development of an alternative explanation of strange (patho)-physiological states began, as we have seen, with the Enlightenment reporters who devised medical explanations to debunk folkloric beliefs, but in later vampire literature, the irrational was elevated as the more comprehensive explanation to account for that which could not be covered by rationalism. In the twentieth century, movies and television amplified this trend toward horror, and week after week in *The X-Files,* the scientific explanation was set up in order to fail or at least to appear less plausible than a more occult explanation. Such failure constitutes a subversive position: the real failure, according to *The X-Files,* is the stale Hoover-McCarthyite modality of investigation adhered to by a traditional and rather moribund white-bread bureaucracy, the FBI. The FBI is incapable of reflection and therefore incapable of looking inward for its own culpability, and it does not understand either the modern world or the ancient. The modern, Carterian monster is (networked) technological complexity, in which ostensible cause-and-effect relations (the truth) are obscured not only by political conspiracy and suppression (rerouting) of fact but by failures of the imagination and lack of empathy with the demonic. The very name of the X-files, according to Agent Arthur Dales, derives from the fact that the file drawer labeled "U" had become so full that the folders for unsolved cases were moved to the roomier drawer labeled "X."[12] Increasingly, the institutions established to investigate crime are impotent to come to terms with either the new techniques of criminal activity or the imaginative powers of the criminals, who now are perceived to be internal to the system. "The Truth is Out There" means that only by engaging the "other world" does it become possible to reveal the complex layers of immorality that are corrupting this one. The vampire slayer has thus become an investigator as well of aliens, less to destroy them than to learn what they might be able to see.

ONE GIRL IN ALL THE WORLD

If *Kolchak* and *The X-Files* suggest the need for a seer not so much to identify and thereby preempt invading monsters as to continually object to the taboos against publicly acknowledging their existence, by the time of the television series *Buffy the Vampire Slayer,* there is no longer any such need. *Buffy* ran for seven seasons (ending in 2003) and spawned at least one spin-off (*Angel*). More interesting, perhaps, is that it also spawned a veritable industry of scholarly (and not-so-scholarly) analysis and criticism, to the extent that an "academic bibliography" of *Buffy* research compiled in mid-2004 contained 273 entries (with the present author's work listed among them).[13] This is a phenomenal amount of discourse pertaining to a suburban mythology developed within a seven-year narrative on a minor television network. While it might be tempting to attempt here a sort of meta-analysis of this phenomenon surrounding a phenomenon, the context of the preceding chapters obliges me to restrict my observations to the ways in which *Buffy* in fact draws on the tradition of the vampire slayer and the witch seer yet adapts those ancient themes to the contemporary American and European post-Goth vampire revival.

In retrospect now, *Buffy* was an almost inexorable product of the purely American television vampire slayer and the purely American comic book superhero(ine). Within that context, *Buffy* expressed, among other things, the deep but repressed political conflict between the angry disaffected youth of white America (alas, racism was not a political theme the show engaged directly)[14] and the increasingly obedient and conformist students in American secondary and college education. Yet for all its seeming novelty, especially relative to other network programming, *Buffy* does not really transcend in any significant way the constraints imposed by the seer-slayer tradition that is grounded in *Dracula* but that actually goes back several centuries before.[15] In fact, Stoker's gentrified posse is more or less replicated in *Buffy*, where the slayer is supported in her exploits by a gang of geeky friends (referred to as the Scooby Gang after the animated television show about teenage ghost chasers, *Scooby-Doo*) who implicitly trust her abilities to destroy vampires and demons but who are willing to lend their own skills to the task whenever possible.[16] However, the mentoring aspect of Van Helsing has been transposed in *Buffy* from a Dutch physician to a British "watcher," in school librarian Rupert Giles. Buffy herself wields the standard vampire-destroying paraphernalia, including a set of always-at-hand pointed spikes.[17] Though she is a girl, Buffy acquires through the phallic symbolism of the spikes a quasi-masculine status, which is exemplified by her adroit kickboxing style of knocking off demons, who are predominantly male.

In *Buffy*, for perhaps the first time in the history of the modern vampire slayer, the slayer's calling is explicit and formal rather than merely circumstantial. Unlike Van Helsing and Mina, Kolchak, or Scully and Mulder, Buffy is marked by more than being an outcast or outsider. Like a *benandante* or *sâbotnik*, she is designated by ritual

Fig. 8. Buffy and Mr. Pointy. *Buffy the Vampire Slayer.* (© 1997 Twentieth Century Fox Television. All rights reserved.)

(folkloric) tradition, and her task is to destroy the inhuman vampires by violent means.[18] However, unlike her folkloric predecessors, whose real task was to recognize which members of the community might conveniently be labeled a witch or a vampire, in the case of Buffy, there is no such requirement: at least when they are enraged or experiencing "the feed," the vampires and demons are visibly different from humans, becoming quite monstrous. Whenever she is fighting these demonic beings, they are unmistakably in beast mode, wearing their "game faces." Thus, while *Buffy* restores, albeit in a highly romanticized fashion, the notion of an inherited ritual marker selecting the slayer, completely gone is any residual ambiguity about the reality of the demonic. In *Buffy*, the demonic is treated as quite real indeed; Gothic subtlety has been exchanged for the possibilities of metaphoric social statement (as well as the possibilities of gathering a larger audience).

Like television serials in general, *Buffy* provides a microcosmic frame for working out relations between a core set of characters within a recycling set of plot structures. In this case, the basic characters are high school (in later years of the series, college-aged) students connected to each other through the myth of the slayer as transmitted by Giles. Through this primary relationship, they test out various modes of accommodation and challenge to authority and morality. Issues of power, corruption, loyalty, nature, intellect, and, of course, sexuality form the more salient themes of at least the critical episodes. Murder, death, and violence are evident in virtually every episode, but unlike the pathological criminal violence depicted in contemporary "adult" programming (e.g., *Law and Order* or *CSI*), the cartoonish death and destruction in *Buffy* serve primarily as *daimon ex machina* techniques for trying on and then discarding the advantages of certain dangerous impulses.

The so-called Buffyverse (the fictional universe of *Buffy*) is not only microcosmic but microcosmological: behind the extended narrative of Buffy and the Scooby Gang is an ever-unfolding backstory that is overtly mythological in its language. Protohistory and ancientness suffuse the grandiose and violent conflicts between middle-class suburban youths and a host of chthonic forces seemingly intent on nothing less than the destruction of the human world. The great battles, which, fortunately for all of us, are always ultimately lost by the forces of darkness, take on enormous proportion in their implications, although they are always fought at the human level. But the most persistent battle, the one that seemingly cannot be won, is that between autonomy and authority. As true mythological narratives reveal the outcomes of the imagined primordial struggles that are antecedent to the formation of the human universe, with its consequent arrangement of laws and perceptual (categorical) limitations, so do the ancient mythological texts[19] kept and transmitted by Giles propose the reasons behind the various forms of adolescent suffering. They also implicitly challenge the transgressive slayer, as hero, to overcome the worldview they encode.

So there is in *Buffy* a natural dramatic tension between tradition and countertradition. Is this anything more than an ordinary reenactment of the myth of the rebellious teenager imagining herself to have the power to reject or off-load the weight of adult tradition in order to eliminate the accretions of evil (usually posited as either hypocrisy or abuse of power) in the world she sees? Buffy's worldview itself is not particularly complex, insofar as it intentionally fails to recognize the many contingencies such futurism would necessarily obliterate. Indeed, magical power improperly used by those who cannot foresee all of the downstream effects tends to backfire on the magician, which is what separates the sorcerer from the apprentice. The *Buffy* character Willow, for example, in the aftermath of the accidental murder of another character, Tara, allows herself to become possessed by both vengeful rage and the will to power, without attenuating her response with any awareness of her own participation in the event, and this almost leads to utter disaster. Such are always the lessons of individuation.

Interesting as this grandiose fantasy of saving the world by ridding it of evil (in the form of excessive control) might be, it is part of the mythological tradition, not a reaction against it. The impulse to reject authority is hardly transgressive; it is anticipated and quaint—especially in today's postmodern world, where revolutionary action is coopted at the outset. We have in Buffy a savior or hero who is a perfect mythological model that the rest of the Sunnydale community might mimic but will never be. The uniqueness of her calling functions as a charm that fascinates and thereby inhibits refocusing on alternate versions of reality.

While *Buffy* scholars have pointed out the ways in which Buffy struggles with the natural desire to be "normal" and the acceptance of the responsibility of being *the* slayer, it seems to have generally gone unrecognized that nowhere in the story is the bias of Giles's tradition-bearing texts ever deconstructed. Certainly Giles is personally rejected at this or that juncture by either the authorities who employ him or by Buffy herself, but the presumed authenticity of the magical/mythological texts in such languages as Sumerian or (ancient?) Romanian and the accuracy of Giles's reading and exegesis of these spells and narratives are never questioned.[20] This constitutes a failure to demand of Giles a more substantive reading of writ that presumably would reveal the nostalgic and primordial understanding of the universal forces that invade our destiny in the form of angels and demons. This acquiescence, this failure to be more demanding of Giles, seems to result from his avuncular status. Unlike Van Helsing, who becomes "authoritarian and despotic" as a defense against inquiry into his presumptions, Giles is nervous and reserved and sympathetically seems to understand the vicissitudes of adolescent life where other grown-up figures do not; indeed, he "develops a genuine fatherly affection for Buffy."[21] Although this lends a certain charm to the show and a certain structural stability to Buffy's fatherless existence, perhaps it also masks a strategy whereby Giles's mythologized assertions about the nature of hidden reality will be accepted without question.[22] Consequently, challenges to true authority are inevitably misdirected, and, once again, the truth remains veiled by the invisible powers that be.

CONCLUSION

The pathway from the shamanic healer to Buffy passes from the image of the seer-healer as a powerful, desirable figure capable of seeing into the world of the dead to that of a humanized slayer who is incapable of seeing very far past the obvious but who at the same time refuses to accept a dualistic attitude regarding the human and the demonic. There are many and obvious changes in the surface structure of the vampire slayer over several centuries, and these changes parallel similar shifts in the shape of the vampire, especially as the vampire moves from the domain of the folkloric to the domain of the metaphoric. Despite these differences, I have attempted to show how the most essential functions of both the vampire and the slayer remain invariant. Furthermore, it is precisely this invariance—this primal scene, if you will—that the historical changes in the contours of the vampire and slayer attempt to conceal.

The forbidden knowledge that lurks behind all tales of vampires and slayers is that both the vampire and the slayer are cut from the same cloth; they are homozygotic and in many ways share the same purpose. This is expressed in the folklore both linguistically and as ambiguity about the conditions under which someone becomes either one or the other type. In Hungarian shamanism, the dual aspect of the *táltos* likewise encodes this ambivalence. Together, the slayer and the vampire form a conspiratorial pair, in which one tacitly covers up the crime done to the other. The projected collective guilt that attaches to the accused dead (the vampire) represents an energizing motive for the enraged vampire's return, the possibility of a reanimated will to vengeance and concomitant exposure of injustice in the name of protecting extant categories of reality and power. The slayer's ability to recognize the vampire is in a sense due to his identification, if not his identity, with the dead person, whose very deadness signals his inability to protest or explain. Immolation silences him forever.

Although the seer or slayer appears from the public perspective to have special insight, such insight is in fact attributed by agreement and projected onto him by a collective that needs to rationalize its right to excommunicate. In the world of *Buffy*'s Sunnydale, where even those who dress funny are mocked as demonic,[23] it only makes sense that the slayer would be someone popular, cute, even normal-seeming, and therefore capable of justifying the wishes of the community to be rid of such negative reflections of their own shallow consumerism.

Since the sixteenth or seventeenth century, if not before, the focus of both folkloric tales and then literature has been on the vampire rather than the slayer. In part, this may be because, as I suggested in chapter 7, the original healing role of the shamanic priest was intentionally obscured by proselytizing Christianizers wishing to eradicate evidence of the pre-Christian divine. I have conjectured that the residual shamanic ability to enter into the world of the dead and return with healing knowledge was thus left in a defective state, unable to permeate the membrane in both directions. The defective healer thus became a folk magician, who was then associated with anathema and was eventually absorbed as a sorcerer into the ontology of the derelict vampire.

The long-term survival of traces of pre-Christian ritual in the context of Orthodoxy eventually led to the reimagination of the heroic or healing aspect of the shaman (or other pre-Christian holy man), but this was necessarily pressed into the service of further suppressing the collective memory of what had been done to the shaman as a person or to shamanism as a religion.

Much of the preceding paragraph, admittedly, is purely speculative, perhaps the result of taking Stephen King too seriously. Nevertheless, except for the twenty-year interlude of *Kolchak* and *The X-Files*, where the seers were clearly countercultural and essentially personae non gratae in the halls of power, the history of the concept of the vampire seer/hunter/slayer seems to reveal a well-developed and extremely subtle mechanism for heroizing that which helps a community bury the traces of injustice committed in the name of preserving things as they are.

APPENDIX

The Alien Vampire

The earliest written reference to the term *vampir* is Old Russian, appearing in the margin of a partially Glagolitic text of the *Book of the Prophets* (*Kniga prorokov*) dated to 1047,[1] a reproduction of which was made in 1499.[2] The actual form of the inscription is попъ оупирь лихъый, [o]*upir'* being the East Slavic variant of South Slavic *vampir*. A problem arises here with the meaning of the (presumed) epithet or nickname оупирь лихъый. Since лихой in modern Russian means "evil," it is natural for modern scholars to assume that the Old Russian phrase лихой упырь would mean something like "evil vampire." From that, it is all too easy to conclude, given contemporary notions about vampires, that the word оупирь meant in the eleventh century pretty much what it means now: a supernatural demon.[3]

Let us, however, examine that facile conclusion a little more closely. Putting aside for a moment the etymology of *vampir/upir'* and concentrating instead on the etymology of Russian лихой provided by Vasmer, we find that in Old Russian, лихъ meant "deprived" (cf. Rus. лишенный), meaning "sad," "evil," "bad," and "courageous." Indeed,

187

the modern Russian verb лишить, "to deprive," is descended directly from Old Slavic лишити, meaning also "to deprive" (Gk. *sterein*), which is related to лихъ. Vasmer provides the Greek gloss *allotrios*, "foreign, estranged, alien"[4] for the word translated by Old Church Slavic (OCS) as лихъ.[5] From this, we may unhesitatingly infer that among the original meanings of the word was something more closely connected with the notion of estrangement, being "outside" or "foreign." Given what I have already said about Christian attitudes toward paganism, we may suppose that the semantic shift from "foreign, estranged" to "bad, evil" follows an analogous logic whereby that which is foreign is considered (in some contexts, at any rate) evil.

Furthermore, лихъий, according to the Bulgarian lexicographer Sabina Pavlova,[6] was sometimes used formulaically in a self-denigrating fashion, meaning "weak" in the sense of "susceptible to (outside, evil) influence." The contexts for this usage were similar to those in which a scribe or scholiast might refer to himself in self-abasement as an "unworthy servant," "a slave," and so on.[7] Since the phrase попъ оупирь лихъий evidently is more of an epithet or nickname than an actual personal name, it is likely that the adjective лихъий was not being used to mean "evil" in the absolute sense. Rather, we may conjecture that it connoted a departure from acceptable behavior, stepping outside the circle of the permissible.[8]

If this is true, then we are quickly liberated from the assumption that оупирь originally designated an evil demon. On the contrary, it is extremely unlikely that a (lapsed) Orthodox monk could ever refer to himself—even in a self-deprecating way—as a demon or a reanimated dead person. To do so would represent a contradiction: since pagan gods presumably have no actuality and hence no power, in effect they have no real existence. The transformation of a living Orthodox monk into a pagan demon, even if it were not a logical contradiction, would certainly represent an irreversible process;[9] it is difficult to imagine the reinstatement of monastic orders for someone who has been a supernatural demon.

Упирь, then, in all likelihood must have designated a category of human, a member of a group whose attributes I am about to examine. Perkowski is of the opinion that the word *vampir* consists of two Slavic roots or at least two morphemes. Furthermore, it is likely that the second part of the word, *pir,* pertains to "feasting" or "libation." The Old Slavonic meaning is particularly associated with wedding feasts.[10] The root itself is cognate with various Slavic and, in general, Indo-European terms having to do with drinking.[11] Although I have admitted in chapter 3 that the version of the "Oration of Saint Gregory" that first contains the word оупирь, *NS,* dates from the fifteenth century, it is significant that the term appears in a diatribe against feasting, particularly the sort that characterizes wedding banquets. This sort of revelry, or пирщество, is behavior that is associated with pagans, with Others—from the Christian perspective, with outsiders.

Summarizing the logic here, I am claiming that the word лихъый in a copy of an eleventh-century manuscript had a meaning that was associated with foreignness or, at any rate, with being estranged from some place or group. Further, I have followed Perkowski in assuming that *vampir/upyr'* contains two Slavic morphemes, the second of which refers to feasting, some aspect of which was anathema to Orthodox Christians. It now remains to determine what the first part of the word meant.

If we assume that the first morpheme in *vampir/upyr'* is also of Slavic origin, then three phonologically plausible possibilities propose themselves before any others.[12] These correspond to OCS вамъ, въ, and вънъ. When combined with the root пиръ, we encounter three hypothetical compounds: (1) вамъ+пиръ, (2) въ+пиръ, and (3) вънъ+пиръ.

Phonologically, the compound that involves the least morphophonemic difference from *vampir* is вамъ+пиръ. In this case, we would have to assume that вамъ represents a dative plural of the Old Slavic second-person plural personal pronoun, вы. In this form, there would be virtually no phonological change except the dropping of a weak back vowel: вамъ+пиръ > вам(ъ)+пир(ъ) > вампир(ъ). Thus, we would probably have to imagine that the original phrase meant something like "a feast (or libation) for/to you [pl.]." As an ethnonym, perhaps, such a word might refer to a group that was known to offer libations to multiple deities (since the Orthodox Christian God was always addressed, in prayers, by the singular, тъы). However, there is some disagreement about whether such an ethnonymic construction follows a productive pattern in Old Slavic. The Russian mythologist Dmitrij Raevskij,[13] for example, objects that ethnonyms never involve pronouns, much less pronouns in oblique cases, such as the dative. Furthermore, a question remains about the order of morphemes: why would we end up with *vam pir* rather than *pir vam*, the more natural Slavic word order? Also, if, as is generally agreed, the Bulgarian form precedes the Russian, then derivation of Russian *u-* from Old Bulgarian *vamъ-* requires us to postulate a slightly more complex sequence of steps, involving first dropping the nasal consonant [m] and reduction of the vowel [a] to [ъ] prior to the Old Slavic-to-Russian sound change from *vъ* to *u* in initial position.[14]

The second possibility, въ пиръ, is a prepositional phrase and requires the assumption of some sort of epenthetic nasal [m] between the reduced back vowel [ъ][15] and the initial [p] in Bulgarian: *vъ pir > vъm pir*.[16] This compound would mean, presumably "in (or into) the feast," въ being a preposition that may be glossed as "in, into, among." In this case, *vъ pir*, designating a member of a group, might refer to someone who participated in feasting. (It is harder to justify the notion that пиръ was ever some sort of *nomen agentis*, such that *vъ pir* would mean "he who drinks in," an etymology proposed by Rudnyćkyj.)[17]

The third proposed compound, въньъ пиръ, is also a prepositional phrase and is phonologically easier to derive than the second alternative. The nasal dental [n] becoming bilabialized to [m] before a bilabial stop [p] following the loss of the "weak" vowel [ъ] is a type of assimilation that is commonplace.[18] However, from a semantic perspective, the meaning of this phrase is a little trickier to explain. The literal meaning of the compound would be "outside the feast." This speculation was offered by Ivan Marazov,[19] who was willing to interpret пиръ in a slightly different way. If we take пиръ to mean not merely a feast or drinking bout but a libation offered at an initiation,[20] then we would arrive at a gloss of въньъ пиръ as something like "uninitiated" or "outside the circle of initiates."

This last hypothesis is attractive, given our understanding of лихъый as "outside, foreign." However, since the word *vampir/upir'* is Slavic and since the writer of the word in *NS* is an Orthodox monk from Novgorod, we would have to infer that the implied self-criticism of оупирь лихъый concerns the writer's uninitiated status: he is "an estranged uninitiate." Since Christianity effectively replaced initiation ceremonies with baptism, seeing in initiation evidence of paganism not very different from sacrifice, we would think that a more potent form of self-abnegation would be for this monk to refer to himself as an initiate, rather than as an outsider relative to the outsiders.

Based on the foregoing discussion, we may more confidently assert that the word *vampir* was a pejorative name for a group or a member of a group whose rituals or behavior were offensive to early Orthodox Christians. It is unlikely that the earliest meaning of the word *vampir* denoted anything supernatural. Rather, I suspect that the term generally designated someone who engaged in *pirštestvo,* that is, in ritual feasting, where sacrifice was performed and wine was drunk to excess and ritually poured out (as libation), sometimes mixed with blood. Alongside activities involving wine were those involving music, of a sort that must have offended the Christian sensibility. Whether such activities were ritually linked with initiation into some cult or secret society cannot be determined on the basis of information available. In all likelihood, the dualist heretical sects—such as the Bogomils—that eventually became associated with the term *vampire* had nothing to do with the term initially. These sects eschewed virtually all formal ritual, since their very philosophy was ascetic or, at the very least, antagonistic to hierarchy.[21] Rather, I propose that the meaning of the term *vampir* was extended from pagan groups to heretical sects, since both were common enemies of the church. Thus, in the case of the East Slavic оупирь лихъый, attested in the eleventh century, we may speculate that the remorseful author had lapsed from Christianity by participating in pagan Slavic feasting (heavily influenced by Norse ritual),[22] of the sort condemned in the later manuscripts against paganism.

Notes

CHAPTER ONE

1. Since the great majority of vampires are male, I shall generally let the use of the masculine pronoun relieve me of the obligation to use infelicitous constructions or laborious periphrasis simply in order to be inclusive.

2. Slavic regions around the northern boundaries of Austria and Hungary, particularly Moravia and Silesia, were also investigated for cases of vampirism in the mid-eighteenth century.

3. Joseph Pitton de Tournefort is usually credited with first reporting on the *vrykolakas* from the Greek island of Mykonos for the Europeans further north, in *Relation d'un Voyage du Levant* (Lyons, 1718). See the English edition, *A Voyage into the Levant . . .* (London: D. Midwinter, 1741), 1:142–48. Pertinent excerpts from the English edition are now easily available on various Web sites, including http://www.thecovenorganization.com/levant.htm.

4. The story of Arnod Paole as it is recounted, for example, by Herbert Mayo in his 1851 essay "Vampyrism" (reprinted in Clive Leatherdale, *The Origins of Dracula: The Background to Bram Stoker's Gothic Masterpiece* [London: William Kimber, 1987], chap. 3), although embellished far beyond what would be reported in the oral context, is clearly just an elaboration of the classic (Bulgarian) motif of the "vampire suitor." Paul Barber notes that "a number of motifs [in a report by Dom Calmet regarding Arnod Paole] are typical instances of vampirism" (*Vampires, Burial, and Death: Folklore and Reality* [New Haven, CT: Yale University Press, 1988], 18). Leatherdale (*Origins,* 58) notes that "most of the folkloric paraphernalia of vampirism are set out" in the episode of poor Arnod. However, both authors are attempting to demonstrate the fanciful nature of the tale without regard for either the meaning of or the cultural constraints on the "motifs."

5. Witness, for example, the fate of the Russian *volkhvy.* See W. F. Ryan, *The Bathhouse at Midnight: Magic in Russia* (University Park: Pennsylvania State University Press, 1999), 70–72.

6. Like the vampire, until Buffy, the antagonists of vampires were predominantly male.

7. Actually, what the slayer does is reestablish the balance of power in favor of the status quo. His mystical "insight" is recognized as such because it is not at odds with the outcome desired by the community.

8. "Capital is dead labour, that, vampire-like, only lives by sucking living labour, and lives the more, the more labour it sucks" (Karl Marx, *Capital: A Critique of Political Economy,* ed. Frederick Engels, trans. Samuel Moore and Edward Aveling [New York: Modern Library, 1906], 257). See Franco Moretti, *Signs Taken for Wonders: Essays in the Sociology of Literary Forms,* trans. Susan Fischer, David Forgacs, and David Miller (London: Verso and NLB, 1983), 91. See also Carol A. Senf, *The Vampire in Nineteenth-Century English Literature* (Bowling Green, OH: Popular Press, 1988), 51, 171 n. 29.

9. Rob Latham, *Consuming Youth: Vampires, Cyborgs, and the Culture of Consumption* (Chicago: University of Chicago Press, 2002).

10. The Bulgarian compound word *krâvopiec,* which literally means "blood drinker," refers to a leech or usurer or extortionist but rarely to a literal vampire. This economic metaphoric usage is most likely borrowed from the Western European sense following Marx.

11. Bruce McClelland, "The Anathematic Vampire: Concepts of Matter and Spirit in Orthodoxy, Dualism, and Pre-Christian Slavic Mythology," *Internet Vampire Tribune Quarterly: De Natura Haeretica's Electronic Journal of Vampire Studies* 1, no. 1 (autumn 1996).

12. Hungarian anthropologist Éva Pócs has discussed the dual aspect of the shamanic *táltos* in Hungarian folklore, in *Between the Living and the Dead: A Perspective on Witches and Seers in the Early Modern Age,* trans. Szilvia Rédey and Michael Webb (Budapest: Central European University Press, 1999). Gábor Klaniczay discusses the merger of the *táltos* with the vampire in the mid-eighteenth century, in *The Uses of Supernatural Power: The Transformation of Popular Religion in Medieval and Early-Modern Europe,* ed. Karen Margolis, trans. Susan Singerman (Princeton, NJ: Princeton University Press, 1990), chap. 9. Although the possible connection between the vampire slayer and the shaman is further discussed in chapter 6 of the present book, without further evidence, I think I ought to stop short of asserting that the dual (good/evil) aspect of the shaman as it occurs in Hungarian folklore is homologous to the vampire/slayer pair in Bulgaro-Macedonian folklore. In any case, I am happier with the perhaps improvable idea that the vampire is the residual empty shell of the abject shaman, onto whom evil has been projected thanks to his association with pre-Christian ritual and his believed ability to enter the world of the dead. The slayer represents a later, absolutely necessary reemergence of the healer's originally beneficent power, in response to the memory of social injustice pricked by the vampire. The apparent good that is done by the slayer is thus not the destruction of the mimetic but the repression of collective memory.

13. Bruce McClelland, "Slawische Religion," in *Religion in Geschichte und Gegenwart: Handwörterbuch für Theologie und Religionswissenschaft,* 4th ed. (Tübingen: Mohr Siebeck, 2004), 8:1392–95.

14. Jan Perkowski, *The Darkling: A Treatise on Slavic Vampirism* (Columbus, OH: Slavica, 1989).

15. Bruce McClelland, "Sacrifice, Scapegoat, Vampire: The Religious and Social Origins of the Bulgarian Folkloric Vampire" (PhD diss., University of Virginia, 1999).

16. René Girard, "Generative Scapegoating," in *Violent Origins: Ritual Killing and Cultural Formation,* ed. Robert G. Hamerton-Kelly (Stanford, CA: Stanford University Press, 1987), 73–105.

CHAPTER TWO

1. John Polidori's novella *The Vampyre* was published under Lord Byron's name in 1819. The translation of this work into French paved the way for the belletristic European vampire that became the basis of Western European vampire literature. The image of the vampire had occurred slightly earlier in English literature (e.g., Robert Southey's poem "Thalaba the Destroyer" appeared in 1797, Stagg's "The Vampire" appeared in 1810, and Lord Byron's "Giaour"—which includes a vampire curse—appeared in 1813), but Polidori's work—which some consider a roman à clef concerning Byron himself, who was Polidori's companion and employer—represents the beginning of what James B. Twitchell calls "a chain reaction that has carried the myth both to heights of artistic psychomachia and to depths of sadistic vulgarity, making the vampire, along with the Frankenstein monster, the most compelling and complex figure to be produced by the gothic imagination" (*The Living Dead: A Study of the Vampire in Romantic Literature* [Durham, NC: Duke University Press, 1981], 103).

2. The contribution of Vambery's knowledge of Transylvanian history to Stoker's plot is controversial. *Dracula* and Stoker specialist Elizabeth Miller points out that there are only two documented encounters between Vambery and Stoker, and there is no indication that Vambery passed on any information about Vlad Dracula or Transylvania. Still, even in the novel, Stoker attributes knowledge of Hungary to "Arminius, of Buda-Pesth University" (291). Stoker's admiration for Vambery's erudition is unquestionable, and it is not at all impossible that Vambery had mentioned, if not Dracula, then perhaps the role of Austro-Hungary in making the vampire known in the West. The effect on Stoker of Vambery's role as a provocateur and as a historian of Hungary have not been thoroughly investigated, in part due to the scarcity of documentation. See Elizabeth Miller's recapitulation of the facts surrounding the relationship between Vambery and Stoker in *Dracula: Sense and Nonsense* (Essex: Desert Island, 2000), 30–31 and passim. A briefer summary is available online at http://www.ucs.mun.ca/~emiller/kalo.htm.

3. Emily Gerard's article "Transylvanian Superstitions" (*Nineteenth Century,*

July 1885, 128–44) had a major influence on Stoker's plotting of *Dracula*. For a review of other sources used by Stoker and of their possible influence, see especially Miller, *Dracula: Sense and Nonsense;* Leatherdale, *Origins.* The latter volume reprints Gerard's article.

4. See, for example, Perkowski, *The Darkling;* McClelland, "Sacrifice, Scapegoat, Vampire."

5. Ethnographic data concerning vampire folklore in Bulgarian archives is rich until about the mid-1950s, after which processes of urbanization gradually eroded the agrarian folk traditions. Nevertheless, older villagers still recall a few vampire tales, and much fieldwork continues in Bulgaria and Macedonia even today.

6. There has recently been some analysis of Dracula from the point of view of European politics of the late nineteenth century. See, for example, Eleni Coundouriotis, "*Dracula* and the Idea of Europe," *Connotations* 9, no. 2 (1999–2000): 143–59; Carol A. Senf, "A Response to '*Dracula* and the Idea of Europe,'" *Connotations* 10, no. 1 (2000–2001): 47–58. Missing from both these discussions, however, is any mention of Stoker's admiration for Arminius Vambery, who was in London attempting to enlist British support for the Turkish cause. Coundouriotis, for example, strangely suggests that Dracula represents "the Ottoman Empire itself" (154). This ignores Vambery's notion of pan-Turkism, which he was promoting to large audiences (often including Stoker) in order to enlist the support of England as a means of blocking the Russian advance into Central Asia and, possibly, further west, across the Balkans and Transylvania into Hungary (a push that could no longer be resisted half a century later).

7. Nina Auerbach, *Our Vampires, Ourselves* (Chicago: University of Chicago Press, 1995), 6.

8. This particular variation of the vampire motif is the subject of an episode of *The X-Files.* See further discussion in chapter 10 of this book.

9. Mircea Eliade, *Zalmoxis: The Vanishing God,* trans. Willard R. Trask, Comparative Studies in the Religions and Folklore of Dacia and Eastern Europe (Chicago: University of Chicago Press, 1972), 35.

10. The response to evident lack of "corruption" may of course relate to religious belief. In both Western (Roman) and Eastern (Orthodox) Christianity, for example, failure of the body to decay postmortem was a miraculous sign of saintliness, because "the grace of God present in the saints' bodies during life remains active in their relics when they have died" (Timothy Ware, *The Orthodox Church* [London: Penguin Books, 1963], 239). However, in the Eastern Church, incorruption could also be considered demonic or a sign of evil. It is in the context of the Eastern Church that notions of the Slavic vampire first arose. This context is described in more detail in chapters 3 and 4 in the present book.

11. Adam Burgess, *Divided Europe: The New Domination of the East* (London: Pluto, 1997), 69ff.

12. The hubristic scientist Victor Frankenstein becomes the prototype for the post–World War II Faustian theme of the mad scientist. After Hiroshima, Japanese monster movies, such as *Rodan* or *Godzilla,* link nuclear violence (created by aberrant scientific endeavor) with a kind of reanimation of long-slumbering (hence, effectively dead) prehistoric (i.e., mythological) creatures, who come back to wreak havoc and violent destruction on the societies that disturbed them. Unlike American monsters, however, the Japanese monsters, mimicking the destruction of the H-bomb, are mass killers; the drama hinges on the threat of immediate and impersonal mass extinction.

13. Another form of humanoid monstrosity that emerged at roughly the same time is the zombie. In *White Zombie* (Universal Studios, 1932), Bela Lugosi played the master of a plantation worked by zombies, who were effectively reanimated dead. This theme, though never quite as popular as the other Universal monsters from the same era, persists in such classic later films as George Romero's *Night of the Living Dead* (1968).

14. It must be pointed out that, unlike in the movie, Victor Frankenstein's creation in Mary Shelley's novel was not only quite articulate but also capable of exquisite reasoning. Still, because of his creator's shame and inability to respond to the creature's accusations, the creature is made to live outside human society. As a result of that forced isolation, there is no social control over his violence and rage. The blind spot of the creator is thus the injustice that provokes revenge.

15. John Cuthbert Lawson, *Modern Greek Folklore and Ancient Greek Religion: A Study in Survivals* (Cambridge: Cambridge University Press, 1909; reprint, New Hyde Park, NY: University Books, 1964), 381, 412ff. The nonborrowed Greek equivalent of the Slavic vampire goes by various names, such as *lampasma* and *sarkomenos.*

16. Michael Taussig, *Mimesis and Alterity: A Particular History of the Senses* (New York: Routledge, 1993), 11.

17. Interestingly, testimony from the Hannover Wendland in the 1850s reveals that a vampire was known as "ein Doppelsauger." Folk etymology links this doubleness to the marker whereby "a child which nurses after weaning is destined to become a vampire" (Perkowski, *The Darkling,* 107). The understanding of the vampire's nature as a double is suppressed in favor of an analysis that relates the disordered sucking behavior to mammalian nature (the German term *Säuger* means "mammal").

18. Wendy Doniger, e-mail message to author, March 31, 2001.

19. Taussig, *Mimesis,* 68.

20. For a discussion of how Orthodox Christianity viewed the threat of dualism theologically, see Jaroslav Pelikan, *The Spirit of Eastern Christendom (600–1700),* vol. 2 of *The Christian Tradition: A History of the Development of Doctrine* (Chicago: University of Chicago Press, 1974), especially the section "Evil and the God of Love," 216–27.

21. The dualist sects proposing these and other alternate (and heretical) views of creation and salvation include Bogomilism, Paulicianism, Manichaeanism, Zoroastrianism, and Marcionism. For a history of the path of dualist religions in Europe, see Yuri Stoyanov, *The Hidden Tradition in Europe: The Secret History of Medieval Christian Heresy* (London: Penguin, 1994). On the history of dualism in general, see P. F. M. Fontaine, *The Light and the Dark: A Cultural History of Dualism,* 20 vols. (Amsterdam: J. C. Gieben, 1986–2004).

22. Critical to notions of the danger posed by witches (and, by extension, vampires) is that witches are "within the gates," members of the community. Philip Mayer states, "the essence of the witchcraft idea is simply this: people believe that the blame for some of their sufferings rests upon a peculiar evil power, embodied in certain individuals in their midst" ("Witches," in *Witchcraft and Sorcery: Selected Readings,* ed. Max Marwick [Harmondsworth, England: Penguin, 1970], 45–64). Norman Cohn goes further, noting that contaminating antihumanness is at the base of accusations against witches (*Europe's Inner Demons: An Enquiry Inspired by the Great Witch-Hunt* [New York: Basic, 1975], 12).

23. Carlo Ginzburg, *The Night Battles: Witchcraft and Agrarian Cults in the Sixteenth and Seventeenth Centuries,* trans. John and Anne Tedeschi (Baltimore: Johns Hopkins University Press, 1992), 6. The caul as a marker of magical power, whether good or bad, has an interesting history. See Thomas Forbes, "The Social History of the Caul," *Yale Journal of Biology and Medicine* (1953):495–508. In the case of the *benandanti,* it is likely that the caul was initially a marker of "good witches," but as they were gradually persecuted as witches, it became associated with evil. Thus, in Poland, a congenital caul is a sign that the individual will become a vampire unless certain rituals are performed. For continuance of the belief regarding cauls and vampires in the New World, see Jan Perkowski, *Vampires of the Slavs* (Cambridge, MA: Slavica, 1976), 137.

24. McClelland, "Sacrifice, Scapegoat, Vampire."

25. Perkowski, *The Darkling,* 81.

26. The paradigm was first elaborated by René Girard ("Generative Scapegoating," 90): in times of crisis or ambiguous guilt, a scapegoat is identified, differentiated from the group, and attacked, so that "insiders feel united as they never did before"; these insiders then "form a new and tighter inside"; at this point, "[t]he alien threat displaces everything else; internal quarrels are forgotten"; finally, "[a] new unity and comradeship prevails among those who, feeling attacked as a group, also feel they must defend themselves as a group." David Nirenberg critiques the limitations of Girard's model of the scapegoating mechanism in focusing communal violence: "It is not concerned with the processes by which difference is identified and maintained, nor does it ask how these processes are affected by the cultural and material structures of a particular place and time" (*Communities of Violence: Persecution of Minorities in the Middle Ages* [Princeton, NJ: Princeton University Press, 1996], 241).

27. In other cultures, such detectives are known by many names. For example,

among the African Gusii, professional witch detectives are called "smellers" (Mayer, "Witches," 49).

28. Indeed, this feature of preying on victims is central to many definitions of the vampire. See, for example, Perkowski, *The Darkling.* Also, René Girard points out that "the persecutors' portrayal of the situation is irrational . . . The responsibility of the victims suffers the same fantastic exaggeration whether it is real or not" (*The Scapegoat,* trans. Yvonne Freccero [Baltimore: Johns Hopkins University Press, 1986], 21).

29. "Fools! Fools! What devil or witch was so great as Attila, whose blood is in these veins?" (*Dracula,* 40). All page numbers from *Dracula* (novel) refer to L. Wolf, *The Essential "Dracula": The Definitive Annotated Edition of Bram Stoker's Classic Novel* (New York: Plume, 1993).

30. In Browning's *Dracula* (1931), the count, played by Bela Lugosi, proclaims, "To die . . . to be *really* dead: that must be *glorious.*"

31. Girard, *The Scapegoat,* 39, 50. Moral oversimplification in support of mob action frequently demands rejection of the obvious fact that confirming evidence is either missing or fundamentally flawed. For example, despite well-documented statements that Saddam Hussein did not have stockpiles of weapons of mass destruction prior to the Iraq War in 2003, those intent on attacking Iraq continued to deny that such weapons did not exist.

32. Curiously, Coppola's version of *Dracula* is thematically as close to the French fairy tale *Beauty and the Beast*—specifically to Jean Cocteau's 1946 film *La Belle et la Bête*—as it is to Stoker's version.

33. Roger Caillois observes: "It is no less remarkable that the tormentor appears simultaneously as the seducer and, if need be, as the comforter. Romantic literature, in exalting Satan and Lucifer, in endowing both with every charm, has merely portrayed their true nature, according to the very logic of the sacred" (*Man and the Sacred,* trans. Meyer Barash [Westport, CT: Greenwood, 1980], 38).

34. Bruce McClelland, "By Whose Authority? The Magical Tradition, Violence, and the Legitimation of the Vampire Slayer," *Slayage* 1 (2001), http://www.slayage.tv/essays/slayage1/bmcclelland.htm.

35. Even Hungary may be included here. In 1750, the Benedictine abbot Dom Augustin Calmet related the story of a vampire in the Moravian village of Liebava who was destroyed by a "Hungarian stranger" passing through the village, who boasted that he could put an end to the vampire's visits and make the vampire disappear. Calmet does not hide his skepticism very well, implying that the Hungarian vampire slayer was something of a fraud or charlatan, since no one in the village could unequivocally confirm the slayer's claim to have destroyed the vampire (by beheading it with a spade). In this tale, the fact of being a "stranger" is the slayer's social marking. See Leatherdale, *Origins,* chap. 4.

36. The scene in Joss Whedon's film in which Buffy is informed by Merrick of her special obligation is rather humorous (http://www.dailyscript.com/scripts/buffy_the_vampire_slayer.html).

BUFFY. What? Oh. I used to do gymnastics. Are you looking for someone?

MERRICK. I'm looking for you, actually.

BUFFY. Am I in trouble or something?

MERRICK. Not at all. My name is Merrick. I was sent to find you some time ago. I should have found you much sooner but there were . . . complications. You should have been taught, prepared.

BUFFY. What are you talking about?

MERRICK. I've searched the entire world for you, Buffy.

BUFFY. Why?

MERRICK. To bring you . . . your birthright.

BUFFY. My birthright? You mean, like a trust fund?

Merrick looks at her.

BUFFY. I had a trust fund [*sic*] my great-grandfather, or maybe it was an inheritance, 'cause he's dead, and I spent it on shoes.

MERRICK. You must come with me. It's much too late already. You must come with me to the graveyard.

BUFFY. Wait a minute. My birthright is in the graveyard? Later not.

MERRICK. Wait!

BUFFY. You're one of those skanky old men that, like, attack girls and stuff. Forget you. My, um, my boyfriend is gonna be here in about thirty seconds, and he's way testy.

MERRICK. You don't understand. You have been chosen.

BUFFY. Chosen to go to the graveyard? Why don't you just take the first runner up, okay?

MERRICK. You must believe me. You must come with me while there's still time.

BUFFY. Time to do what?

MERRICK. To stop the killing. To stop the vampires.

BUFFY. Let me get this straight. You're like, this greasy bum, and I have to go to the graveyard with you 'cause I'm chosen, and there's vampires.

37. Buffy's gang is similarly comprised of losers and geeks. Consider the following description of Willow in the shooting script for the first episode of the show (1996): "WILLOW. She is shy, bookish, and very possibly dressed by her mother. The intelligence in her eyes and the sweetness of her smile belie a genuine charm that is lost on the unsubtle high school mind" (*Buffy the Vampire Slayer: The Script Book*, vol. 1 [New York: Pocket Books, Pocket Pulse, 2000], 10).

38. Some Slavic languages have a gender marker for animate versus inanimate objects under certain grammatical conditions. Thus, in Russian, a deceased person (*pokoinik*) is marked as animate, while the soulless corpse (*trup*) is marked morphologically as inanimate.

CHAPTER THREE

1. The earliest written reference to the term *vampir* is Old Russian, appearing in the margin of a partially Glagolitic text dated to 1047 (Kniga Prorokov s Tolkovanijam: ["Book of Prophets, with Interpretations"]), a copy of which was made in 1499, in the Gennadiev Bible (Gennad'evskaja biblija [1499]. Reprint ed. Moscow: Moscow Patriarchate, 1992). The actual form of the inscription is попъ оупирь лихъый, transliterated *popŭ oupirĭ lixyj, [o]upir'* being the East Slavic variant of the South Slavic *vampir.*

2. Manichaeism was a dualist religion founded in the third century AD by a Persian nobleman, Mani (216–77). The syncretic religion spread to the Roman Empire, where it lasted until the persecution of dualist heresies under the Byzantine emperor Justinian (527–65). Manichaean philosophy and mythology were borrowed, to one degree or another, by later dualist religions, particularly Bogomilism. See Janet Hamilton and Bernard Hamilton, eds., *Christian Dualist Heresies in the Byzantine World, c. 650–c. 1450* (Manchester, England: Manchester University Press, 1998), 1–2.

3. Orphism was a Thracian mystery religion in which belief in immortality seems to have played a part. The religion was "democratized" after the fifth century BC via the cult of Dionysus in southern Thrace. See Aleksandâr Fol, *Trakijskijat dionis* [The Thracian Dionysus], book 2, *Sabazij* (Sofia: Universitetsko izdatelstvo "Sv. Kliment Oxridski," 1994), 367. The figure of Orpheus seems to represent the reform of an eastern Mediterranean solar-chthonic cult from the early Iron Age. Orphism spread to Greece from southern Thrace. See Lewis Richard Farnell, "Sacrifice (Greek)," in *Encyclopaedia of Religion and Ethics,* ed. James Hastings (Oxford: Oxford University Press, 1970).

4. Neli Miteva, "Ethnocultural Characteristics of the Population in the Thracian Lands in the 4th–6th cc.," *Byzantino-Bulgarica* VIII (1994): 241–52.

5. Gilles Quispel, "The Origins of the Gnostic Demiurge," in *Kyriakon: Festschrift Johannes Quasten*, ed. Patrick Granfield and Josef A. Jungmann (Münster Westf.: Verlag Aschendorff, 1970), 1:271–76.

6. Hamilton and Hamilton, *Christian Dualist Heresies,* 1.

7. Stoyanov, *The Hidden Tradition in Europe,* 113.

8. Pelikan, *The Spirit of Eastern Christendom,* 217.

9. Ramsay MacMullen, *Christianity and Paganism in the Fourth to Eighth Centuries* (New Haven, CT: Yale University Press, 1997), 34.

10. Alfred C. Rush, *Death and Burial in Christian Antiquity* (Washington, DC: Catholic University of America Press, 1941), viii.

11. Georges Bataille, *The Accursed Share: An Essay on General Economy,* vol. 1, *Consumption,* trans. Robert Hurley (New York: Zone, 1991), 27–44.

12. Royden Keith Yerkes, *Sacrifice in Greek and Roman Religions and Early Judaism* (New York: Charles Scribner's Sons, 1952), 202.

13. Georges Florovsky, *Creation and Redemption* (Belmont, MA: Nordland, 1976), 220.

14. *Чудото на св. Георги с българина.*

15. "Аз съм от новопокръстения български народ, когото бог просвети със свето кръщение тези години чрез своя избраник Бориса който го отвърна от тъмните и измамни и смрадни и богоумразни жертви и отхвърли смрадните и нечисти жертвени храни" (Evgenij K. Teodorov, *Drevnotrakijsko nasledstvo v bâlgarskija folklor* [Sofia: Izdatelstvo nauka i izkustvo, 1972], 84).

16. "И когато дойде денят да тръна на война, поканих свещеник и извърших света служба; заклах най-скъпия (си) вол и от овцете и свинете по десет и раздадох на бедните" (ibid.).

17. Ibid.

18. Perkowski notes that in certain Muslim communities in Bulgaria, the *kurban* still has the quality of an offering in exchange for a desired object or outcome: "The core ritual performed at the Tekke is the 'kurban' or animal sacrifice, which is promised if something wished for is received . . . When it is received, the dedicated male animal is taken to a picnic area over the spring" ("On the Legend of Demir Baba, the Iron Father," *Zeitschrift für Balkanologie* 34, no. 2 [1998]: 1–8).

19. *Слово Григория Богослова како погани суще языци кланялся идоломъ.*

20. The most comprehensive paleographic discussion of these texts is to be found in E. V. Aničkov, *Jazyčestvo i drevnjaja Rus': Xristianizacija varvarskix narodov Evropy* (St. Petersburg: Tipografija M. M. Stasjulevič, 1914). A fragment of the original eleventh-century text was published by Budilovič, A. "Slov Grigorija Bogoslova drevneslavjanskom perevode po rukopisi Imperatorskoj publičnoj biblioteki XI veka." St. Petersburg, 1875. p. 2. Cited in Zubov, M. I. "Slovo Grigorija Bogoslova i spiski jogo davn'oruskoi pererobki." Available online at http://www.textology.ru/public/zubov.html.

21. Editions of the text are available in Aničkov, *Jazyčestvo i drevnjaja Rus',* 380–86, and N. M. Gal'kovskij, ed., *Bor'ba xristianstva s ostatkami jazyčestva v drevnej Rusi,* vol. 2, *Drevnye russkie slova i poučenija, napravlennye protiv jazyčestva v narode* (Moscow, 1913), 17–35. The manuscript resides in the library of the Kirillo-Belozerskij Monastery (MS no. 4/1081).

22. MS no. 1295.

23. MS no. 43/1120.

24. Aničkov, *Jazyčestvo i drevnjaja Rus',* 28.

25. *Slovar' knižnikov i knižnosti drevnej Rusi XI–pervaja polovina XIV v* (Leningrad, 1987), 437.

26. Pelikan, *The Spirit of Eastern Christendom,* 249, 323.

27. Ibid., 156.

28. On Christian "responsibility" as incorporation and repression of the "secret" of the orgiastic, see Jacques Derrida, *The Gift of Death,* trans. David Wills (Chicago: University of Chicago Press, 1995), chap. 1. Derrida cites a passage by Patočka regarding enthusiasm as a threat to responsibility: "This is of course an en-

thusiasm that, in spite of the cult of reason, retains its orgiastic character, one which is undisciplined or insufficiently disciplined by the personal relation to responsibility. The danger of a new fall into the orgiastic is imminent" (*The Gift of Death,* 22).

29. Peter Brown, *The Body and Society: Men, Women, and Sexual Renunciation in Early Christianity,* Lectures on the History of Religions (New York: Columbia University Press, 1988), 140.

30. Presumed survivals of Dionysiac rituals in the Balkans are widely discussed in the literature. See, for example, Mixail Arnaudov, *Studii vârxu bâlgarskite obredi i legendi,* vol. 1 (Sofia: Izdatelstvo na bâlgarskata akademija na naukite, 1971), especially chap. 4, "Sâvremennen karnaval i drevni Dionisii," 80–127; C. A. Romaios, *Cultes populaires de la Thrace* (Athens, 1949); R. M. Dawkins, "The Modern Carnival in Thrace and the Cult of Dionysus," *Journal of Hellenic Studies* XXVI (1906): 191–206; F. K. Litsas, "Rousalia: The Ritual Worship of the Dead," in *The Realm of the Extra-Human: Agents and Audiences,* ed. Agehananda Bharati (The Hague: Mouton, 1976), 447–65; Teodorov, *Drevnotrakijsko nasledstvo;* Ivanička Georgieva, "Survivances de la religion des Thraces dans la culture spirituelle du peuple Bulgare," in *Actes du IIᵉ Congrès International de Thracologie, Bucarest, 1976.* Bucuresti, 1980. Vol. 3. 217–76; Lawson, *Modern Greek Folklore.*

31. Aničkov (*Jazyčestvo i drevnjaja Rus',* 65) says that the original translation from Gregory was "very literal, exhibiting no understanding of Greek thought, but rather attempting merely to represent paganism in the worst light."

32. Ibid.

33. See, for example, F. Miklosich, *Lexicon Paleoslovenico-Graeco-Latinum, Emendatum auctum* (Vindobonae: Guilelmus Braumueller, 1865); I. I. Sreznevskij, *Materialy dlja slovarja drevne-russkago jazyka po pismennym pamjatnikam,* vol. 3 (St. Petersburg: Rossijskaja Akademija Nauk, 1903).

34. Regis Boyer reads an unspecified variant of this text as meaning that vampires preceded the other Slavic deities and demons: "Known as *The Story of How Pagans Honored Their Idols,* it states that the Eastern Slavs 'first' offered sacrifice to the *rody* and to the *rožanicy* . . . , 'then' to Perun, 'their god,' whereas 'before that time' they were devoted to a cult of vampires and *beregyni* (nature spirits)" ("Slavic Myths, Rites, and Gods," in *American, African, and Old European Mythologies,* ed. Yves Bonnefoy, translated under the direction of Wendy Doniger [Chicago: University of Chicago Press, 1993], 241–48). Boyer does not point out that the date of the inserted fragment is no earlier than the fifteenth century. For additional discussion, see McClelland, "Slawische Religion."

35. Felix Oinas, "Heretics as Vampires and Demons in Russia." *Slavic and East European Journal* 22 (winter 1978): 433–41.

36. Linda Ivanits, *Russian Folk Belief* (Armonk, NY: M. E. Sharpe, 1989), 78; N. I. Tolstoy, "Берегини," in *Slavjanskie Drevnosti: Etnolingvističeskij Slovar'* (Moscow: Meždunarodnye otnošenija, 1995), vol. 1. 155–56.

37. Perkowski, *The Darkling,* 10; Jan Perkoswki, "The Vampires of Bulgaria and Macedonia—an Update," *Balkanistica* (Sofia) 12 (1999): 151–62.

38. A more detailed treatment of the etymological problems surrounding the term *vampir* is reserved for the appendix.

39. For a comprehensive history of this sect in English, see Dmitri Obolensky, *The Bogomils: A Study in Balkan Neo-Manichaeism* (Cambridge: Cambridge University Press, 1948); Steven Runciman, *The Medieval Manichee: A Study of the Christian Dualist Heresy* (Cambridge: Cambridge University Press, 1947; reprint, 1955). In Bulgarian, K. Gečeva has recently compiled a bibliography of Bogomilism, *Bogomilstvoto: Bibliografija* (Sofia, 1997). Stoyanov's *The Hidden Tradition in Europe* discusses both the ancestors and the descendants of Bogomilism and similar medieval dualisms.

40. Oinas, "Heretics as Vampires and Demons."

41. P. V. Vladimirov, *Poučenija protiv jazyčestva i narodnyx sueverij,* 3rd ed. (St. Petersburg, 1897), 198.

42. "The Discourse of the Priest Cosmas against the Bogomils," in Hamilton and Hamilton, *Christian Dualist Heresies,* 120.

43. The tract is available in French in Henri-Charles Puech and André Vaillant, eds. and trans., *Le traité contre les Bogomiles de Cosmas le Prêtre* (Paris: Imprimerie nationale, 1945). An English excerpt appears in Hamilton and Hamilton, *Christian Dualist Heresies,* 112–34.

44. Hamilton and Hamilton, *Christian Dualist Heresies,* 117.

45. Ibid.

46. Paul Veyne, ed., *A History of Private Life,* vol. 1, *From Pagan Rome to Byzantium,* trans. Arthur Goldhammer (Cambridge, MA: Belknap, 1992), 636–39.

47. Ample discussion of the dissident aspect of Bogomilism exists, especially in Marxist literature. See, for example, Drajan Taškovski, "Klasniot i socijalniot karakter na Bogomilstvoto" [The Class and Social Character of Bogomilism], in *Bogomilstvoto na Balkanot vo svetlinata na najnovite istražuvanja: Materiali od simpoziumot održan vo skopje na 30, 31 maj i 1 juni 1978 godina* (Skopje: Makedonska akademija na naukite i umetnostite, 1982), 41–54. In English, an extremely Marxist-Leninist discussion is to be found in Dragan Tashkovski [Drajan Taškovski], *Bogomilism in Macedonia,* trans. Alan McConnell (Skopje: Macedonian Review Editions, 1975), especially chap. 5, "The Spirit of National Liberation in the Bogomil Movement in Macedonia," 79–92.

48. Garth Fowden notes, "The doctrinal rigidification we observe in the Church from the fourth century, the vain search for precise definitions guaranteed to exclude old heresies and preclude new, would even so have been slower to set in had it not been for another of Christianity's supposed advantages over polytheism, namely its professional priesthood" (*Empire to Commonwealth: Consequences of Monotheism in Late Antiquity* [Princeton, NJ: Princeton University Press, 1993], 107).

49. Hamilton and Hamilton, *Christian Dualist Heresies,* 106. Accusations of sacrifice of flesh and blood from umbilical cords may not actually be so far-

fetched. Even in the twentieth century, it was a Slavic practice to incinerate the congenital membrane known as a caul and mix the ashes with the child's food in later life to prevent the child from becoming a vampire. For further discussion of the significance of the caul and marking vampires (or slayers), see chapter 7 in the present book.

50. The time between Christmas and New Year's Eve is often laden with taboos and rituals. These days are often referred to as the "Unclean Days" or "Pagan Days," and are a period during which vampires and other demons roam.

51. Hamilton and Hamilton, *Christian Dualist Heresies,* 106.

52. Ibid., 122.

53. Pelikan, *The Spirit of Eastern Christendom,* 216.

54. Hamilton and Hamilton, *Christian Dualist Heresies,* 119.

55. Bogomils in eleventh-century Byzantium had developed a sort of initiation ceremony to distinguish the elect from the common believers. The Byzantine writer Euthymius describes these ceremonies, sufficient evidence that the earlier, Balkan form of Bogomilism was devoid of rites, while later Bogomilism became slightly more hierarchical (see Hamilton and Hamilton, *Christian Dualist Heresies,* 33).

CHAPTER FOUR

1. This interpretation of Christian sacrifice is put forth by René Girard in *The Scapegoat,* chaps. 9–12.

2. Girard, *The Scapegoat,* 74.

3. Ibid., 53; E. E. Evans-Pritchard, "Witchcraft," *Africa* 8 (1955): 418–19.

4. Mary Douglas, *Natural Symbols: Explorations in Cosmology* (New York: Pantheon, 1970), 113.

5. Ibid.

6. Girard, *The Scapegoat,* 14ff.

7. So are witches. See Douglas, *Natural Symbols,* 107.

8. It can be argued that a powerful individual, such as a king or president, may play the role either of sacrificial victim or of scapegoat. While this is true, the role ascribed is different in the two circumstances: in the case of sacrifice, the destruction of the king is an honor and often part of the kingly function; in the case where the king is a scapegoat (as in the case of Oedipus), he has already lost his power and been dishonored. The recent case of impeachment proceedings against U.S. president Bill Clinton is an interesting example: in this case, the scapegoating mechanism was not completely successful, in part because there was no real catastrophe to invoke the operation of the scapegoat mechanism, which must operate both blindly and without dissension; also, the taboo violated by the president was no longer in great force, so that he was not greatly enough dishonored to be marginalized as a scapegoat, except by that portion of the population conservatively desiring to restore an earlier taboo.

9. Mary Douglas has written at great length about the notion of contamination, especially in her book *Purity and Danger: An Analysis of the Concepts of Pollution and Taboo* (London: Routledge, 1966). Of more specific relevance to the present topic are two essays in her book *Natural Symbols,* "Sin and Society" and "The Problem of Evil." In the latter, Douglas discusses the scapegoat mechanism in terms of social control: "In a community in which overt conflict cannot be maintained, witchcraft fears are used to justify expulsion and fission. Beyond a certain size, they cannot persist without introducing sharper definition into the structure of roles. Only certain limited targets can be achieved by their low level of organization. Expulsion of dissidents is one method of control, fission of a group a more drastic one" (114).

10. Ivanička Georgieva, *Bâlgarska narodna mitologija* [Bulgarian Folk Mythology] (Sofia: Nauki i izkustvo, 1983), 153.

11. Bruce Lincoln, e-mail communication to author, September 1998.

12. Arnold van Gennep, *The Rites of Passage,* trans. Monika Vizedom and Gabrielle Caffee (Chicago: University of Chicago Press, 1960), 147.

13. Evgenija Georgieva Miceva, "Narodni predstavi za brodešti noštem svrâx-estestveni sâštestva" [Popular Conceptions of Supernatural Beings That Go about at Night] *Bâlgarski Folklor* (Sofia) 7, no. 2 (1981): 62.

14. Ivan Snegarov notes: "Dominic, the translator for the mission, told St. Gerlach that in Bulgaria and Greece some dead people, excommunicated from the church, did not decay and at night the devil entered them." (*Istorija na oxridskata arxiepiskopija-patriaršija* [Sofija, 1931], 292).

15. Slobodan Zečević notes: "It is believed that at their death righteous people depart easily, while sinners on that occasion suffer greatly. It is thought that such people will become vampires." (*Mitska bića srpskih predanja* [Mythical Beings of Serbian Legends] [Beograd: Vuk Karadžić, 1981], 127).

16. Ibid., 123.

17. Evgenija Georgieva Miceva, "Demonični predstavi i personaži v bâlgarski folklor" [Demonic Representations and Personages in Bulgarian Folklore] (PhD diss., Bâlgarska akademija na naukite, Institut za folklor, 1984), 139.

18. Račko Ivanov Popov notes: "After death, unbelievers, the godless, excommunicates and the anathematized become vampires. St. Gerlach's notes from the XVI c. attest to this." ("Bâlgarski demonologični i mitologični vjarvanija: Kraja na XIX–sredata na XX v" [PhD diss., Ethnographic Institute and Museum, Bulgarian Academy of Sciences, Sofia, 1983], 36). Cf. note 14 in the present chapter: Popov here may be referring to the same text cited by Snegarov, in which case perhaps Popov means the seventeenth century rather than the sixteenth.

19. According to Račko Popov ("Bâlgarski demonologični," 34) the class of "secular" vampires includes robbers, bloodsuckers (i.e., extortionists), thieves, drunks, liars, men and women with easy behavior, and tavern keepers. On outlaws as demonic, see Bruce Lincoln, "The Living Dead: Of Outlaws and Others," review of *Die Toten Lebenden: Eine religionsphänomenologische Studie zum sozialen*

Tod in archaischen Gesellschaften; Zugleich ein kritischer Beitrag zur sogenannten Strafopfertheorie, by Hans-Peter Hasenfratz, *History of Religions* 23, no. 4 (May 1984): 387–89.

20. Among the Eastern Slavs, where the vampire has generally been supplanted, these individuals are destined to become members of the "unquiet dead." See D. K. Zelenin, *Očerki russkoj mifologii* (Petrograd: Tipografija D. V. Orlova, 1916), 1ff.

21. On these Орисници, or Fates, see Georgieva, *Bâlgarska narodna mitologija*, 137–45.

22. These names in Bulgarian are Погани дни, пепелин дни, некръстени дни, вампирясани дни. See Ivanička Georgieva, ed., *Kalendarni praznici i običai na Bâlgarite: Enciklopedija* [Calendar Holidays and Customs of the Bulgarians: An Encyclopedia] (Sofia: Prof. Marin Drinov, 1998), 20; Račko Ivanov Popov, "Kâm xarakteristikata na bulgarskite narodni vjarvanija, svârzani s periodite na prexod kâm zimata i proletta" [On the Characteristics of Bulgarian Folk Beliefs Connected with Times of Transition to Winter and Spring], in *Etnografski problemi na narodnata duxovna kultura* [Ethnographic Problems of Folk Spiritual Culture] (Sofia: Izdatelstvo "Club," 1992), 1:55; AIF 241.

23. The modern date of Christmas on December 25 was fixed to coincide with a pagan Roman holiday, Brumalia, "the feast of the Birth of the Unconquered Sun—*Natalis Invicti Solis*" (Alan Watts, *Myth and Ritual in Christianity* [Boston: Beacon, 1968], 122). Thus, Christmas and a major pagan holiday begin at the same time, a clear case where Christianity intentionally supplanted pre-Christian ritual.

24. Ember Days also occurred at other seasonal transition points. For the quote in text and for further information, see Ginzburg, *The Night Battles,* 43.

25. Cf. Aničkov, *Jazyčestvo i drevnjaja Rus',* 169: ". . . пиры как слишком плотское празнвание."

26. In his chapter "Beliefs about the Unseen World," Dimitâr Marinov includes vampires under the heading "Invisible Beings, Which Originally Were Human" (*Narodna vjara i religionzni narodni običaj* [Folk Belief and Folk Religious Customs] [1914; 2nd reprint, Sofia: Izdatelstvo na bâlgarskata akademija naukite, 1994], 811). One might speculate that demons are thought to be invisible when they simply represent the function subtending a class of events and a class of responses. Thus, the form of the demon is irrelevant or at least not central. With regard to the vampire, being a dead scapegoat is equivalent to being an invisible one: in either case, no direct action is taken against a living being, nor is there ever direct perception of the demon being engaged in the activity attributed to him.

27. The term *vampirdžia* has a Bulgarian root with a Turkish suffix.

28. These abilities are amplified, in some reports, by an "herb" that the *vampirdžia* keeps in his mouth. See Xristo Vakarelski, *Bâlgarski pogrebalni običai: Sravnitelno izučavane* [Bulgarian Burial Customs: A Comparative Study] (Sofia: Izdatelstvo na Bâlgarskata Akademija na Naukite, 1990), 166; G. V. Angelov, "Ot Bitolsko," *SbNU* XII (1895): 127. To date, there does not seem to be any published

research on the connection between *vampirdžii* and hallucinogens. However, mystical substances that provide special insight are often associated with shamanic practice. Further discussion regarding vampires and shamanism appears in chapter 6 in the present book.

29. Girard (*The Scapegoat*, 18) notes that scapegoats are sometimes chosen from among those "who have difficulty adapting, someone from another country or state, an orphan, an only son, someone who is penniless." Illegitimacy may easily be used as a reason for marginalization and scapegoating. Thus, by birth the *vampirdžia* would ordinarily be outcast.

30. Reports from Târnovo and Oxrid at the end of the nineteenth century state that *vampirdžii* often charged money for their vampire-hunting services. See Vakarelski, *Bâlgarski pogrebalni običai*, 167.

31. In the Strandja region, it is believed that when children who were conceived or born on Saturday die, they become vampires (*ustreli*) nine days after burial. See Georgieva, *Bâlgarska narodna mitologia*, 154 n. 5.

32. In general, dogs and wolves are considered enemies of the vampire (see, e.g., Georgieva, *Bâlgarska narodna mitologia*, 156.) Although it will not be investigated here, this notion may have to do with initiatory groups whose totem animal was the wolf (see Mircea Eliade, "The Dacians and Wolves," in Eliade, *Zalmoxis*, chap. 1). Curiously, in Central Europe, we find a case, cited by Ginzburg, regarding the Livonian werewolf Thiess, who was accused of witchcraft and consort with the devil in 1692. According to Thiess himself, werewolves "cannot tolerate the devil," because they are the "hounds of God" (Ginzburg, *The Night Battles*, 29). Such evidence runs contrary to the usual opinion of werewolves, which are considered similar in some ways to the vampire. See Perkowski, *The Darkling*, chap. 3.

33. The first instances in the New Testament where we find that Sunday is replacing Saturday as the Christian Sabbath are at Acts 20:7 and 1 Corinthians 16:2.

34. Brown, *The Body and Society*, 439.

35. K. Telbizov and M. Vekova-Telbizova, "Tradicionen bit i kultura na banatskite Bâlgari," *SbNU* LI (1963): 20.

36. In Bulgaria, a given day does not necessarily end at midnight; the morning of the following day begins at some unspecified time after around 2 a.m. Thus, if a vampire emerges on Saturday after sundown, some time after that he would be about on Sunday morning, well before cockcrow.

37. Such a broad statement requires qualification. Justinian, for example, hated both heretics and the Jews in Palestine more than pagans, and he persecuted both of the former vigorously (see MacMullen, *Christianity and Paganism*, 27). In general, however, since Judaism was monotheistic and since Jesus was a Jew and the Christian tradition was formally linked to the Old Testament, Jews did not represent as great a threat to Christianity as did heresy (which was increasing) or paganism. Polytheism constituted an affront to the expansion of Byzantine imperialism, which was inextricably tied to the notion of a single god. See Fowden, *Empire to Commonwealth*, 3.

38. Another link, which might deserve further investigation, is the connection between the *sâbotnik* and the sabbats of witches in Western Europe. The *benandanti,* who were said to attend the witches' sabbats in their sleep in order to do battle with them, occupied the Friuli region of northeastern Italy, not far from Slovenia. The *benandanti* were witch-hunters par excellence, and folklore may have reached further south into the Balkans. However, such a link is purely speculative. The connection between the *benandanti* and the vampire slayer is discussed in chapter 7 in the present book.

39. Aničkov, *Jazyčestvo i drevnjaja Rus',* 166 (my translation).

40. Račko Popov notes, "According to N. Veletskaya, the Soviet ethnographer, there are traces of the one-time ritual of slaying old men in the custom of Gherman, so that their souls may be sent as emissaries to the cosmic world of the forefathers" (*Butterfly and Gherman: Bulgarian Folk Customs and Rituals,* trans. Marguerite Alexieva [Sofia: Septemvri State Publishing House, 1989], 81).

41. Ibid., 75.

42. Girard notices the similarity in effect that natural disasters and certain social crimes, such as incest, have on social order: "All these crimes seem to be fundamental. They attack the very foundation of cultural order, the family and the hierarchical differences without which there would be no social order" (*The Scapegoat,* 14).

43. R. Popov, *Butterfly,* 81.

44. Evidence for a personified demon considered the origin of all diseases, the *nežit,* goes back to the tenth century. For discussion of early amulets with prayers against this demon, see Kazimir Popkonstantinov and Otto Kronsteiner, "Starobâlgarski nadpisi," *Die slawischen Sprachen* 36 (1994): 113–26. On a possible connection between the *nežit* and the vampire, see Bruce McClelland, "Pagans or Heretics? The Scapegoat Process, *Nezhit,* and the Bulgarian Folkloric Vampire," in *Bâlgaristikata v zorata na dvadeset i pârvi vek: Bâlgaro-amerikanskata perspektiva za naučni izsledvanija* (Sofia: Gutenberg, 2000), 132–37.

45. That vampires might cause epidemics should not be confused with the non-Slavic notion of "vampire contagion," discussed in more detail in chapter 5.

46. Girard (*The Scapegoat,* 43) maintains: "Admittedly, scapegoats cure neither real epidemics nor droughts nor floods. But the main dimension of every crisis is the way in which it affects human relations . . . As long as external causes exist, such as an epidemic of plague for example, scapegoats will have no efficacy. On the other hand, when these causes no longer exist, the first scapegoat to appear will bring an end to the crisis by eliminating all the interpersonal repercussions in the concentration of all evildoing in the person of one victim." This process seems to have been at work in the response to the terrorist attacks on the United States on September 11, 2001.

47. I have argued that the ritual symbolism surrounding the destruction of a vampire contains elements of sacrifice, suggesting that the vampire is as much a sacrificial victim as a scapegoat.

48. Girard, *The Scapegoat,* 53. Henri Hubert and Marcel Mauss, it should be noted, see expulsion as the simplest case of expiation and therefore do not really distinguish between sacrifice and scapegoating: "The most elementary form of expiation is elimination pure and simple. The expulsion of Azazel's goat, and that of the bird in the sacrifice for purification of a leper, is of this kind" (*Sacrifice: Its Nature and Functions,* trans. W. D. Halls [Chicago: University of Chicago Press, 1964; reprint, Midway Reprint, 1981], 53).

49. Certainly the level of "medical literacy" in rural Balkan villages was extremely low when compared with urban centers. Nevertheless, one does not have to understand a pathological process to realize that it is medical in nature.

50. Contra my assertion, see Barber, *Vampires, Burial, and Death,* 88 and passim.

51. See, for example, AIF 217, 97 (Mixailovgradski region, E. Miceva, coll., 1982).

52. Jordan Zaxariev, "Kamenica," *SbNU* XL (1935): 260–64; AIF 216, 239; AIF 217, 108; AIF 239, 2; Vakarelski, *Bâlgarski pogrebalni običai,* 86.

53. Rush, *Death and Burial,* 212.

54. In the Judeo-Christian tradition, this high value placed on blood is first explicitly stated in Leviticus 17:2: "For the life of the flesh is in the blood." The Mosaic prohibition against eating the blood follows immediately the story of Aaron and the scapegoat, and we may thus observe that the prohibition against eating or drinking blood represents an early step in the elimination of blood sacrifice among the Hebrews.

55. Walter Burkert, *Homo Necans: The Anthropology of Ancient Greek Sacrificial Ritual and Myth,* trans. Peter Bing (Berkeley: University of California Press, 1985), 2, 12; *Creation of the Sacred: Tracks of Biology in Early Religions* (Cambridge, MA: Harvard University Press, 1996), 9ff.

56. Joseph Henninger explains: "Originally what was sacrificed was either something living or an element or symbol of life. In other words, it was not primarily food that was surrendered, but life itself" ("Sacrifice," in *The Encyclopedia of Religion,* ed. Mircea Eliade [New York: Macmillan, 1987] 12:544–57). Concerning pouring sacrificial blood into the earth, cf. Bruce Lincoln, "Death and Resurrection in Indo-European Thought," *Journal of Indo-European Studies* 5 (1977): 247–64.

57. Farnell, "Sacrifice (Greek)."

58. Dirk Obbink, "Dionysus Poured Out: Ancient and Modern Theories of Sacrifice and Cultural Formation," in *Masks of Dionysus,* ed. Thomas H. Carpenter and Christopher A. Faraone (Ithaca, NY: Cornell University Press, 1993), 65–88.

59. Rush, *Death and Burial,* 116.

60. However, an early twentieth-century Russian ethnographer, N. S. Deržavin, records a curious anti-Semitic belief among Bulgarians who had been repatriated to East Slavic regions (present-day Moldova and Kherson): "Jews drink Christian blood instead of the Eucharist, guard against Jews!" [Еврея пьют христианскую кровь вместо причастия, опасайся еврей!] ("Bolgarskie kolonii v Rossii (tavričeskaja, xersonskaja i bessarabskaja gubernii)," *SbNU* XXIX [1914]: 175–90.)

61. In one of the insertions into the "Oration of Saint Gregory," we find a curious Russian charge against "the Bulgarians" (by which is probably meant the Bogomils): "Bulgarians eat the foul vileness that flows from private parts" [. . . бо-лгары . . . от срамных уд истекшюю скверну вкушают] (Aničkov, *Jazyčestvo i drevnjaja Rus',* 59). It is intentionally ambiguous which "vileness" (скверна) the Bulgarians supposedly prefer to eat, in the opinion of the Russians, but menstrual blood certainly might have been included. Such a strange aspersion, however, is more likely a charge against sexual practices than an accusation against blood drinking per se.

62. The period is usually forty days (see, e.g., AIF 216, 65) or six months (see R. Popov, "Bâlgarski demonologični," 39).

63. I mentioned in chapter 2 (n. 15) that among the names of the modern Greek revenant is *sarkomenos. Sarx* is the (ancient) Greek word for "flesh," and *menos* would mean something like "spirit" in this compound. It remains to be determined whether the Bulgarian word *plâtenik* might be a loan translation of *sarkomenos.*

64. Miceva, "Demonični predstavi i personaži," 110.

65. The absence of a skeleton may have a couple of interpretations. First, since bones survive the decomposition process, the absence of bones prevents any inquiry into the physical residue of a vampire's existence, once he has been destroyed. Second, bones generally play no role in sacrifice, while skin, meat (muscle and fat), and blood do. Finally, it is the skeleton that provides higher animals with their individual structures; absence of skeletal structure prevents the vampire from being categorized as an actual member of any species. The fact that vampires are thought to take on human or animal shape is not contradicted by their amorphousness in the Bulgarian popular imagination.

66. Georgieva (*Bâlgarska narodna mitologija,* 157) cites folklore in which a vampire that lasts for three years becomes "a handsome man."

67. Marcel Detienne, "Culinary Practices and the Spirit of Sacrifice," in *The Cuisine of Sacrifice among the Greeks,* trans. Paula Wissing (Chicago: University of Chicago Press, 1989), 1–20.

68. Hubert and Mauss, *Sacrifice,* 34. It should also be noted that the *gajda* is made from the gut of an animal that is commonly sacrificed.

69. Hubert and Mauss (ibid., 68–69) point out that in the Greek sacrificial ritual known as *Bouphonia,* "the flesh of the bullock was shared among those present, the skin, after having been filled with straw, was sewn up again, and the stuffed animal was harnessed to a plough." They interpret this event, in which the skin was stuffed, as a means of bringing the sacrificial victim back to life. There would seem to be some similarity between the Greek and Bulgarian images. Burkert (*Homo Necans,* 16) also sees postsacrificial processes (e.g., gathering the bones, raising the skull, or stretching the skin) as "an attempt at restoration, a resurrection in the most concrete sense." This need for resurrection, he posits, is associated with the "comedy of innocence," a means of quelling the "underlying anxiety about the continuation of life in the face of death."

70. V. Čajkanović, "The Killing of a Vampire," in *The Vampire: A Casebook,* ed. Alan Dundes (Madison: University of Wisconsin Press, 1998), 72–84.

71. Rush, *Death and Burial,* 169.

72. Yerkes, *Sacrifice,* 54.

73. A precaution against a corpse becoming a vampire is to prick the skin, which destroys its integrity. This is done, according to folk belief, so that "the Devil cannot make a bagpipe [*gajda*]" (Georgieva, *Bâlgarska narodna mitologija,* 154).

74. Aničkov, *Jazyčestvo i drevnjaja Rus',* 160. *Vampirdžii* are known to entice vampires with music so they can kill them. See Georgieva, *Bâlgarska narodna mitologija,* 157.

75. Actually, in Bulgarian vampire lore, "pissing image" might also be an appropriate phrase. In material collected from around Mixajlovgrad in 1982, a woman who had been wasting away found the postvampiric jelly, *pixtija,* in her garden and went out to piss on it. ("Жена пикала на пихтия," AIF 217, 193). Spitting as an apotropaic in the face of simulacra is common among the Slavs.

76. Georgieva, *Bâlgarska narodna mitologija,* 158.

77. R. Popov, "Bâlgarski demonologični," 42. Liudmil Getov lists the sites as Vratsa, Kazanluk, and Panagurište ("Observations sur les rites funéraires des Thraces aux époques hellénistique et romaine," in *Actes du IIe Congrès International de Thracologie, Bucarest, 4–10 September 1976,* vol. 2, *History and Archaeology* [Bucharest: Editura academiei republicii socialiste Romania, 1980], 221). See also R. F. Hoddinott, *The Thracians* (London: Thames and Hudson, 1981), 33ff.

78. Vakarelski (*Bâlgarski pogrebalni običai,* 168) cites Slavomíri Wollman (1921) as describing a West Slavic report from 1252: "On account of fratricide Duke Abel of Schezvig was considered a vampire and was transfixed in the chest with a stake." We should bear in mind that Wollman is using the term *vampire* somewhat loosely, applying it retrospectively. It is doubtful that any word cognate with *vampir* was used in West Slavic regions in the thirteenth century, but many "relatives" of the Balkan vampire that go by different names are attested in many areas of Eastern and Central Europe, especially those contiguous to the regions settled by the Slavs. I have not seen the original thirteenth-century manuscript.

79. Perkowski, *The Darkling,* 102, 106, passim.

80. Vakarelski, *Bâlgarski pogrebalni običai,* 85.

81. Vakarelski (*Bâlgarski pogrebalni običai,* 86) writes, "In a list of apocryphal books as proof against the sect of the Bogomils, Jeremiah says, 'бъілъвъ навѣхъ на Верзноуловъ колоу,' which is interpreted as piercing the dead person with a stake [кол] against vampirism."

82. T. Atanasova et al., *Bâlgarsko-anglijski rečnik* [Bulgarian-English dictionary], (Sofia: Nauka i izkustvo, 1975) s.v. заколвам.

83. Liddell and Scott, *A Lexicon: Abridged from Lidell and Scott's Greek-English Lexicon,* (Oxford: Oxford University Press, 1966), s.v. ΣΦΑΖΩ.

84. Dimitâr Marinov, *Živa Starina* (Russe: Pečatnica Sv. Kiril i Metodii, 1891), 41.

85. On the cosmogonic symbolism of dismemberment in sacrifice, see Bruce Lincoln, *Myth, Cosmos, and Society: Indo-European Themes of Creation and Destruction* (Cambridge, MA: Harvard University Press, 1986), chap. 2, 41–63.

86. Fol, *Trakijskijât dionis,* 373.

87. Чувал is also frequently used to describe the baglike vampire.

88. Telbizov and Vekova-Telbizova, "Tradicionen bit," 201. Cf., in C. Ginčov's "Ot Târnovsko" (*SbNU* II [1890]: 189–91), "The Tale of the Vampire Suitor," in which a betrothed girl cuts off the finger of her exhumed suitor because he was "bloated" (надул; i.e., a vampire) and she could not retrieve his engagement ring.

89. The folklore concerning throwing a finger into the water may in fact represent a Bulgarian pun. In a similar tale, earth from the grave is thrown into the river, with the same result: the vampire goes in after it and drowns (see Georgieva, *Bâlgarska narodna mitologija,* 159). In Bulgarian, the word пръст means both "finger" and "earth." The liturgical phrase Лека му пръст means "May he rest in peace." Removing earth from the grave and removing fingers and then using either as a means of attracting the vampire are both common themes.

90. Mary Durham, discussing the Balkan (Serbian) ritual known as *Vodokrsche,* a blessing of the waters that takes place on January 6, the final day of the "Unclean Days," writes, "A human victim was in ancient days sacrificed in the Nile and the throwing of the cross, representing Christ, into the river suggests that the custom is a relic of a human sacrifice" (M. E. Durham, "Some Balkan Festivals," *Folk-Lore* 51 [1940]: 83–89). Of course, we may also view throwing things in rivers as a form of purification. See, for example, François de Polignac, *Cults, Territory, and the Origins of the Greek City-State,* trans. Janet Lloyd (Chicago: University of Chicago Press, 1994), 70. Girard (*The Scapegoat,* 176) notes that the Greek *pharmakos,* or scapegoat, "was made to throw himself into the sea from such a height that death was inevitable."

91. Yerkes, *Sacrifice,* 52.

92. R. Popov, "Bâlgarski demonologični," 36.

93. Rush, *Death and Burial,* 140, 236, 244.

94. Examples are the Greek *holocaust* or the Hebrew *olah,* burnt offerings in which no residue was consumable by humans.

95. Erwin Rohde, *Psyche: The Cult of Souls and Belief in Immortality among the Greeks,* trans. W. B. Hillis (1920; reprint, New York: Books for Libraries Press, 1972), 165.

96. Hubert and Mauss, *Sacrifice,* 25.

97. Anani Stojnev, ed., *Bâlgarska mitologija: Enciklopedičen rečnik* (Sofia: Izdatelska grupa 7M, 1994), s.v. трън.

98. Ibid.

99. Mention of the crown of thorns is in Mark 15:18.

100. Čajkanović, "The Killing of a Vampire," 75.

101. Sir James George Frazer, *The Golden Bough: A Study in Magic and Religion,* abridged ed. in 1 vol. (New York: Macmillan, 1922), 646.

102. Thorn and garlic are often woven or mixed together as a protective measure in contemporary folklore (cf. AIF 216, 68, 193, 316). One informant (68) refers to an old saying that the thorn is used "so there will be red wine, and a good harvest for the year" [Да има червено вино, е така, старите поговорки, да и берекет на годината, те така. На трън].

103. Georgieva, *Bâlgarska narodna mitologija,* 155.

104. Ginzburg (*The Night Battles,* 90) remarks on a similar tradition, in Western European witchcraft accusations, of imputing stupidity and ignorance to "the villain."

105. Burkert, *Homo Necans,* 11.

106. The offering of bread to a vampire is conserved even in folk songs. In an interview recorded in Sakar in 1983, an informant recalled the following partial ditty: "Вампир ходи, раде / Из село ходи. / И у нас дойди. / Дадох парча ляб, / Парча зелник" [A vampire left the village and came to us. I gave him a piece of bread, a piece of leek] (AIF 216, 227).

107. Georgieva, *Bâlgarska narodna mitologija,* 157.

108. Cf. the Greek practice. Yerkes (*Sacrifice,* 108) notes: "Libations were of common occurrence throughout the history of Greek religions. Wine, blood and wine, oil and honey were used for various purposes; if these were lacking, water could be used as a surrogate."

109. Yerkes, *Sacrifice,* 99.

110. Slavic folklorist Natalie Kononenko suggests that the compulsive acts demanded of demons represent a means of imposing order on them (personal communication with author, Charlottesville, VA, April 14, 1999). The general threat posed by the demonic, of course, is disorder.

111. Yerkes, *Sacrifice,* 58.

112. Zaxariev ("Kamenica," 260) notes, "When the body is moved, they drive a nail [пирон] where his head was, and above it they place an axe to frighten the soul that it won't return to the house."

113. Vakarelski, *Bâlgarski pogrebalni običai,* 87; Georgieva, *Bâlgarska narodna mitologija,* 155. In the Ukraine, according to Vakarelski, scythes and sickles may also be placed at the site of death.

114. E. E. Levkievskaja, personal conversation, Institute for Slavistics and Balkanistics, Russian Academy of Sciences, Moscow, April 1997.

CHAPTER FIVE

1. Katharina M. Wilson, "The History of the Word *Vampire,*" in Dundes, *The Vampire,* 3–11. Wilson too easily accepts Bruckner's dismissal of the usefulness of the citation in the *Liber Prophetarum* (*Kniga prorokov*) for drawing conclusions about the etymology of the word *vampir* (*upyr'*), on the grounds that the term

was a proper name. Bruckner failed to recognize that the proper name was in fact a self-deprecating nickname that provides significant evidence about the original meaning of the term.

2. McClelland, "Sacrifice, Scapegoat, Vampire," 165.

3. Eliade, *Zalmoxis,* 31ff.

4. For accessible discussions of the Orthodox view of the soul in the afterlife, see Fr. Seraphim Rose, *The Soul after Death* (Platina, CA: St. Herman of Alaska Brotherhood, 1995); Ware, *The Orthodox Church,* especially 258–60.

5. The groundwork for scapegoating nobility by accusations of witchcraft may be seen in the accusations against the Bathory family of Hungary, especially the infamous Erzebet, who was tried and convicted in 1611. For further discussion of the pattern of witchcraft accusations against members of nobility, see chapter 9.

6. Bruce Lincoln points out that this process of "semantic folklorization" is not without precedent: "This is the semantic shift of the term 'Magi,' originally a Median tribe that performed priestly functions (as per Herodotus 1.101), but which came to denote Oriental sages, charlatans (already in Heraclitus, as quoted by Clement of Alexandria, *Protepticus* 22.2), and royalty (thus the Gospel narratives) of various sorts, ultimately 'magicians' in general (with a -*ko*- suffix in Greek)" (e-mail message to author, December 10, 2002).

7. It may be objected that there are early references to vampirelike demons in West Slavic regions as well, and cognate forms of *vampir* certainly exist in Czech and Polish. Furthermore, in Greek folklore, there is the revenant figure of an ambulatory corpse. However, the semantic merger of *vampir* with the names of demons from neighboring regions, such as the Serbian *vrkolak,* is a later development and evidences a process Perkowski terms "demon contamination."

8. Wilson, "History of the Word *Vampire,*" 6.

9. In some areas, to see a vampire is to die. This folkloric strategy actually eliminates the possibility of anyone ever seeing a vampire and being able to report it.

10. The perception of the northernmost region of the Ottoman Empire, which was separated from Hungary by a military frontier at the end of the sixteenth century, was that it was a source of disease and contamination. Concerning the period under the rule of Maria Theresa, Barabara Jelavich reports: "because of the prevalence of plague and other dangerous, communicable diseases in the Ottoman Empire, the Habsburg government kept a strict quarantine along the frontiers. Travelers entering the monarchy were forced to remain in seclusion for up to three weeks, and all letters and goods were disinfected by the primitive means of the time" (*History of the Balkans,* vol. 1, *Eighteenth and Nineteenth Centuries* [Cambridge: Cambridge University Press, 1983], 147).

11. Quoted in Wilson, "History of the Word *Vampire,*" 7.

12. See, for example, Perkowski, *The Darkling;* Barber, *Vampires, Burial, and Death;* John Fine, "In Defense of Vampires," in Dundes, *The Vampire,* 57–66.

13. See, for example, Barber, *Vampires, Burial, and Death.* The problem with

this approach is that it superimposes medical materialism onto folklore without any consideration for the ways in which folklore develops and is disseminated. It assumes that the primary motive of folklore is to explain the otherwise inexplicable.

14. Wolf, *Dracula,* 28.

15. Contemporary Bulgarian folklorists and ethnographers are able even to supply phone numbers of known vampires (Margarita Karamihova, personal communication with author, Sofia, 1998; no mention was made of how such vampires became known).

16. Klaniczay, *The Uses of Supernatural Power,* 169.

17. Ibid., 170.

18. The timing of Van Swieten's venture into Moravia was probably motivated as well by more strategic goals than are usually mentioned. The Seven Years' War, which began in 1756, concerned primarily possession of Habsburg territories, in particular Silesia, which Austria had been forced to surrender in 1748. See Jelavich, *History of the Balkans,* 133.

19. Vampire beliefs in Poland and Bohemia (i.e., West Slavic regions) were also of interest to Western reporters, but it was the outbreaks occurring primarily in Serbia that initially drew the most attention.

20. Note that the "justice" brought against Count Dracula is determined by exactly these two modalities of evidence.

21. The trials were usually against those who carried out grave desecration. See, for example, the account from the island of Lastovo in Croatia in 1737 in Perkowski, *The Darkling,* 85. Perkowski (ibid., 125) points out that this transcript is "the missing link between actual Slavic vampire cult practices and their reflexion [*sic*] in Western European literature" and, further, that the "court testimony provides a clear presentation of vampire activity which presents no primary, firsthand evidence which cannot be explained by natural causes."

22. Perkowski (*The Darkling,* 30) notes, "The people also assert that all those who have been killed by vampires must in turn become the same thing."

CHAPTER SIX

1. Miceva, "Demonični predstavi i personaži," 103, 110ff.; Evgenija Georgieva Miceva, *Nevidimi noštni gosti: Podbor i naučen komentar* (Sofia: Nauka i Izkustvo, 1994), 17–18.

2. Miceva, "Demonični predstavi i personaži," 121. In some narratives, the vampire does acquire a skeleton as a last step in his final "reincarnation." He can live up to three years as a complete human simulacrum.

3. Walter Burkert discusses the difference between sacrificial violence and the form of expulsion that takes place within the scapegoat mechanism, or what he calls the "pharmakos complex." He identifies the focus of the scapegoating ritual as "the separation of the victim bound for annihilation from all those others destined for salvation." He adds: "there need not be direct killing in the phar-

makos complex, though it must be ensured that the scapegoat does not return: this would mean catastrophe. Hence instead of slaughter we often find other forms of annihilation, such as drowning or burning" ("The Problem of Ritual Killing," in *Violent Origins: Walter Burkert, René Girard, and Jonathan Z. Smith on Ritual Killing and Cultural Formation,* ed. Robert G. Hamerton-Kelly [Stanford, CA: Stanford University Press, 1987], 173). The homology of the dynamics of Burkert's "pharmakos complex" with that of the annihilation of the vampire should be clear.

4. Račko Popov ("Bâlgarski demonologični," 43) reports an interesting case where the vampire was dispatched by three women.

5. In some cases, the priest may be willing to say prayers over the severed head of a suspected vampire, without any qualms. Tanja Boneva, *Smoljansko,* field report, AEIM 110-III, folder II (Sofia, 1987).

6. The enforcement of a relationship between ritual accuracy and efficacy naturally opens the door to blaming any ritual failure on some probable misstep during the performance of the rite.

7. Tihomir R. Đorđević, "Vampir i druga mitska biħa u narodnom verovanju i predanju" [The Vampire and Other Mythical Beings in Folklore and Legend], in *Srpski etnografski zbornik* LXVI (Belgrade, 1963), 5–255. See also Vakarelski, *Bâlgarski pogrebalni običai,* 67, 86.

8. Pócs, *Between the Living and the Dead,* 121.

9. Carlo Ginzburg, *Ecstasies: Deciphering the Witches' Sabbath,* trans. Raymond Rosenthal (New York: Penguin, 1991), 212.

10. The Balkan portion of the Ottoman Empire was partitioned by the major European powers at the Congress of Berlin in July 1878. See Jelavich, *History of the Balkans,* 360.

11. S. D. Božev, "Ot Demir-Xisarsko," *SbNU* IV (1891): 111.

12. I shall here from time to time use the contemporary term *vampire slayer* generically, when the distinction is not particularly significant, to refer to various South Slavic individuals with the capacity to see and destroy vampires and related demons. While there are good reasons for keeping the regional nomenclature distinct—retaining such terms as *glog, sâbotnik, vâpirar, dhampir,* and *vampirdžia*— the colorful and admittedly popular term *slayer* has the advantage of succinctly encapsulating a semantic cluster in a convenient form.

13. Evgenija Miceva ("Demonični predstavi i personaži," 110) notes that the territory that demons inhabit is a marginal world, similar to earthly existence, but where everything is antisymmetrical.

14. In both Bulgarian and Greek funeral customs, mirrors and other image-replicating surfaces (e.g., glasses of water) are covered or removed or otherwise made incapable of reflecting the dying or dead person. In popular belief, the mirror was said to be able to "capture the soul" of the deceased, which would naturally interrupt the soul's journey. Here is a direct link between a belief about the natural path of the soul in the afterlife and the categorical problem of simulacra.

15. In the Bulgarian apocryphal book of Jeremiah from the Middle Ages, there is mention of piercing the excommunicate dead with a stake to prevent them from roaming.

16. D. Matov, "Ot Veles," *SbNU* IX (1893): 130.

17. G. V. Angelov, "Ot Bitolsko," 126.

18. Drums are used in shamanic magic to alter the perceptions: "The Hungarian *táltos* used a drum while exercising his magic. By beating it he was able to discern malicious persons" (B. Gunda, "Survivals of Totemism in the Hungarian *táltos* Tradition," in *Folk Beliefs and Shamanistic Traditions in Siberia,* ed. Vilmos Diószegi and Mihály Hoppál, trans. S. Simon [Budapest: Akadémiai Kiadó, 1996], 15–25). See also, in the same volume, J. Balázs, "The Hungarian Shaman's Technique of Trance Induction." I examine a proposed connection between Central European shamanism and certain aspects of Balkan vampire folklore in the discussion that follows in text.

19. Vakarelski, *Bâlgarski pogrebalni običai,* 166.

20. Xristo Gandev, *Ranno vâzraždane 1700–1860.* Studia Historica Philologica Serdicensia, suppl. 3 (Sofia, 1939), 32.

21. Konstantin Ireček, "Stari pâtešestvija po Bâlgarija ot 15–18 stoletie," in *Periodičesko spisanie na bâlgarskoto knižovno družestvo v Sredec,* book iv (Sofia: Dâržavna pečatica, 1883), 162.

22. Ibid.

23. Whereas Jesus's divinity is confirmed by his resurrection, the negative mirror image of that event confirms the demonic in the ambulatory corpse, which, by virtue of being anathema, cannot enter the world after life. That vampires are in some sense evil mirrors of Christ is shown by the belief that vampires are reincarnated on the Saturday before Easter (see Telbizov and Vekova-Telbizova, "Tradicionen bit," 46). The wilting of the vampire when confronted with an image of Christ (in the form of an icon, usually) attests to the inferiority of the simulacrum.

24. In discussing the annihilation of the scapegoat, Burkert (*Creation of the Sacred,* 53) notes: "the tolerable loss may nevertheless leave the survivors with a bad conscience. This can be countered by an alternative projection: the being chosen to perish was guilty, polluted and detestable; the positive effect is enhanced by the negative criteria of selection."

25. Deržavin, "Bolgarskie kolonii v Rossii"; Panajot Madžarov, "'Poganoto' (Pogani Dni) vâv vjarvanijata i bita na strandžanskite sela," *Bâlgarski Folklor* (Sofia) 4 (1982): 91–101. In Russian lower mythology, forces of spiritual evil are labeled unclean. Furthermore, there is a Russian homologue to the South Slavic vampire known as the "unquiet dead" (*založnyj pokojnik*). The relationship between this class of demons and the Bulgarian vampire deserves greater attention. For a good general discussion of the Russian folklore in this area, see Ivanits, *Russian Folk Belief,* especially chap. 3.

26. The nature of this conflict is complex, but in general it exemplifies the

same tensions between Christianity and paganism that occur wherever the two belief systems come into contact. For a discussion of how these two religious systems interacted and influenced each other in late antiquity, see MacMullen, *Christianity and Paganism.* For a more specific discussion of the conflict between the two views of time in Slavic areas, as codified in the rituals of the Unclean Days, see McClelland, "The Anathematic Vampire."

27. Gandev, *Ranno vâzraždane,* 33.

28. Amusingly, the advance of light-bringing electricity into the mountain village is held responsible for the falloff in the number of vampires. "We stopped having so many vampires after we got electric lights," says one informant in the late 1980s (Boneva, *Smoljansko,* AEIM 110-III, folder II 77). Here, an attribute of the vampire—namely, fear of light—is incorporated into a folk rationalization regarding the larger process of urbanization.

29. Evgenija Miceva, Folklorni materiali ot mixajlovgradski okrâg, mixajlovgradski rajon, 22.xi.–27.xi. 1982. AIF 216-I, 62.

30. Actually, this is not quite true. While researching cultural beliefs among the Kashub population in Canada, Jan Perkowski encountered a respondent who, in response to the question "What is a vampire?" on a sociological questionnaire, answered, "I am a vampire." I would argue that since in the West Slavic tradition, which has been strongly influenced by Western European witch beliefs, there are rituals that can be performed to prevent a marked child from becoming a vampire after death, the negativity attached to the *wupij* (Kashubian vampire) is not as strong as in the Balkan tradition. Furthermore, this confession was obtained in the New World, where the influence of the literary or cinematic vampire can less easily be discounted. Because of the conflation of the vampire and the vampire slayer in some areas, confessions of being a vampire do occur, but only when they are effectively also confessions to being a seer. Ginzburg (*Ecstasies,* 172) cites the case of the Ukrainian Semyen Kallenichenko, who in 1727 confessed to being a vampire, able to recognize witches.

31. In the Hungarian *táltos* tradition, the confusion between the witch (homologous here to the vampire) and the *táltos* (homologous to the vampire slayer) can be reduced by "one characteristic fact": "that no one confesses he is a witch, whereas one does admit that one is a *táltos*" (Gunda, "Survivals," 15).

32. Boneva, *Smoljansko,* AEIM 110-III, folder II.

33. Girard, *Scapegoat,* chap. 10.

34. AIF 1983, 251; Vakarelski, *Bâlgarski pogrebalni običai,* 165.

35. Račko Ivanov Popov, *Sakar-Xarmanlijsko,* AEIM 313-III (Sofia, 1995).

36. This is a type of legend encountered also in Romanian werewolf folklore. See, for example, Harry Senn, *Were-Wolf and Vampire in Romania* (Boulder, CO: East European Monographs, 1982), app. A, 79ff.

37. The story provides a folk etiology for the presence of red thread, which is present in a great deal of folklore and taboos connected with burial and vampires.

38. This hydrophobia, of which the medical materialists make far too much,

is probably due as much to water's purifying value in Christian initiation (i.e., baptism) as to its reflective surface. As an example of a medical "explanation" of the vampire's origins that ignores virtually all folkloric evidence and history, see Alonso J. Gomez, "Rabies: A Possible Explanation for the Vampire Legend," *Neurology* 51, no. 3 (September 1998): 856–59.

39. Tanja Boneva, *Pazardžik.*

40. R. Popov, "Bâlgarski demonologični," 47; Račko Ivanov Popov, "Za vârkolaka v bâlgarskite narodni vjarvanija (istoričeski koreni i mjasto v narodnata kultura)" [On the Werewolf in Bulgarian Folk Belief (Historical Roots and Its Place in Folk Culture)] (Sofia: n.d.).

41. Vakarelski, *Bâlgarski pogrebalni običai.*

42. The term *männerbund* was coined in 1902 by Heinrich Schurtz to designate a hierarchically organized company of men, bound by oaths and certain rituals and having a common purpose.

43. Perkowski speaks of "demon contamination" where a historical linguist would refer to "semantic merger." The increasing identity between the terms *vukodlak* and *vampir,* which originate in separate areas of the Balkans and have completely different etymological roots, suggests that the terms had something in common—such as referring to outlaws (as in the case of the wolf) and excommunicates (as in the case of the vampire)—and that this commonality grew as the original referents disappeared and the linguistic groups came increasingly into contact or became increasingly difficult to differentiate. This analysis is pure conjecture, since there is hardly enough historical data to support a convincing analysis.

44. Anani Stojnev, *Bâlgarska mitologija,* s.v. *vâlči praznici.*

45. R. Popov, "Bâlgarski demonologični," 44.

46. Ireček, "Stari pâtešestvija po Bâlgarija," book 2, 116–18.

47. Georgieva, *Bâlgarska narodna mitologija,* 155.

48. Dimitâr Popov points to an ecstatic ritual from Thrace in the third century BC in which men and women walked around the hearth inhaling the smoke produced from throwing the seeds of certain grasses and herbs on the fire. There is no mention of whether any sort of hawthorn was included, but perhaps the folklore of throwing *glog* into the hearth or the oven derives from such a ritual.

CHAPTER SEVEN

1. This is of course a matter of perception. The usual sense of the vampire is that spirit has somehow (re)entered the inanimate corpse, so this might be termed *enstasis.* Still, folkloric narratives tend to focus on the vampire's ability to leave the grave (i.e., the world of the dead) in order to enter the world of the living.

2. It is possible that these character defects attributed to the vampire in late folklore are indications of a general weakening of belief in vampires from the late nineteenth century forward. However, I believe that these traits are more specifi-

cally linked to the vampire's role as a sacrificial victim. This connection is worked out in more detail in McClelland, "Sacrifice, Scapegoat, Vampire."

3. Ginzburg, *Ecstasies,* 214.

4. Ibid., 195.

5. Ibid. See also Cohn, *Europe's Inner Demons,* 217, 232. Cohn argues persuasively that the sabbats never actually took place, contra Margaret Murray and Montague Summers.

6. Ginzburg, *Ecstasies,* 93.

7. Klaniczay, *The Uses of Supernatural Power,* 131.

8. Senn (*Were-Wolf,* 64), following Roman Jakobson's analysis of Slavic epic, points out that in Slavic cultures, the caul frequently indicates good fortune, while in Norse Icelandic mythology, it bestows second sight and the ability to change into an animal (*Selected Writings IV: Slavic Epic Studies* [The Hague: Mouton, 1966]).

9. "Ember Days," in *Catholic Encyclopedia,* vol. 5 (New York: Robert Appleton, 1909), available online at http://www.newadvent.org/cathen/05399b.htm (2003).

10. Klaniczay, *The Uses of Supernatural Power,* 140.

11. The claim is attributed to Mrs. Demeter Paskuly in Pócs, *Between the Living and the Dead,* 146.

12. Klaniczay, *The Uses of Supernatural Power,* 145.

13. Ibid., 134.

14. Ibid., 136.

15. Ibid., 129–50.

16. Carlo Ginzburg, e-mail message to author, June 2003.

17. Stoyanov, *The Hidden Tradition in Europe,* 207ff.

18. Cohn, *Europe's Inner Demons,* 23.

19. See, for example, "Punishment of the Dead and Inanimate Objects and in Effigy," in *Criminal Justice through the Ages: From Divine Judgment to Modern German Legislation,* trans. John Fosberry, Publications of the Mediaeval Crime Museum, vol. 4 (Rothenburg ob der Tauber, 1981).

CHAPTER EIGHT

1. Frank T. Brechka, *Gerard van Swieten and His World, 1700–1772* (The Hague: Martinus Nijhoff, 1970), 132.

2. Ibid., 2.

3. The Catholic Habsburgs did not rush to mobilize the empire's forces to assist the Calvinist Hungarians in pushing back the Turks until 145 years after major Hungarian cities had come under the dominion of the Ottoman Empire. See Arminius Vambery, *The Story of Nations: Hungary in Ancient, Mediaeval, and Modern Times* (London: T. Fisher Unwin, 1887), chap. 11.

4. It is uncertain whether Van Swieten actually attended lectures by Van Espen. See Brechka, *Gerard van Swieten,* 43.

5. Ibid., 36. Here is an explicit demand within the southern Dutch and, by implication, Austro-Hungarian sphere for the separation of church and state.

6. Ibid., 61.

7. Vambery, *Hungary,* 369–70.

8. Brechka, *Gerard van Swieten,* 151.

9. Ibid., 125–26.

10. Klaniczay, *The Uses of Supernatural Power,* 161; Vambery, *Hungary,* 368.

11. Cited in Brechka, *Gerard van Swieten,* 131 n. 106.

12. Gerard van Swieten, *Vampyrismus* (Palermo: S. F. Flaccovio, 1988), 15.

13. The rough English translation herein of all passages from Van Swieten's text is by the author, on the basis of the Italian translation *Considerazione intorno alla pretesa magia postuma per servire alla storia de' Vampiri presentata al supremo Direttorio di Vienna,* trans. Signor Barone (Naples: Presso Giuseppe Maria Porcelli, 1787). The text and annotation have been reprinted (in Italian) as Gerhard van Swieten, *Vampyrismus,* ed. Piero Violante (Palermo, Italy: S. F. Flaccovio, 1988), 9–10.

14. Van Swieten, *Vampyrismus,* 11.

15. Ibid., 11–12.

16. In the Balkans, the term *haiduk* (which has various spellings, according to region and alphabet, and is probably of Turkish origin) has the sense of a brigand who was also something of a mercenary who fought against the Turks. In Hungary, the term came to refer to a class of mercenary foot soldiers who were rewarded around 1605 with political positions for their defense of Protestantism. In Austro-Hungary, *haiduk* had the meaning that is familiar to Van Swieten—namely, an assistant to the court.

17. Ibid., 12–13.

18. Ibid., 15–16.

19. Ibid., 16.

20. Ibid., 17–19.

21. Ibid., 19.

22. "Bericht des Regimetfeldschers Flückinger an die Belgrader Oberkommandautur" (26.1.1732) in *Mortuus non mordet; Kommentierte Dokumentation zum Vampirismus,* Klaus Hamberger, 49–54. See also http://www.paranormal.de/vampir/quellec.html.

CHAPTER NINE

1. Perkowski reminds us that within Islamic cosmology, reanimation of the corpse is an untenable concept, since Islamic demons are always disembodied. There is no evidence that any of the English writers on vampires attribute the origin of the idea to the Turkish or Arabic Muslims. Rather, it seems they presume an earlier pagan substratum, which is closer to the truth than they perhaps realized.

2. Carol Senf points out that Polidori expressly cites both Tournefort and

Dom Calmet in the introduction to *The Vampyre* (London: Sherwood, Neely, and Jones, 1819), xxiv.

3. I mentioned in the introduction the influence of Marx on the reception of the economic metaphor of the vampire. For further discussion, see Terrell Carver, *The Postmodern Marx* (University Park: Pennsylvania State University Press, 1998), especially chap. 1, "Spectres and Vampires: Marx's Metaphors," 7–23. Auerbach (*Our Vampires,* 31) notes that Marx's *Capital* (originally published in 1867) "sealed the vampire's class descent from mobile aristocrat to exploitative employer," though it is hard to see Bram Stoker's Count Dracula as an example of the latter rather than the former. For a broader discussion of the social climate in which the vampire of English literature arose, see Senf, *The Vampire in Nineteenth-Century English Literature.* Here, Senf, discussing James Malcolm Rymer's *Varney the Vampyre* (1847), points out, for example, that "much of the evil in *Varney* centers on money, for Varney is at least in some ways a perfectly ordinary economic parasite" (44). I discuss the syllogism of the economic metaphor shortly in text.

4. Auerbach (*Our Vampires,* 64) suggests that "Dracula . . . is less the culmination of a tradition than the destroyer of one."

5. Auerbach's claim that "Dracula . . . is the first vampire we have met who is not visibly a corpse" (*Our Vampires,* 95) is somewhat misleading. In earlier English literature, the vampires engage in various types of intercourse with ordinary humans, who in fact take them as being unquestionably alive. Thus, the vampire is not abject in the same way that the folkloric vampire is, as a resident of a desecrated or unhallowed grave.

6. Klaniczay, *The Uses of Supernatural Power,* chap. 10, "The Decline of Witches and the Rise of Vampires under the Eighteenth-Century Habsburg Monarchy," 168–88.

7. An excerpted English translation (by M. Cooper) of Dom Augustin Calmet's *Vampires of Hungary, Bohemia, Moravia, and Silesia* is to be found in Perkowski, *Vampires of the Slavs.* Perkowski's book is to be reprinted as *Vampire Lore* (Indianapolis: Slavica, forthcoming).

8. Klaniczay (*The Uses of Supernatural Power,* 162) notes, "Even the rapid extension of witchcraft accusations from lower social circles to socially more elevated targets conforms very much to Western European witch scares."

9. Klaniczay, *The Uses of Supernatural Power,* 159.

10. A predominance of sensationalism over factual investigation can be seen in the titles of some recently published books on Elizabeth Báthory: *The Blood Countess, Erzebet Bathory of Hungary* (Robert Peters, 1987), *Countess Dracula: The Life and Times of Elisabeth Bathory, the Blood Countess* (Tony Thorne, 1998), and *The Bloody Countess: The Atrocities of Erzsebet Bathory* (Valentine Penrose, 1996).

11. Immediately following the terrorist attack against U.S. symbols on September 11, 2001, President George W. Bush proposed an attack on "terrorists" that was fueled by a similarly reductive equation: "You are either with us or against us," he said, "in the fight against terror" (http://www.cnn.com/2001/US/11/06/gen

.attack.on.terror/). Such a simplistic, dualistic orientation may actually be a prerequisite for scapegoating, since the availability of nuance and context tends to mitigate social aggression. Clearly, the attack on Saddam Hussein, who was a more available scapegoat than the more amorphous (and vampiric) al-Qaeda, could not have been carried out if a rational explanation for doing so had been demanded by the public.

12. Ioan Couliano discusses the ways in which, beginning at the end of the Renaissance, the forces of ecclesiastical Christianity and Cartesian politics jointly attacked the remnant images of Neoplatonism. Couliano correctly interprets this as an attack on the power of the imagination. It is my belief that the Enlightenment destruction of vampire beliefs in the name of eradicating injustice is a similar attack. See Ioan P. Couliano, *Eros and Magic in the Renaissance,* trans. Margaret Cook (Chicago: University of Chicago Press, 1987), especially chaps. 7 ("Demonomagic") and 9 ("Censoring Phantasy").

13. Senf, *The Vampire in Nineteenth-Century English Literature,* 44.

14. Leonard Wolf, ed., *The Essential Dracula: The Definitive Annotated Edition of Bram Stoker's Classic Novel* (New York: Plume, 1993), 367. Subsequent citations of *Dracula* appear in parentheses in text and refer to Wolf's edition.

15. Martin Luther, *A Commentary on St. Paul's Epistle to the Galatians,* reprinted in *Witchcraft in Europe, 1100–1700: A Documentary History,* ed. Alan C. Kors and Edward Peters (Philadelphia: University of Pennsylvania Press, 1972), 195–201.

16. Seward, we learned in chapter 8, struggles against addiction to the sedative-hypnotic chloral hydrate. Perhaps this explains his willingness to bring in someone else to help him with his confusion. Or perhaps there is another reason; see note 19 in the present chapter.

17. In the late nineteenth century, hysteria (a condition whose name derives from the Greek word for "womb") affected primarily women and was thought to be connected with the "death trance" or "suspended animation," a physiological state often misdiagnosed and resulting in premature burial. Lucy certainly qualifies as a candidate for the "death trance" diagnosis, according to Herbert Mayo, whose article "Vampyrism" Stoker had read. Mayo explains: "But in any form of disease, when the body is brought to a certain degree of debility, death-trance may supervene. Age and sex have to do with its occurrence; which is more frequent in the young than in the old, in women than in men—differences evidently connected with greater irritability of the nervous system." Death trance may occur, according to Mayo, "after incomplete poisoning, after suffocation in either of its various ways" (Mayo, "Vampyrism," in Leatherdale, *Origins,* 57–74). Concerning incomplete poisoning, consider the substances that are put into Lucy's body and her room, including laudanum and morphine, as well as garlic laced with some sort of soporific. Lucy comments: "I never liked garlic before, but tonight it is delightful! There is peace in its smell. I feel sleep coming already" (*Dracula,* 171).

18. Actually, Lucy's symptoms more resemble those that would have called to mind the presence of another Bulgarian folkloric demon, known as *zmeja* (ser-

pent). An attack by this demon would cause an adolescent girl to become morose or depressed, to be drained of energy, and to lose her appetite.

19. For example, anemia is a common complication of pregnancy, usually occurring toward the twentieth week of gestation. Its symptoms include fatigue, weakness, pale skin, palpitations, breathlessness, and fainting spells.

20. Elizabeth Miller (*Dracula: Sense and Nonsense,* 88–89) does not include Van Swieten in her list of candidates for possible models for the character of Van Helsing. But then, she also in my opinion is overly cautious about the relationship between Stoker and Arminius Vambery. Considering that Vambery was a historian of Hungary, he certainly would have known about Van Swieten's work on vampires, and he may have mentioned him during one of his conversations with Stoker. The red herring appears to be the speculation that Van Helsing is based on Vambery himself, which is, as Miller says, nonsense.

21. Miller, *Dracula: Sense and Nonsense,* 74.

22. At the time Van Helsing begins assembling for himself the evidence that a vampire is afoot, he has not yet become familiar with the hallucinatory journal of Jonathan Harker, who (in my interpretation) had been suffering from bacterial meningitis caused by infection of a cut he obtained while shaving.

23. For recent discussion of the "idea of Europe" and its influence in *Dracula,* see Coundouriotis, "*Dracula* and the Idea of Europe." Cf. also note 6 in chapter 2 of the present study. For an interesting polemical discussion of how the political situation in the occupied Balkans has affected Western perceptions of Eastern Europe, see Burgess, *Divided Europe.*

24. Even today, Eastern Europe is constructed as a disease needing to be quarantined: "The threatening 'otherness' of Eastern Europe today is expressed in new ways. There is a discernible medical emphasis, more particularly a suggestion of disease, in several of the principal themes through which the region is understood . . . The conception of 'the East' as metaphorically diseased, has disposed analysts to exaggerate all manner of real medical conditions, to the extent that they may even infect the West" (Burgess, *Divided Europe,* 55–56).

25. Freud begins his famous essay on "the uncanny" ("Das Unheimliche," 1925) with mention of how "Jentsch has taken as a very good instance [of this sensation] 'doubts whether an apparently animate being is really alive; or conversely, whether a lifeless object might not be in fact animate'" (219–52). The second, converse term of such doubt represents the psychological ambiguity in which the vampire may exist and in which the vampire slayer may therefore also exist. Freud is referring here to Ernst Jentsch's 1906 essay "The Psychology of the Uncanny." Clearly, such topics were in the air around the time *Dracula* was published.

26. Frazer's *The Golden Bough* was first published in 1890.

27. Richard Webster, "Freud, Charcot, and Hysteria: Lost in the Labyrinth," 2003, http://www.richardwebster.net/freudandcharcot.html.

28. If there is literary mastery here, it lies in Stoker's brilliantly subversive arrangement of circumstances or the circumstantial. The reader of *Dracula* never

questions the sequencing of the independent blocks of narrative that seem to lead to an inexorable conclusion, and the reader thus comes to sympathize with the heroes according to the same dynamic that caused the heroes to unquestioningly accept Van Helsing's explication.

29. For more on the nuptial aspect of the relationship between Dracula and Mina, see Wolf's several footnotes in *The Essential Dracula,* 343ff.

30. Such techniques of public persuasion are not unknown in today's political discourses.

CHAPTER TEN

1. Bruce Lincoln makes the point in various essays that sacrifice is a "ritual which effectively repeats the cosmogony" (*Death, War, and Sacrifice: Studies in Ideology and Practice* [Chicago: University of Chicago Press, 1991], 170). Cosmogony, furthermore, is the primary myth of origins, in which it is explained for a people how things came to be the way they are.

2. For a fuller elaboration of the dramatic structures of contemporary horror, see Noel Carroll, *The Philosophy of Horror, or Paradoxes of the Heart* (New York: Routledge, 1990), especially chap. 3, "Plotting Horror" (99).

3. Latinized names may be used in horror films to suggest a learned person of Central European origin. In *Bride of Frankenstein* (1935), the strange Dr. Pretorius (portrayed by Ernest Thesiger) is a neglected and unappreciated genius who has been rejected for his hubristic, Faustian incursions into creation of life. It would seem that in the surname *Abronsius* used in *The Fearless Vampire Killers,* Polanski or his coauthor, Gerard Brach, is combining the first syllable of the name *Abraham* with a Latin-sounding ending that is reminiscent of the name *Arminius* (as in the historian Arminus Vambery, admired by Bram Stoker). The name of the vampire in *The Fearless Vampire Killers,* Count Krolock, is clearly a reference to Count Orlock, the vampire in the 1922 film *Nosferatu,* who is based loosely on Bram Stoker's Dracula character.

4. I think Kirk J. Schneider's observation on the essence of evil as framed by the horror tale is apropos: "Evil, according to classic horror, is constrictive or expansive *excess;* it is infinitude which cannot be managed" (*Horror and the Holy: Wisdom Teachings of the Monster Tale* [Chicago: Open Court, 1993], 130).

5. The crimes of Dracula were linked in the public mind with the violence of at least two real, presumably psychopathic or sociopathic serial killers: David Trenton Chase, aka the Dracula Killer and the Vampire of Sacramento (whose literally bloodthirsty, sadistic crimes are detailed in the exposé by Lt. Ray Biondi and Walt Hecox, *Dracula Killer* [New York: Pocket Books, 1992]), and, much earlier (1913), Peter Kürten, whose eroticized blood drinking accompanying child sexual abuse and murder earned him the title of the Vampire of Düsseldorf (see Richard Monaco and Bill Burt, *The Dracula Syndrome*). These serial killers were linked with vampires because of their fondness for blood drinking, a psy-

chopathological compulsion that itself probably drew on the popular image of the vampire.

6. There was some controversy concerning the screenplays, which were based on the then unpublished novel *The Kolchak Papers* (1970) by Jeff Rice. Rice was not properly compensated by the producer, Dan Curtis (who had also produced *Dark Shadows*), for Matheson's use of the idea that became a successful, if short-lived, Friday-night television series. Additional tensions between Curtis and the show's star, Darren McGavin (who felt the weekly format should involve an ongoing hunt for the vampire Janos Skorzeny, similar to the successful 1960s program *The Fugitive*), contributed to the premature demise of the program.

7. Matheson advanced the idea of vampirism as a disease as early as 1954, in his novel *I Am Legend* (159), which was later made into the film *The Omega Man* (1971). In this plot, Robert Neville is the last nonvampire human alive, everyone else having been turned into a vampire by airborne bacteria. The motif of the vampire as outsider is thus turned on its head: at the end of the novel, Neville realizes that it is he who is the outcast, the social anomaly: "Robert Neville looked out over the new people of the earth. He knew that he did not belong to them; he knew that, like the vampires, he was anathema and black terror to be destroyed."

8. Alain Silver and James Ursini, *The Vampire Film from "Nosferatu" to "Bram Stoker's Dracula,"* rev. ed. (New York: Limelight Editions, 1994), 75.

9. Ibid.

10. Frank Lovece, *The X-Files Declassified* (Secaucus, NJ: Carol, 1996), 1.

11. The first was "Travelers," airdate March 29, 1998. Carter had originally planned to get McGavin into the show during its second season, as Agent Mulder's father, but scheduling problems prevented this. A third episode, "The Professionals," was written around the character of Arthur Dales, but Darren McGavin was unable to appear in the role due to illness. See the online discussion of "The Travelers" episode of *The X-Files* at http://www.tvtome.com/tvtome/servlet/GuidePageServlet/showid-61/epid-602.

12. Ibid.

13. Derek A. Badman, "Buffy Bibliography," http://www.madinkbeard.com/buffyology.html (updated April 20, 2005).

14. Mimi Marinucci, "Feminism and the Ethics of Violence: Why Buffy Kicks Ass," in *Buffy the Vampire Slayer and Philosophy: Fear and Trembling in Sunnydale,* ed. James B. South (Peru, IL: Open Court, 2003), chap. 5, 61–75.

15. Contra this assertion, however, see Stacey Abbott, "A Little Less Ritual and a Little More Fun: The Modern Vampire in *Buffy the Vampire Slayer,*" *Slayage* 3 (2001), http://www.slayage.tv/essays/slayage3/sabbott.htm. Abbott speaks of a subversion of the vampire tradition that "is gradual from season to season." I am of the opinion that the ostensible subversion of tradition is illusory and that *Buffy* is in fact a very traditional program.

16. For a more thorough discussion of the relationship between Dracula and Buffy the Vampire Slayer, see Michelle Callander, "Bram Stoker's *Buffy:* Traditional

Gothic and Contemporary Culture," *Slayage* 3 (2001), http://www.slayage.tv/ essays/slayage3/callander.html. The editor of *Slayage* notes that the article was written before the airing of the *Buffy* episode "Buffy vs. Dracula" (September 26, 2000, season 5).

17. Mimi Marinucci ("Feminism and the Ethics of Violence," 73) observes that Buffy refers to her own stake as "Mr. Pointy" in such episodes as "Helpless" (January 19, 1999), "Choices" (May 4, 1999), and "The Freshman" (October 5, 1999). Although Marinucci is discussing the masculine penetrating nature of the stake in the context of "sexualized violence," she fails to note that the intimate personal naming of the object suggests that the phallus may also coyly signify a dildo. Among Buffy's more frequent complaints about her life early in the series is her inability to get close to (ordinary) boys, despite her ordinary attraction to them. This is of course a general problem among superheroes, whose "secret identity" would be exposed were they to have consort with ordinary mortals. Alas, Buffy's identity is not that secret.

18. It has been pointed out that Buffy actually rejects the mandate to kill all vampires and demons, and this is taken as evidence that the moral code in *Buffy the Vampire Slayer* is more sophisticated than that handed down by the Watcher's Council (the show's governing body of slayers): "Despite her title, Buffy does not simply slay all vampires and demons; rather, she establishes a set of penalties for certain infringements that vary from the most extreme (death to vampires who feed on the living) to the relatively mild and necessary (werewolves must be locked up during a full moon)" (Martin Buinicki and Anthony Enns, "Buffy the Vampire Disciplinarian: Institutional Excess and the New Economy of Power," *Slayage* 4 (2001), http://www.slayage.tv/essays/slayage4/buinickienns.htm).

19. The ostensibly magical texts consulted by Giles and, later, the budding witch Willow to provide the antidotes to spells cast by demons are inquisitional fantasies. They are frequently in a kind of television-style ecclesiastical Latin (it being presumed that no one knows enough Latin anymore to know better). Latin would have been the official language of the Inquisitors' demonological documents but would certainly not have been the language of documents written by people accused of paganism or heresy or witchcraft—assuming they could write documents at all.

20. Neither is their monetary value considered. One would think that the possessor of primary (cuneiform?) manuscripts that were over three thousand years old might not have to earn his keep as a high school librarian.

21. Coralline Dupuy, "Is Giles Simply Another Dr Van Helsing? Continuity and Innovation in the Figure of the Watcher in *Buffy the Vampire Slayer.*" *Refractory: A Journal of Entertainment Media* 2. (March 2003). http://www.refractory .unimelb.edu.au/journalissues/vol2/cDupuy.pdf.

22. I am reminded of the problem of the Fisher King in the Arthurian romances, where failure to ask the (chthonic) Fisher King, "Whom does the Grail serve?" leads to five years of desolation. The Fisher King's debility is in fact a sign of strength, not weakness, insofar as it inhibits aggressive or invasive inquiry.

23. Against *Buffy's* southern California suburban backdrop, fashionable clothing is mandatory for social acceptance, so clearly not only are vampires unacceptable, but the unacceptable are vampiric. The following scene is from scene 29D, episode 1: "Welcome to the Hellmouth," rev. September 6, 1996, in *Buffy the Vampire Slayer™: The Script Book, Season One, Volume One.* 46–47. New York: Pocket Books, 2000.

> GILES. But will you be ready? There's so much you don't know, about them and about your own powers. A vampire appears to be a normal person, until the feed is upon them. Only then do they reveal their true demonic visage.
> BUFFY. You're like a textbook with arms! I know this!
> GILES. The point is, a Slayer should be able to see them anyway. Without looking, without thinking. Can you tell me if there's a vampire in this building?
> BUFFY. Maybe?
> GILES. You should know! Even through this mass and this din you should be able to sense them. Try. Reach out with your mind.
>
> *She looks down at the mass of kids on the floor. Furrows her brow.*
>
> GILES. You have to hone your senses, focus until the energy washes over you, till you can feel every particle of—
> BUFFY. There's one.
>
> *Giles stops, nonplussed.*
>
> GILES. What? Where?
> BUFFY (*pointing*). Down there. Talking to that girl.
>
> *In the corner stands a good-looking young man, talking to a girl we can't really see.*
>
> GILES. But you don't know—
> BUFFY. Oh, please. Look at his jacket. He's got the sleeves rolled up. And the shirt . . . Deal with that outfit for a moment.
> GILES. It's dated?
> BUFFY. It's carbon dated! Trust me: only someone who's been living underground for ten years would think that was the look.

APPENDIX

1. The entry in Miklosich's *Lexicon* concerning this manuscript states that it was produced ten years before the Ostromir Gospel, which was written in Novgorod in 1056–57: "Prophetae cum commentariis, duo codd. I cod saec XV. Musei Rumjancov; II cod chart. Saec. XV. in fol. Russ. descriptus e cod anni 1047,

scripto a 'попъ оупирь лихъый' pro principe novgorodensi Vladimir Jaroslavičo, decem annis ante Ostromiri evengelium."

2. Archimandrite Leonid explains: "The margin note [приписката] of the priest Upir Likij from 1047 was reproduced in the Russian Gennadiev bible from 1499:

слава тебѣ гн црю небс҇ныи . ıако сподоби на написати книги си ис коурилоцѣ

It is supposed that this concerns the List of Interpretative Prophecies [*Spisok tolkovyx prorokov*], in which isolated Glagolitic words are encountered. P. Šafařík assumes that the OCS original was Glagolitic. Archimandrate Leonid does not agree with this; he believes that "ис коурилоцѣ" is a genitival form of OCS коурѣлъкъ, meaning "form, prototype, literary original." This is not accepted by contemporary scholars. ("Zametka o slove 'is kouriloce,'" *Rossiskij filosofskij vestnik* XXV [1891]: 135–37).

3. Felix Oinas ("Heretics") agrees that the word *upir'* most likely had a different meaning: "Since *upir'* was used as a personal name in the earliest period of Russian history, it could be inferred that the term for 'vampire' originally did not denote an extremely bloodthirsty and detestable being." It is probable that *upir' likhyj* was not a "personal name" but, rather, a nickname. Vladimirov (*Poučenija*, 204) refers to the phrase as a *prozvišče* as early as 1897.

4. Liddell and Scott, *Greek-English Lexicon,* abridged ed., s.v. ἀλλοτρίος.

5. Of course, even within the period of OCS, the meaning of the word varies across manuscripts. Thus, in the glossary provided by Auty in the *Handbook of Old Church Slavonic,* the term лихъ is glossed as "vain, excessive," as it is found in Zografensis, Matthew V: 37.

6. Personal communication with author, September 1998.

7. For example, in an Old Bulgarian inscription from the tenth century, we find a similar signature, нерадъ грешьн, which is incorrectly translated into German by Kronsteiner as "Nerad, der Suender" (as if *Nerad* were a proper name). We may take the compound word нерадъ to mean "unhappy," the phrase itself thus meaning something like "unhappy sinner." Such a formula is structurally identical and semantically similar to the meaning we propose for оупирь лихъый, оупирь being equivalent to "sinner." See Popkonstantinov and Kronsteiner, "Starobâlgarski nadpisi," 113.

8. An interesting parallel is the relationship between the eligibility for last rites and the sinfulness of sacrificing. Rush (*Death and Burial,* 96) retells an account by Dionysius of Alexandria concerning the reception of *viaticum* (the eucharistic host given at the deathbed) by Serapion: "Serapion was an old man who had *lapsed by sacrificing.* On his deathbed he called his grandson to summon one of the priests. Dionysius, the bishop, had already stipulated that those who lapsed should be absolved on their deathbed if they had made supplication for it beforehand."

9. Similar processes that are reversible are known as shape-shifting, that is, transformation into an animal, sometimes associated with a particular god or cult.

It is true that in folklore, vampires are often associated with shape-shifters. Be that as it may, there is no reason to imagine that оупирь referred to any such being. Furthermore, the ability of a shape-shifter to oscillate between the human and the nonhuman is still a characteristic of the demonic; reversibility of form does not imply reversibility of metaphysical status.

10. Maks Fasmer, *Etimologičeskij slovar' russkogo jazyka v četyrex tomax*, trans. O. N. Trubančeva, 3rd ed. (St. Petersburg: Azbuka, 1996), s.v. пир.

11. Examples are modern Russian пить, "to drink"; Bulgarian пирувам, "to feast"; and English *beverage, beer.* Perkowski (*The Darkling,* 33) glosses OCS пиръ as "revelry, drinking bout."

12. Other possibilities exist. See, for example, Perkowski's earlier proposed etymology concerning the Armenian god Vaghan (*The Darkling,* 33). However, the effort here is to determine if it is possible to propose a reconstruction that is semantically not so difficult to justify.

13. Personal communication with author, September 1998.

14. Terence R. Carlton, *Introduction to the Phonological History of the Slavic Languages* (Columbus, OH: Slavica, 1990), 299.

15. Another possibility not considered here would require the word *vampir,* if derived from this prepositional phrase, to have a much earlier origin—namely, at a point before the back nasal in Common Slavic emerged as the reduced back vowel in Bulgarian. In East Slavic, back nasal emerges as [u]. See Carlton, *Phonological History,* 305, 295.

16. There are cognates in other Slavic languages that do not involve a nasal consonant, including Russian.

17. Jaroslav B. Rudnyćkyj, *An Etymological Dictionary of the Ukrainian Language* (Winnipeg: Ukrainian Free Academy of Sciences, 1962), s.v. упир.

18. The final vowel (a so-called back jer) of the preposition would have dropped out according to a historical phonological process known as Havelik's Law.

19. Personal communication with author, September 1998.

20. If we take the primary meaning of *pir* as "libation," the link between feasting and initiation is supported by Greek ritual. Yerkes (*Sacrifice,* 108) points out: "libations were of common occurrence throughout the history of Greek religions. Wine, blood and wine, oil and honey were used for various purposes; if these were lacking, water could be used as a surrogate. They are found in all sacrifices, before the mysteries, at visits to tombs, before a journey, before and after meals, before retiring at night, at marriages, for purposes of purification, and as accompaniment to simple, private and family devotions." Here we see the drinking of blood linked with initiation, sacrifice, and feasting.

21. Hamilton and Hamilton, *Christian Dualist Heresies,* 10.

22. Regis Boyer, "The Kinship of Slavic and Norse Mythologies: The Problem of Perun-Perkun-Perkunas-Fjörgyn(n)," in *American, African, and Old European Mythologies,* compiled by Yves Bonnefoy, translated under the direction of Wendy Doniger (Chicago: University of Chicago Press, 1993), 250.

Bibliography

ABBREVIATIONS

AEIM   Arxiv na Etnografskija institut i muzej (Sofia)
AIF   Arxiv na Instituta za folklor
NBKM   Narodna Biblioteka "Sv. Sv. Kirill i Metodij" (Sofia)
SbNU   *Sbornik za bâlgarski narodni umotvorenija*

ARCHIVAL AND MANUSCRIPT SOURCES

Boneva, Tanja. *Blagoevgrad.* Field report. AEIM 113-III. Sofia, 1987.

———. *Haskovo.* Field report. AEIM 111-III. Sofia, 1987.

———. *Kârdžali.* Field report. AEIM 114-III. Sofia, 1987.

———. *Pazardžik.* Field report. AEIM 112-III. Sofia, 1987.

———. *Smoljansko.* Field report. AEIM 110-III, folders I–II. Sofia, 1987.

———. *Smoljansko.* Field report. AEIM 110-IIIA, folder II. Sofia, 1987.

Kuzmanova, Magdalena. *Dobrič* and *Povadija.* AEIM 271-III. Sofia, 1991.

Miceva, Evgenija. "Folklorni materiali ot mixajlovgradski okrâg, mixajlovgradski rajon," 22.xi.–27.xi.1982. AIF 216. Sofia, 1982.

"Molitva ot Nežita." NBKM MS.273, *Sborniče sâ apokrifni molitvi, XVII v,* fols. 70r–73r. Sofia. Available online (in Bulgarian) in Donka Petkanova, "Stara bâlgarska literatura. Apokrifi" http://knigite.abv.bg/bg_ap/dp_45.html.

"Molitva ot prokletago Nežita." NBKM MS.622, *Trebnik ot XVII v, red. srâbska.* Reprinted in: B. Conev, *Opis na râkopisite i staropečatnite knigi na Narodnata biblioteka B Sofija.* vol 2, 133. Sofia, 1923. Available online (in Bulgarian) in Donka Petkanova "Stara bâlgarska literatura. Apokrifi" http://knigite.abv.bg/bg_ap/dp_45.html.

Popov, Račko Ivanov. *Loveško.* AEIM 251-III. Sofia, 1992.

———. *Sakar-Xarmanlijsko.* AEIM 313-III. Sofia, 1995.

Vaseva, Valentina. *Kârdžali.* AEIM 115-III. Sofia, 1987.

PUBLISHED FIELD REPORTS
(BULGARIA AND MACEDONIA)

Angelov, G. V. "Ot Bitolsko." *SbNU* XII (1895): 125–28.
Božev, S. D. "Ot Demir-Xisarsko." *SbNU* IV (1891): 111.
Cepenkov, M. K. "Ot Prilep." *SbNU* III (1890): 155–57.
———. "Ot Prilep." *SbNU* VII (1892): 146–50.
Deržavin, N. S. "Bolgarskie kolonii v Rossii (tavričeskaja, xersonskaja i bessarab-
    skaja gubernii)." *SbNU* XXIX (1914): 175–90.
Ginčov, C. "Ot Târnovsko." *SbNU* II (1890): 189–91.
———. "Ot Târnovsko: Cerenie nežitja sâ med." *SbNU* IV (1891): 97.
Lâžev, Georgi. "Ot Voden." *SbNU* III (1890): 147–53.
Martinov, Aleksandâr P. "Narodopisni materiali ot Graovo." *SbNU* XLIX (1958).
Matov, D. "Ot Veles." *SbNU* IX (1893): 130–31.
Nastev, N. "Ot Lerinsko." *SbNU* V (1891): 142–43.
Prostranov, E. "Ot Oxrid." *SbNU* XV (1898): 59–69.
Russev, St. S. "Ot Burgazsko." *SbNU* V (1891): 131–34.
Sprostranov, E. "Ot Oxrid." *SbNU* XV (1898): 59–69.
Stamboliev, S. "Ot Berkovsko." *SbNU* XXI (1905): 35–62.
Stančev, N. "Ot Kotlensko." *SbNU* XIV (1897): 101.
Telbizov, K., and M. Vekova-Telbizova. "Tradicionen bit i kultura na banatskite
    Bâlgari." *SbNU* LI (1963): 1–361.
Virčev, Georgi. "Ot dupnička Džumaja." *SbNU* X (1894): 141–43.
Zaxariev, Jordan. "Kamenica." *SbNU* XL (1935): 260–64.
———. "Kjustendilsko krajšte." *SbNU* XXXII (1927): 146.

SLAVIC RESOURCES

Angelov, Dimitâr. *Bogomilstvoto v Bâlgarija.* 3rd ed. Sofia: Nauka i izkustvo, 1980.
Aničkov, E. V. *Jazyčestvo i drevnjaja Rus': Xristianizacija varvarskix narodov Evropy.*
    St. Petersburg: Tipografija M. M. Stasjulevič, 1914.
Antik, Vera. "Dualistički elementi vo makedonskijot folklor." In *Bogomilstvoto na
    balkanot vo svetlinata na najnovite istražuvanja: Materiali od simpoziumot
    održan vo skopje na 30, 31 maj i 1 juni 1978 godina,* 113–26. Skopje: Makedon-
    ska akademija na naukite i umetnostite, 1982.
Antoljak, Stjepan. "Makedonski heretici u zapadnim izvorima 11 i 12 stolječa." In
    *Bogomilstvoto na balkanot vo svetlinata na najnovite istražuvanja: Materiali od
    simpoziumot održan vo skopje na 30, 31 maj i 1 juni 1978 godina,* 55–66. Skopje:
    Makedonska akademija na naukite i umetnostite, 1982.
Arnaudov, Mixail. *Očerki po bâlgarskija folklor.* Vols. 1 and 2. 1934. 3rd phototype
    ed., Sofia: Prof. Marin Drinov, 1998.
———. *Studii vârxu bâlgarskite obredi i legendi.* Vol. 1. Sofia: Bâlgarskata
    akademija na naukite, 1971.

Begunov, Ju. K. "Bolgarskie bogomily i russkie strigol'niki." *Byzantino-Bulgarica* VI (1980): 63–72.

Dal', V. I. *O poverijax, sueverijax, i predrassudkax russkogo naroda: Materialy po russkoj demonologii.* 1880. Reprint, St. Petersburg: Litera, 1994.

Danov, Xristo Milošev. *Drevna Trakija.* Sofia: Nauka i ízkustvo, 1968.

Daskalova-Perkovska, Liliana, et al. *Bâlgarski folklorni prikazki: Katalog.* Sofia: Universitetsko izdatelstvo "Sv. Kliment Oxridski," 1994.

Dimitrov, Xr. Review of "Prinjatie xristianstva narodami central'noj i jugo-vostočnoj Evropy i kreščenie Rusi," by G. G. Litvarin, ed. *Byzantino-Bulgarica* IX (1995): 214–15.

Đorđevič, T. P. *Vampir i druga biča i našem narodnom verovanju i predanju.* Beograd, 1953.

Dragojevič, Ivan. *Vukodlaci.* Zagreb, 1969.

Dragojlovič, Dragoljub. *Bogomilstvo na balkanu i u maloj aziji.* Vol. 1, *Bogomilski rodonačalnici.* Beograd: Srpska akademija nauka i umetnosti, balkanološki institut, 1974.

———. *Bogomilstvo na balkanu i u maloj aziji.* Vol. 2, *Bogomilstvo na pravoslavnom istoku.* Beograd: Srpska akademija nauka i umetnosti, balkanološki institut, 1980.

Dukova, Ute. "Etimologični aspekti v izsledvaneto na mitologijata." In *Problemi na bâlgarskija folklor, 8: Bâlgarskijat folklor v slavjanskata i balkanskata kulturna tradicija,* 186–89. Sofia: Bâlgarskata akademija na naukite, 1991.

Eremina, V. I. *Ritual i fol'klor.* Leningrad: Nauka, 1991.

Etnografija na Bâlgarija. Vol. 3, *Duxovna kultura.* Sofia: Bâlgarskata akademija na naukite, 1985.

Fasmer, Maks. *Etimologičeskij slovar' russkogo jazyka v četyrex tomax.* Trans. O. N. Trubančeva. 3rd ed. St. Petersburg: Azbuka, 1996.

Fol, Aleksandâr. *Politika i kultura vâ drevna Trakija.* Sofia: Nauka i izkustvo, 1990.

———. *Trakijskijat dionis.* Book 2, *Sabazij.* Sofia: Universitetsko izdatelstvo "Sv. Kliment Oxridski," 1994.

Funk, D. A., ed. *Shamanizm i rannie religioznye predstavlenija.* Moscow: Institute of Ethnology and Anthropology, Russian Academy of Sciences, n.d.

Gal'kovskij, N. M., ed. *Bor'ba xristianstva s ostatkami jazyčestva v drevnej Rusi.* Vol. 2, *Drevnye russkie slova i poučenija, napravlennye protiv jazyčestva v narode.* Moscow, 1913.

Gandev, Xristo. *Ranno vâzraždane 1700–1860.* Studia Historica Philologica Serdicensia, suppl. 3. Sofia, 1939.

Gečeva, Krâstina, ed. *Bogomilstvoto: Bibliografija.* Sofia: Prof. Marin Drinov, 1997.

Genčev, Stojan. "Etnografsko edinstvo i regionalni različija v običaite pri pogrebenie u Bâlgarite." In *Etnogenezis i kulturno nasledstvo na bâlgarskija narod, Sbornik,* 111–14. Sofia: Bâlgarskata akademija na naukite, 1971.

Georgieva, Ivanička. *Bâlgarska narodna mitologija.* Sofia: Nauka i izkustvo, 1983.

————. "Edin starinen kult v Rodopite, Strandža i Meždirečieto na Struma i mesta." *Rodopski Sbornik*. Sofia: Bâlgarskata akademija na naukite, 1972.

————, ed. *Kalendarni praznici i običai na Bâlgarite: Enciklopedija*. Sofia: Prof. Marin Drinov, 1998.

————. "Sur certaines influences Thraces dans la culture spirituelle du peuple Bulgare." In *Thracia*, (Sofia) 2 (1974): 213–17.

————. "Survivances de la religion des Thraces dans la culture spirituelle du peuple Bulgare." In *Actes du II-e Congrès International de Thracologie, Bucarest. 1976*. Bucharest, 1980. 3:217–76.

Gergova, Diana, ed. *Obredât na obezsmârtjavaneto v drevna Trakija: Izkustvo i mitologija*. Sofia: Agato, 1996.

Gerov, Boris. "Vâprosât za romanizacija na trakijskoto naselenie v bâlgarskite zemi." *Etnogenezis i kulturno nasledstvo na bâlgarskija narod, Sbornik*, 33–37. Sofia: Bâlgarskata akademija na naukite, 1971.

Institut slavjanovedenija i balkanistiki, Rossijskaja akademija nauk. *Slavjanskij i balkanskij fol'klor: Verovanija, tekst, ritual*. Moscow: Nauka, 1994.

Ireček, Konstantin. "Stari pâtešestvija po Bâlgarija ot 15–18 stoletie." In *Periodičesko spisanie na bâlgarskoto knižovno družestvo v Sredec*, book 2, 116–18; book 4, 67–105; book 6, 1–44. Sofia: Dâržavna pečatica, 1883.

Ivanov, Jordan. *Bâlgarski starini iz Makedonija*. 1931. Reprint, Sofia: Nauka i izkustvo, 1970.

————. *Bogomilski knigi i legendi*. Ed. Dimitâr Angelov. Sofia: Pridvorna pečatnica, 1925. Reprint, Sofia: Nauka i izkustvo, 1970.

Jacimirskij, A. I. *Bibliografičeskij obzor apokrifov v južnoslavjanskoj i russkoj pismennosti (spiski pamjatnikov)*. vol. 1, *Apokrify vetxozavetnye*. Petrograd: Otd. Russkogo jazyka i slovesnosti, Rossijskaja akademija nauk, 1921.

Kabakova, G. I. "K probleme distribucii mifologičeskix personažej v kalendarnom cikle." In *Materialy k VI meždunarodnomu kongressu po izučeniju stran jugo-vostočnoj evropy: Problemy kul'tury, Sofia, 30.viii.89–6.ix.89*. Moscow: Institut slavjanovedenija i balkanistiki AN SSSR, 1989.

————. "Materialy po rumynskoj demonologii." In *Materialy k VI meždunarodnomu kongressu po izučeniju stran jugo-vostočnoj evropy: Problemy kul'tury, Sofia, 30.viii.89–6.ix.89*, 133. Moscow: Institut slavjanovedenija i balkanistiki AN SSSR, 1989.

"Kak raspoznat' vampira." *Itogi* (Moscow) 51–52, December 30, 1997.

Kalojanov, Ančo. *Bâlgarski mitove*. Sofia: Izdatelstvo na CK na DKMC, 1979.

Konstantinova, Velička. "Ezikovi beležki vârhu tekstove ot njakolko starobâlgarski amuleta." In *Prislavska knižovna škola*, 2:153–73. Šumen: Šumenski universitet "Episkop Konstantin Preslavski" naučen centâr, 1997.

Kotljarevskij, A. A. *O pogrebal'nyx običajax jazyčeskix Slavjan*. Moscow: Sinodal'naja Tipografija, 1868.

Leonid, Archimandrite. "Zametka o slove 'is kouriloce.'" *Rossiskij filosofskij vestnik* XXV (Moscow, 1891): 135–37.

Levkievskaja, E. E. "вампир." In *Slavjanskie Drevnosti: Etnolingvističeskij Slovar'*, vol. 1, А–Г, ed. N. I. Tolstoj. Moscow: Meždunarodnye otnošenija, 1995, 283–86.

Litvarin, G. G. "O social'nix vozzrenijax Bogomilov." In *Bogomilstvoto na Balkanot vo svetlinata na najnovite istražuvanja: Materiali od simpoziumot održan vo skopje na 30, 31 maj i 1 juni 1978 godina*, 31–39. Skopje: Makedonska akademija na naukite i umetnostite, 1982.

———. *Slavjane i ix sosedi: Imperskaja ideja v stranax central'noj, vostočnoj i jugovostočnoj evropy*. Tezisy XIV konferencii. Moscow: Institut slavjanovedenija i balkanistiki, Akademija nauk RAN, 1995.

Madžarov, Panajot. "'Poganoto' (Pogani Dni) vâv vjarvanijata i bita na strandžanskite sela." *Bâlgarski folklor* (Sofia) 4 (1982): 91–101.

Maksimov, S. V. *Nečistaja, nevedomaja i krestnaja sila*. 1903. Reprint, St. Petersburg: Policet, 1994.

Marazov, Ivan. *Mitologija na Trakite*. Sofia: IK Sekor, 1994.

———. "'Žertvoprinošenie na oven' v trakijskija šlem ot Kocofenešti." In *Obredi i obreden folklor, Sbornik*, 173–94. Sofia: Bâlgarskata akademija na naukite, 1981.

Mareva, Tanja. *Rodopski survakari*. Sofia: Septemvri, 1989.

Marinov, Dimitâr. *Izbrani proizvedenija*. Sofia: Nauka i izkustvo, 1984.

———. *Narodna vjara i religionzni narodni običaj*. 1914. 2nd reprint, Sofia: Bâlgarskata akademija na naukite, 1994.

———. *Živa Starina*. Russe: Pečatnica Sv. Kiril i Metodii, 1891.

Miceva, Evgenija Georgieva. "Demonični predstavi i personaži v bâlgarski folklor." PhD diss., Bâlgarska akademija na naukite, Institut za folklor, 1984.

———. "Demonologični personaži v južnoslavjanskija folklor." *Bâlgarski folklor v slavjanskata i balkanskata kultura tradicija* (Sofia) 8 (1991): 190–94.

———. "Narodni predstavi za brodešti noštem svrâxestestveni sâštestva." *Bâlgarski folklor*, Yr. 7, bk. 2 (Sofia, 1981).

———, ed. *Nevidimi noštni gosti: Podbor i naučen komentar*. Sofia: Nauka i izkustvo, 1994.

Miltenova, Anisava, ed. *Stara bâlgarska literatura*. Vol. 5, *Estestvoznanie*. Sofia: Bâlgarski pisatel, 1992.

Mirčev, Krasimir. *Vampiri, Gunduraci, Zmej*. With drawings by Viktor Paunov. Sofia: Panorama, 1998.

Mladenov, Oleg. *Bâlgarski prazničen naroden kalendar, ili narâčnik po tradicionni praznenstva, sueverija i veselija 1998; 1999; 2000*. Sofia: DIOS, 1997.

Motsious, Iannis. "Vstreča fol'klora i xristianskoj religii v obrjade poxoron i pominok." In *Problemi na bâlgarskija folklor, 8: Bâlgarskijat folklor v slavjanskata i balkanskata kulturna tradicija*, 235–46. Sofia: Bâlgarskata akademija na naukite, 1991.

Panajotov, Veselin. "Personifikacija na zloto v slavjanskoto srednovekovete. I: Demonologijata v apokrifa zaveti na dvanadesete patriarci (po arxivski prepis ot

XV vek)." In *Preslavska knižovna škola*, 2:151–62. Šumen: Šumenski universitet "Episkop Konstantin Preslavski" naučen centâr, 1997.

Pomeranceva, E. V. *Mifologičeskie personaži v russkom fol'klore*. Moscow: Nauka,
1975.

Popov, Dimitâr. "Čoveštite žertvoprinošenija na Zalmoksis." *Godišnik na Sofijski
Universitet, Istoričeski fakultet*. No. 76, II: *Proučvanie vârxu trakijskata religija*
(Sofia, 1995): 59–106.

———. *Zalmoksis: Religija i obštestvo na Trakite*. Sofia, 1989.

Popov, Račko Ivanov. "Bâlgarski demonologični i mitologični vjarvanija: Kraja na
XIX–sredata na XX v." PhD diss., Etnografski institut s muzej-BAN, Sofia,
1983.

———. "Kâm xarakteristikata na bulgarskite narodni vjarvanija, svârzani s periodite na prexod kâm zimata i proletta." In *Etnografski problemi na narodnata
duxovna kultura*, 1:52–74. Sofia: Club, 1992.

———. "Svetci demoni." In *Etnografski problemi na narodnata duxovna kultura*,
2:78–100. Sofia: Club '90, 1994.

———. "Za vârkolaka v bâlgarskite narodni vjarvanija (istoričeski koreni i mjasto
v narodnata kultura)." Sofia: n.d.

Popov, Račko, and Valentina Vaseva, eds. *Trakiecât i negovijat svjat*. Materiali ot
VIII-ta nacionalna konferencija na bâlgarskite etnolozi, Xaskovo '95. Sofia:
Etnografski institut s muzej-BAN, 1997.

Popovič, M. B. *Mirovozzrenie drevnix Slavjan*. Moscow: Naukova dumka, 1985.

Popruženko, M. G. "Kosma Presviter: Bolgarskij pisatel' X veka." In *Bâlgarski
starini*, book 12. Sofia: Bâlgarskata akademija na naukite, 1936.

Propp, V. Ja. *Russkie agrarnye prazdniki*. Leningrad: Leningrad University, 1963.

Romaïos, C. A. *Cultes populaires de la Thrace*. Athens: Institut Français, 1949.

Rybakov, B. A. *Jazyčestvo drevnix Slavjan*. Moscow: Nauka, 1981.

Savel'ev, Igor' Vasil'evič. *Vampiri vo sne i najavu*. Moscow: Russian Society of
Doctors and Men of Letters, 1995.

Slovar' knižnikov i knižnosti drevnej Rusi XI–pervaja polovina XIV v. Leningrad,
1987.

Snegarov, Ivan. *Istorija na oxridskata arxiepiskopija-patriaršija*. Sofia, 1931.

Spirinovska, Leposava, and Tanas Vražinovski, eds. *Vampirite vo makedonskite
veruvanja i predanija*. Skopje: Institut za folklor "Marko Cepenkov," 1988.

Sreznevskij, I. I. *Materialy dlja slovarja drevne-russkago jazyka po pismennym pamjatnikam*. Vol. 3. St. Petersburg: Rossijskaja Akademija Nauk, 1903.

Sterligov, M., ed. *Russkoe koldovstvo, vedovstvo, znaxarstvo*. St. Petersburg: Litera,
1994.

Stojanovič-Lafazanovska, Lidija. *Tanatološkiot pravzor na životot: Fenomenot
žrtvuvanje vo makedonskata narodna književnost*. Special Editions, vol. 23.
Skopje: Institut za folklor "Marko Cepenkov," 1996.

Stojnev, Anani, ed. *Bâlgarska mitologija: Enciklopedičen rečnik*. Sofia: Izdatelska
grupa 7M, 1994.

————. *Bâlgarskite slavjani: Mitologija i religija.* Sofia: Narodna prosveta, 1988.

Taškovski, Drajan. "Klasniot i socijalniot karakter na Bogomilstvoto." In *Bogomil-stvoto na Balkanot vo svetlinata na najnovite istražuvanja: Materiali od simpoz-iumot održan vo skopje na 30, 31 maj i 1 juni 1978 godina,* 41–54. Skopje: Make-donska akademija na naukite i umetnostite, 1982.

Teodorov, Evgenij K. "Altthrakische Erbschaft in der bulgarischen Folklore." In *Thracia* (Sofia) I (1972): vol. 1, 315–25. Sofia, 1972.

————. *Drevnotrakijsko nasledstvo v bâlgarskija folklor.* Sofia: Nauka i izkustvo, 1972.

Tokarev, S. A., ed. *Kalendarnye obyčai i obrjady v stranax zarubežnoj Evropy: Istor-ičeskie korni i razvitie obyčaev.* Moscow: Nauka, 1983.

Tolstoj, N. I. *Jazyk i narodnaja kul'tura: Očerki po slavjanskoj mifologii i etno-lingvistike.* Moscow: Indrik, 1995.

Vakarelski, Xristo. *Bâlgarski pogrebalni običai: Sravnitelno izučavane.* Sofia: Bâl-garskata akademija na naukite, 1990.

————. *Ethnografija na Bulgarija.* Sofia: Nauka i izkustvo, 1977.

Vaklinov, Stančo. *Formirane na starobâlgarskata kultura, VI–XI vek.* Sofia: Nauka i izkustvo, 1977.

"Vampir pedofil tormozi Cigančeta." *168 časa,* year 6, no. 29:1 (Sofia, July 17–23, 1995).

Veleckaja, N. N. "Elementy indoevropejskix i drevnebalkanskix ritualov v slavjan-sko-balkanskov obrjadnosti mediacii sil prirody." *Makedonski folklor* 12, no. 23 (1979): 87–95.

————. *Jazyčeskaja simvolika slavjanskix arxaičeskix ritualov.* Moscow: Nauka, 1978.

Vladimirov, P. V. *Poučenija protiv jazyčestva i narodnyx sueverij.* 3rd ed. St. Peters-burg, 1897.

Zabylin, M. *Russkij narod: Ego obyčai, obrjady, predanija, sueverija i poezija.* 1880. Reprint, St. Petersburg: Brajt Lajt, 1994.

Zečević, Slobodan. *Mitska biča srpskix predanja.* Beograd: Vuk Karadžič, 1981.

Zelenin, D. K. *Očerki russkoj mifologii.* Petrograd: Tipografija D. V. Orlova, 1916.

"Zombi i Vampiri Sred Nas?! Mojat Ljubovnik e Prizrak." *Vsičko za Vseki* (Sofia) 29, no. 91 (August 3–9, 1994): 1.

OTHER RESOURCES

Abbott, George Frederick. *Macedonian Folklore.* Cambridge: Cambridge Univer-sity Press, 1903.

Abbott, Stacey. "A Little Less Ritual and a Little More Fun: The Modern Vampire in *Buffy the Vampire Slayer.*" *Slayage* 3 (2001). http://www.slayage.tv/essays/slayage3/sabbott.htm.

Auerbach, Nina. *Our Vampires, Ourselves.* Chicago: University of Chicago Press, 1995.

Auty, Robert. *Handbook of Old Church Slavonic.* Vol. 2, *Texts and Glossary.* London: Athlone Press, 1960.

Badman, Derek A. "Buffy Bibliography." http://www.madinkbeard.com/buffyology .html (updated April 20, 2005).

Balázs, J. "The Hungarian Shaman's Technique of Trance Induction." In *Folk Beliefs and Shamanistic Traditions in Siberia,* ed. Vilmos Diošzegi and Mihály Hoppál. 26–48. Budapest: Akadémiai Kiadó, 1996.

Barber, Paul. *Vampires, Burial, and Death: Folklore and Reality.* New Haven, CT: Yale University Press, 1988.

Baring-Gould, Sabine. *The Book of Werewolves: Being an Account of a Terrible Superstition.* London: Smith, Elder & Co., 1865. Reprint, Detroit: Gale Research, 1981.

Bataille, Georges. *The Accursed Share: An Essay on General Economy.* Vol. 1, *Consumption.* Trans. Robert Hurley. New York: Zone, 1991.

———. *The Accursed Share: An Essay on General Economy.* Vol. 2, *The History of Eroticism;* vol. 3, *Sovereignty.* Trans. Robert Hurley. New York: Zone, 1993.

———. *Theory of Religion.* Trans. Robert Hurley. New York: Zone, 1992.

Battis, Jes. "'She's Not All Grown Yet': Willow as Hybrid/Hero in *Buffy the Vampire Slayer.*" *Slayage* 8 (2003). http://www.slayage.tv/essays/slayage8/Battis.htm.

Baudrillard, Jean. *Symbolic Exchange and Death.* Trans. Iain Hamilton Grant. Theory, Culture, and Society Series. London: Sage, 1993.

Bauer, Walter. *Orthodoxy and Heresy in Earliest Christianity.* Ed. Robert A. Kraft and Gerhard Krodel. 2nd German ed., trans. Philadelphia Seminar on Christian Origins. Philadelphia: Fortress, 1971.

Belmont, Nicole. "Superstition and Popular Religion in Western Societies." In *Between Belief and Transgression: Structuralist Essays in Religion, History, and Myth,* ed. Michel Izard and Pierre Smith, trans. John Leavitt, 9–23. Chicago: University of Chicago Press, 1982.

Bennett, W. H. "Death and Disposal of the Dead." In *Encyclopaedia of Religion and Ethics,* ed. James Hastings, 497–500. New York: Charles Scribner's Sons, 1924.

Beynen, G. K. "The Vampire in Bulgarian Folklore." In *Vtori meždunaroden kongres po bâlgaristika: Dokladi,* vol. 15, *Folklor,* 456–65. Sofia: Bâlgarska akademija na naukite, 1988.

Bianchi, Ugo. "Dualistic Aspects of Thracian Religion." Trans. Richard Horowitz. *History of Religion* 10, no. 3 (February 1971): 228–33.

Biondi, Ray, and Walt Hecox. *Dracula Killer.* New York: Pocket Books, 1992.

Bonet-Maury, G. "Commemoration of the Dead." In *Encyclopaedia of Religion and Ethics,* ed. James Hastings.

Bourdieu, Pierre. *The Logic of Practice.* Stanford, CA: Stanford University Press, 1990.

———. *The Weight of the World: Social Suffering in Contemporary Society.* Stanford, CA: Stanford University Press, 1999.

Boyer, Regis. "The Kinship of Slavic and Norse Mythologies: The Problem of Perun-Perkun-Perkunas-Fjörgyn(n)." In *American, African, and Old European Mythologies,* compiled by Yves Bonnefoy, translated under the direction of Wendy Doniger, 248–51. Chicago: University of Chicago Press, 1993.

———. "Slavic Myths, Rites, and Gods." In *American, African, and Old European Mythologies,* compiled by Yves Bonnefoy, translated under the direction of Wendy Doniger, 241–48. Chicago: University of Chicago Press, 1993.

Bradney, Anthony. "Choosing Laws, Choosing Families: Images of Law, Love, and Authority in *Buffy the Vampire Slayer.*" *Web Journal of Current Legal Issues* 2 (2003). http://webjcli.ncl.ac.uk/2003/issue2/bradney2.html.

Brechka, Frank T. *Gerard van Swieten and His World, 1700–1772.* The Hague: Martinus Nijhoff, 1970.

Briggs, Robin. *Witches and Neighbors: The Social and Cultural Context of European Witchcraft.* New York: Viking Penguin, 1996.

Brown, Peter. *The Body and Society: Men, Women, and Sexual Renunciation in Early Christianity.* Lectures on the History of Religions. New York: Columbia University Press, 1988.

Browning, Robert. *Byzantium and Bulgaria: A Comparative Study across the Early Medieval Frontier.* London: Temple Smith, 1975.

Buffy the Vampire Slayer: The Script Book. Vols. 1 and 2. New York: Pocket Books, Pocket Pulse, 2000–2001.

Buinicki, Martin, and Anthony Enns. "Buffy the Vampire Disciplinarian: Institutional Excess and the New Economy of Power." *Slayage* 4 (2001). http://www.slayage.tv/essays/slayage4/buinickienns.htm.

Bunson, Matthew, ed. *The Vampire Encyclopedia.* London: Thames and Hudson, 1993.

Burgess, Adam. *Divided Europe: The New Domination of the East.* London: Pluto, 1997.

Burkert, Walter. *Creation of the Sacred: Tracks of Biology in Early Religions.* Cambridge, MA: Harvard University Press, 1996.

———. *Homo Necans: The Anthropology of Ancient Greek Sacrificial Ritual and Myth.* Trans. Peter Bing. Berkeley: University of California Press, 1985.

———. "The Problem of Ritual Killing." In *Violent Origins: Walter Burkert, René Girard, and Jonathan Z. Smith on Ritual Killing and Cultural Formation,* ed. Robert G. Hamerton-Kelly, 149–76. Stanford, CA: Stanford University.

Burkhart, Dagmar. *Kulturraum Balkan.* Berlin: Studien zur Volkskunde und Literatur Südosteuropas, 1989.

———. "Vampirglaube und Vampirsage auf dem Balkan." In *Beitrage zur Südosteuropa-Forschung,* 211–52. Munich, 1966.

Bynum, Caroline Walker. *The Resurrection of the Body in Western Christianity, 200–1336.* New York: Columbia University Press, 1995.

Caillois, Roger. *Man and the Sacred.* Trans. Meyer Barash. Westport, CT: Greenwood, 1980.

Čajkanović, V. "The Killing of a Vampire." In *The Vampire: A Casebook,* ed. Alan Dundes, 72–84. Madison: University of Wisconsin Press, 1998.

Callander, Michelle. "Bram Stoker's *Buffy:* Traditional Gothic and Contemporary Culture." *Slayage* 3 (2001). http://www.slayage.tv/essays/slayage3/callander.html.

Cankova-Petkova, G. "Contribution au sujet de la conversion des Bulgares au Christianisme." *Byzantino-Bulgarica* IV (1973): 83–94.

Carlton, Terence R. *Introduction to the Phonological History of the Slavic Languages.* Columbus, OH: Slavica, 1990.

Carpenter, Thomas H., and Christopher A. Faraone, eds. *Masks of Dionysus.* Ithaca, NY: Cornell University Press, 1993.

Carroll, Noel. *The Philosophy of Horror, or Paradoxes of the Heart.* New York: Routledge, 1990.

Carver, Terrell. *The Postmodern Marx.* University Park: Pennsylvania State University Press, 1998.

Chandler, Holly. "Slaying the Patriarchy: Transfusions of the Vampire Metaphor in *Buffy the Vampire Slayer.*" *Slayage* 9 (August, 2003). http://www.slayage.tv/essays/slayage9/Chandler.htm.

Christie-Murray, David. *A History of Heresy.* London: New English Library, 1976.

Clark, Daniel A., and P. Andrew Miller. "Buffy, the Scooby Gang, and Monstrous Authority: *BtVS* and the Subversion of Authority." *Slayage* 3 (June, 2001). http://www.slayage.tv/essays/slayage3/clarkmiller.html.

Cohn, Norman. *Cosmos, Chaos, and the World to Come: The Ancient Roots of Apocalyptic Faith.* New Haven, CT: Yale University Press, 1993. Paperback ed., 1995.

————. *Europe's Inner Demons: An Enquiry Inspired by the Great Witch-Hunt.* New York: Basic, 1975.

Cole, Susan Guettel. "Voices from beyond the Grave: Dionysus and the Dead." In *Masks of Dionysus,* ed. Thomas H. Carpenter and Christopher A. Faraone, 276–96. Ithaca, NY: Cornell University Press, 1993.

Colloque de Cerisy. *Les Vampires.* Paris: Albin Michel, 1993.

Couliano, Ioan P. *Eros and Magic in the Renaissance.* Trans. Margaret Cook. Chicago: University of Chicago Press, 1987.

————. *The Tree of Gnosis: Gnostic Mythology from Early Christianity to Modern Nihilism.* Trans. H. S. Wiesner and Ioan P. Couliano. San Francisco: HarperSanFrancisco, 1992.

Coundouriotis, Eleni. "*Dracula* and the Idea of Europe." *Connotations* 9, no. 2 (1999–2000): 143–59.

Criminal Justice through the Ages: From Divine Judgement to Modern German Legislation. Trans. John Fosberry. Publications of the Mediaeval Crime Museum, vol. 4. (Rothenburg ob der Tauber, 1981).

Cross, Samuel Hazzard. *Slavic Civilization through the Ages.* Cambridge, MA: Harvard University Press, 1948. Reprint, New York: Russell and Russell, 1963.

Cumont, Franz. *After Life in Roman Paganism.* Lectures Delivered at Yale University on the Silliman Foundation. New Haven, CT: Yale University Press, 1922.

Dawkins, R. M. "The Modern Carnival in Thrace and the Cult of Dionysus." *Journal of Hellenic Studies* XXVI (1906): 191–206.

Derrida, Jacques. *The Gift of Death.* Trans. David Wills. Chicago: University of Chicago Press, 1995.

Detienne, Marcel. "Culinary Practices and the Spirit of Sacrifice." In *The Cuisine of Sacrifice among the Greeks,* trans. Paula Wissing, 1–20. Chicago: University of Chicago Press, 1989.

———. "Rethinking Mythology." In *Between Belief and Transgression: Structuralist Essays in Religion, History, and Myth,* ed. Michel Izard and Pierre Smith, trans. John Leavitt, 43–52. Chicago: University of Chicago Press, 1982.

Diószegi, Vilmos, and Mihály Hoppál, eds. *Folk Beliefs and Shamanistic Traditions in Siberia.* Selected Reprints. Trans. S. Simon. Budapest: Akadémiai Kiadó, 1996.

Douglas, Mary. *Natural Symbols: Explorations in Cosmology.* New York: Pantheon, 1970.

———. *Purity and Danger: An Analysis of the Concepts of Pollution and Taboo.* London: Routledge, 1966.

Dragomanov, M. P. *Notes on the Slavic Religio-ethical Legends: The Dualistic Creation of the World.* Trans. Earl Count. The Hague: Mouton, 1961.

Dundes, Alan, ed. *The Vampire: A Casebook.* Madison: University of Wisconsin Press, 1998.

Dupuy, Coralline. "Is Giles Simply Another Dr. Van Helsing? Continuity and Innovation in the Figure of the Watcher in *Buffy the Vampire Slayer.*" *Refractory: A Journal of Entertainment Media* 2 (March 2003): http://www.refractory.unimelb.edu.au/journalissues/vol2/cDupuy.pdf.

Durham, M. E. "Some Balkan Festivals." *Folk-Lore* 51 (1940): 83–89.

———. *Some Tribal Origins, Laws, and Customs of the Balkans.* London: Allen and Unwin, 1928.

Durkheim, Emile. *The Division of Labor in Society.* Trans. W. D. Halls. New York: Free Press, 1984.

———. *The Elementary Forms of the Religious Life.* Trans. Joseph Ward Swain. London: Allen and Unwin, 1915. Paperback ed., New York: Free Press, 1965.

Dvornik, Francis. *Les Slaves, Byzance et Rome au IXe siècle.* Hattiesburg, MS: Academic International, 1970.

———. *The Slavs: Their Early History and Civilization.* Boston: American Academy of Arts and Sciences, 1956.

Eisler, Robert. *Man into Wolf: An Anthropological Interpretation of Sadism, Masochism, and Lycanthropy.* London: Spring, 1950.

Eliade, Mircea. *Myth and Reality.* Trans. Willard R. Trask. New York: Harper Torchbooks, 1963.

———. *The Myth of the Eternal Return, or Cosmos and History.* Trans. Willard R Trask. Princeton, NJ: Princeton University Press, 1971.

———. *Rites and Symbols of Initiation: The Mysteries of Birth and Rebirth.* Trans. Willard R. Trask. New York: Harper and Row, 1958. Reprint, New York: Harper Torchbooks, 1965.

———. *Shamanism: Archaic Techniques of Ecstasy.* Trans. Willard R. Trask. Bollingen Series LXXVI. New York: Pantheon, 1964.

———. *Zalmoxis: The Vanishing God.* Trans. Willard R. Trask. Comparative Studies in the Religions and Folklore of Dacia and Eastern Europe. Chicago: University of Chicago Press, 1972.

"Ember Days." In *Catholic Encyclopedia,* vol. 5 (New York: Robert Appleton, 1909). Available online at http://www.newadvent.org/cathen/05399b.htm (2003).

Esin, E. "The Conjectural Links of Bogomilism with Central Asian Manicheism." In *Bogomilstvoto na Balkanot vo svetlinata na najnovite istražuvanja: Materiali od simpoziumot održan vo skopje na 30, 31 maj i 1 juni 1978 godina,* 105–12. Skopje: Makedonska akademija na naukite i umetnostite, 1982.

Evans-Pritchard, E. E. "Sorcery and Native Opinion." In *Witchcraft and Sorcery: Selected Readings,* ed. Max Marwick, 21–26. Harmondsworth, England: Penguin, 1931.

———. "Witchcraft amongst the Azande." In *Witchcraft and Sorcery: Selected Readings,* ed. Max Marwick, 27–37. Harmondsworth, England: Penguin, 1929.

Farnell, Lewis Richard. *Greek Hero Cults and Ideas of Immortality.* Oxford: Clarendon, 1921. Reprint, Oxford: Oxford University Press, 1970.

———. "Sacrifice (Greek)." *Encyclopaedia of Religion and Ethics,* ed. James Hastings. Vol. 11:12–18. New York: Charles Scribner's Sons, 1922.

Fine, John V. A., Jr. *The Early Medieval Balkans: A Critical Survey from the Sixth to the Late Twelfth Century.* Paperback ed. Ann Arbor: University of Michigan Press, 1991.

———. "In Defense of Vampires." In *The Vampires: A Casebook,* ed. Alan Dundes, 57–66.

Firth, Raymond. "Reason and Unreason in Human Belief." In *Witchcraft and Sorcery: Selected Reading,* ed. Max Marwick, 38–40. Harmondsworth, England: Penguin, 1956.

Fol, Alexander, and Ivan Marazov. *Thrace and the Thracians.* London: Cassell, 1977.

Florovsky, Georges. *Creation and Redemption.* Belmont, MA: Nordland, 1976.

Fontaine, P. F. M. *The Light and the Dark: A Cultural History of Dualism.* 20 vols. Amsterdam: J. C. Gieben, 1986–2004.

Forbes, Thomas. "The Social History of the Caul." *Yale Journal of Biology and Medicine* 25 (6) (1953): 495–508.

Forsyth, Neil. *The Old Enemy: Satan and the Combat Myth.* Princeton, NJ: Princeton University Press, 1987.

Foucault, Michel. *Discipline and Punish: The Birth of the Prison.* Trans. Alan Sheridan. 2nd ed. New York: Vintage, 1995.

Fowden, Garth. *Empire to Commonwealth: Consequences of Monotheism in Late Antiquity.* Princeton, NJ: Princeton University Press, 1993.

Frazer, Sir James George. *The Golden Bough: A Study in Magic and Religion.* Abridged ed. in 1 vol. New York: Macmillan, 1922.

Freud, Sigmund. *The Standard Edition of the Complete Psychological Works of Sigmund Freud.* Vol. 17. Ed. and trans. James Strachey. London: Hogarth, 1953.

Geertz, Clifford. *The Interpretation of Cultures: Selected Essays.* New York: Basic, 1973.

Georgieva, Ivanichka. *Bulgarian Mythology.* Trans. Vessela Zhelyazovka. Sofia: Svyat, 1985.

Georgieva, Rumjana. "La nourriture dans les rites Thraces (fin du IIe–Ier mill. av. J.-C.)." In *Actes 2e Symposium International des Etudes Thraciennes,* vol. 1, *Thrace Ancienne,* 222–24. Komotini, Greece: L'association culturelle de Komotini, 1997.

Georgoudi, Stella. "Sanctified Slaughter in Modern Greece: The 'Kourbánia' of the Saints." In *The Cuisine of Sacrifice among the Greeks,* ed. Marcel Detienne and Jean-Pierre Vernant, trans. Paula Wissing, 183–203. Chicago: University of Chicago Press, 1989.

Gerard, Emily. *Land across the Forest.* New York: Harper, 1888.

———. "Transylvanian Superstitions." *Nineteenth Century,* July 1885, 128–44.

Getov, Liudmil. "Observations sur les rites funéraires des Thraces aux époques hellénistique et romaine." In *Actes du IIe Congrès International de Thracologie. Bucarest, 4–10 September 1976,* vol. 2, *History and Archaeology.* Bucharest: Editura academiei republicii socialiste Romania, 1980.

Gimbutas, Maria. "Proto Indo-European Culture." In *Indo-European and the Indo-Europeans,* ed. George Cardona and Heinrich Hoenigswald, 155–98. Philadelphia: University of Pennsylvania Press, 1970.

———. *The Slavs.* New York: Praeger, 1971.

Ginzburg, Carlo. *Ecstasies: Deciphering the Witches' Sabbath.* Trans. Raymond Rosenthal. New York: Penguin, 1991.

———. *The Night Battles: Witchcraft and Agrarian Cults in the Sixteenth and Seventeenth Centuries.* Trans. John and Anne Tedeschi. Baltimore: Johns Hopkins University Press, 1992.

Girard, René. "Generative Scapegoating." In *Violent Origins: Ritual Killing and Cultural Formation,* ed. Robert G. Hamerton-Kelly, 73–105. Stanford, CA: Stanford University Press, 1987.

———. *The Scapegoat.* Trans. Yvonne Freccero. Baltimore: Johns Hopkins University Press, 1986.

———. *Things Hidden since the Foundation of the World.* Trans. Michael Metteer (book 1) and Stephen Bann (books 2 and 3). American ed. Stanford: Stanford University Press, 1987.

———. *Violence and the Sacred.* Trans. Patrick Gregory. Baltimore: Johns Hopkins University Press, 1979.

Gomez, Alonso J. "Rabies: A Possible Explanation for the Vampire Legend." *Neurology* 51, no. 3 (September 1988): 856–59.

Gorazd, Archimandrite. "La religion des Thraces et ses resonances dans la vie des peuples chretiens et non-chretiens." In *Thracia,* (Sofia) II (1974): 173–82.

Gordon, Joan, and Veronica Hollinger, eds. *Blood Read: The Vampire as Metaphor in Contemporary Culture.* Philadelphia: University of Pennsylvania Press, 1997.

Graebner, M. "The Slavs in Byzantine Europe: Absorption, Semi-autonomy, and the Limits of Byzantinization." *Byzantino-Bulgarica* V (1978): 41–55.

Graf, Fritz. "Dionysian and Orphic Eschatology: New Texts and Old Questions." In *Masks of Dionysus,* ed. Thomas H. Carpenter and Christopher A. Faraone, 239–58. Ithaca, NY: Cornell University Press, 1993.

Gunda, B. "Survivals of Totemism in the Hungarian *táltos* Tradition." In *Folk Beliefs and Shamanistic Traditions in Siberia,* Vilmos Diószegi and Mihály Hoppál, trans. S. Simon, 15–25. Budapest: Akadémiai Kiadó, 1996.

Guthrie, W. K. C. *Orpheus and Greek Religion: A Study of the Orphic Movement.* London: Methuen, 1952. Reprint, Princeton, NJ: Princeton University Press, 1993.

Gyuzelev, Vassil. *The Proto-Bulgarians: Pre-history of Asparouhian Bulgaria.* Sofia: Sofia Press, 1979.

Hamerton-Kelly, Robert G., ed. *Violent Origins: Walter Burkert, René Girard, and Jonathan Z. Smith on Ritual Killing and Cultural Formation.* Stanford, CA: Stanford University Press, 1987.

Hamilton, Janet, and Bernard Hamilton, eds. *Christian Dualist Heresies in the Byzantine World, c. 650–c. 1450.* Manchester, England: Manchester University Press, 1998.

Heller, Terry. *The Delights of Terror: An Aesthetics of the Tale of Terror.* Urbana: University of Illinois Press, 1987.

Henninger, Joseph. "Sacrifice." In *The Encyclopedia of Religion,* vol. 12, ed. Mircea Eliade, 544–57. New York: Macmillan, 1987.

Henrichs, Albert. "Pagan Ritual and the Alleged Crimes of the Early Christians: A Reconsideration." In *Kyriakon: Festschrift Johannes Quasten,* vol. 1, ed. Patrick Granfield and Josef A. Jungmann, 18–35. Münster Westf.: Verlag Aschendorff, 1970.

Herrenschmidt, Olivier. "Sacrifice: Symbolic or Effective?" In *Between Belief and Transgression: Structuralist Essays in Religion, History, and Myth,* ed. Michel Izard and Pierre Smith, trans. John Leavitt, 24–42. Chicago: University of Chicago Press, 1982.

Hoddinott, R. F. *The Thracians.* London: Thames and Hudson, 1981.

Hosch, Edgar. *Orthodoxie und Häresie im alten Russland.* Schriften zur Geistes-geschichte des Östlichen Europa, vol. 7. Weisbaden: Otto Harrassowitz, 1975.

Hubert, Henri, and Marcel Mauss. *Sacrifice: Its Nature and Functions.* Trans. W. D. Halls. Chicago: University of Chicago Press, 1964. Reprint, Midway Reprint, 1981.

Hussey, J. M. *Church and Learning in the Byzantine Empire, 867–1185.* London: Oxford University Press, 1937.

Ivanits, Linda. *Russian Folk Belief.* Armonk, NY: M. E. Sharpe, 1989.

Jakobson, Roman. *Selected Writings IV: Slavic Epic Studies.* The Hague: Mouton, 1966.

————. "Slavic Mythology." In *Funk and Wagnalls Standard Dictionary of Folk-lore, Mythology, and Legend,* ed. Maria Leach and J. Fried, vol. 2, 1025–28. New York: Funk and Wagnalls, 1949–50.

Jakobson, Svatava Pirkova. "Slavic Folklore." In *Funk and Wagnalls Standard Dic-tionary of Folklore Mythology and Legend,* ed. Maria Leach and J. Fried, vol. 2, 1019–24. New York: Funk and Wagnalls, 1949–50.

Jelavich, Barbara. *History of the Balkans.* Vol. 1, *Eighteenth and Nineteenth Cen-turies.* Cambridge: Cambridge University Press, 1983.

Jellinek, A. L. "Zur Vampyrsage." *Zeitschrift des Vereins für Volkskunde* 14 (Berlin, 1904): 322–28.

Jurginis, J. M. "Relics of Paganism among the Baltic Peoples after the Introduc-tion of Christianity." In *The Realm of the Extra-Human: Ideas and Actions,* ed. Agehananda Bharati, 483–91. The Hague: Mouton, 1976.

Klaniczay, Gábor. *The Uses of Supernatural Power: The Transformation of Popular Religion in Medieval and Early-Modern Europe.* Ed. Karen Margolis. Trans. Susan Singerman. Princeton, NJ: Princeton University Press, 1990.

Kligman, Gail. *The Wedding of the Dead: Ritual, Poetics, and Popular Culture in Transylvania.* Berkeley: University of California Press, 1988.

Koledarov, Petâr. "On the Initial Hearth and Centre of the Bogomil Teaching." *Byzantino-Bulgarica* VI (1980): 237–42.

Konrad, Alexander N. *Old Russia and Byzantium: The Byzantine and Oriental Origins of Russian Culture.* Vienna: Wilhelm Braumueller, 1972.

Kors, Alan C., and Edward Peters, eds. *Witchcraft in Europe, 1100–1700: A Docu-mentary History.* Philadelphia: University of Pennsylvania Press, 1972.

Kristeva, Julia. *Powers of Horror: An Essay on Abjection.* Trans. Leon S. Roudiez. New York: Columbia University Press, 1982.

Kungl, Carla T., ed. *Vampires: Myths and Metaphors of Enduring Evil.* At the In-terface, vol. 6. Oxford: Inter-Disciplinary Press, 2003.

Laistner, M. L. W. *Christianity and Pagan Culture in the Later Roman Empire, to-gether with an English Translation of John Chrysostom's Address on Vainglory and the Right Way for Parents to Bring Up Their Children.* Ithaca, NY: Cornell Uni-versity Press, 1951.

Latham, Rob. *Consuming Youth: Vampires, Cyborgs, and the Culture of Consumption*. Chicago: University of Chicago Press, 2001.

Lawson, John Cuthbert. *Modern Greek Folklore and Ancient Greek Religion: A Study in Survivals*. Cambridge: Cambridge University Press, 1909. Reprint, New Hyde Park, NY: University Books, 1964.

Leach, Edmund. "The Logic of Sacrifice." In *Anthropological Approaches to the Old Testament*, ed. Bernhard Lang, 136–62. Philadelphia: Fortress, 1985.

Leatherdale, Clive. *The Origins of Dracula: The Background to Bram Stoker's Gothic Masterpiece*. London: William Kimber, 1987.

Lévi-Strauss, Claude. *Anthropology and Myth: Lectures, 1951–1982*. Trans. Roy Willis. London: Basil Blackwell, 1987.

———. *The Raw and the Cooked: Introduction to a Science of Mythology*. Trans. John and Doreen Weightman. New York: Harper and Row, 1975.

Lincoln, Bruce. "Death and Resurrection in Indo-European Thought." *Journal of Indo-European Studies* 5 (1977): 247–64.

———. *Death, War, and Sacrifice: Studies in Ideology and Practice*. Chicago: University of Chicago Press, 1991.

———. *Discourse and the Construction of Society: Comparative Studies of Myth, Ritual, and Classification*. New York: Oxford University Press, 1989.

———. "The Living Dead: Of Outlaws and Others." Review of *Die Toten Lebenden: Eine religionsphänomenologische Studie zum sozialen Tod in archaischen Gesellschaften; Zugleich ein kritischer Beitrag zur sogenannten Strafopfertheorie*, by Hans-Peter Hasenfratz. *History of Religions* 23, no. 4 (May 1984): 387–89.

———. *Myth, Cosmos, and Society: Indo-European Themes of Creation and Destruction*. Cambridge, MA: Harvard University Press, 1986.

———. *Theorizing Myth: Narrative, Ideology, and Scholarship*. Chicago: University of Chicago Press, 1999.

Linedecker, Clifford L. *The Vampire Killers*. New York: St. Martin's Paperbacks, 1998.

Litsas, F. K. "Rousalia: The Ritual Worship of the Dead." In *The Realm of the Extra-Human: Agents and Audiences*, ed. Agehananda Bharati, 447–65. The Hague: Mouton, 1976.

Locklin, Reid B. "*Buffy the Vampire Slayer* and the Domestic Church: Revisioning Family and the Common Good." *Slayage* 6 (2002). http://www.slayage.tv/essays/slayage6/Locklin.htm.

Loos, Milan. *Dualist Heresy in the Middle Ages*. Trans. Iris Lewitova. The Hague: Martinus Nijhoff, 1974.

Lovece, Frank. *The X-Files Declassified*. Secaucus, NJ: Carol, 1996.

Lozovan, E. "Aux origines du christianisme daco-scythique." In *Geschichte Der Hunnen*, vol. 4, *Die Europäischen Hunnen*, 146–65. Berlin, 1975.

Macalister, R. A. S. "Sacrifice (Semitic)." In *Encyclopaedia of Religion and Ethics*, ed. James Hastings (1910).

Macfarlane, A. D. J. "Definitions of Witchcraft." In *Witchcraft and Sorcery: Se-*

lected Readings, ed. Max Marwick, 41–44. Harmondsworth, England: Penguin, 1970.

MacMullen, Ramsay. *Christianity and Paganism in the Fourth to Eighth Centuries.* New Haven, CT: Yale University Press, 1997.

———. *Paganism in the Roman Empire.* New Haven, CT: Yale University Press, 1981.

Malina, Bruce J. *Christian Origins and Cultural Anthropology: Practical Models for Biblical Interpretation.* Atlanta: John Knox, 1986.

Malinowski, Bronislaw. *Magic, Science, and Religion, and Other Essays.* 1948. Reprint, Prospect Heights, IL: Waveland, 1992.

Marazov, Ivan. "Sacrificial Crisis and Cultural Change." In *Thracia,* (Sofia) XI (1995): 353–64.

Marinucci, Mimi. "Feminism and the Ethics of Violence: Why Buffy Kicks Ass." In *"Buffy the Vampire Slayer" and Philosophy: Fear and Trembling in Sunnydale,* ed. James B. South, 61–75. Peru, IL: Open Court, 2003.

Marwick, Max. *Witchcraft and Sorcery: Selected Readings.* Penguin Modern Sociology Readings. Harmondsworth, England: Penguin, 1970.

Marx, Karl. *Capital: A Critique of Political Economy.* Ed. Frederick Engels. Trans. Samuel Moore and Edward Aveling. New York: Modern Library, 1906.

Matheson, Richard. *I Am Legend.* New York: Gold Medal, 1954.

Mauss, Marcel. *The Gift: The Form and Reason for Exchange in Archaic Societies.* Trans. W. D. Halls. New York: W. W. Norton, 1990.

Mayer, Philip. "Witches." In *Witchcraft and Sorcery: Selected Readings,* ed. Max Marwick, 45–64. Harmondsworth, England: Penguin, 1970.

McClelland, Bruce. "The Anathematic Vampire: Concepts of Matter and Spirit in Orthodoxy, Dualism, and Pre-Christian Slavic Mythology." *Internet Vampire Tribune Quarterly: De Natura Haeretica's Electronic Journal of Vampire Studies* 1, no. 1 (autumn 1996). http://www.Generation.Net/~valmont/ivtq/ivtq11.Html (accessed autumn 1996).

———. "By Whose Authority? The Magical Tradition, Violence, and the Legitimation of the Vampire Slayer." *Slayage* 1 (2001). http://www.slayage.tv/essays/slayage1/bmcclelland.htm.

———. "Pagans or Heretics? The Scapegoat Process, *Nezhit,* and the Bulgarian Folkloric Vampire." In *Bâlgaristikata v zorata na dvadeset i pârvi vek: Bâlgaro-amerikanskata perspektiva za naučni izsledvanija,* 132–37. Sofia: Gutenberg, 2000.

———. Review of *Between the Living and the Dead: A Perspective on Witches and Seers in the Early Modern Age,* by Éva Pócs. *History of Religions* 40, no. 4 (May 2001): 381–84.

———. Review of *The Bathhouse at Midnight: Magic in Russia,* by W. F. Ryan. *History of Religions* 42, no. 2 (February 2003): 273–75.

———. "Sacrifice, Scapegoat, Vampire: The Social and Religious Origin of the Bulgarian Folkloric Vampire." PhD diss., University of Virginia, 1999.

————. "Slawische Religion." In *Religion in Geschichte und Gegenwart: Hand-wörterbuch für Theologie und Religionswissenschaft,* 4th ed., 8: 1392–95. Tübingen: Mohr Siebeck, 2004.

McGinn, Bernard. *Anti-Christ: Two Thousand Years of the Human Fascination with Evil.* San Francisco: HarperSanFrancisco, 1994.

McNally, Raymond T., and Radu Florescu. *In Search of Dracula: A True History of Dracula and Vampire Legends.* Greenwich, CT: New York Graphic Society, 1972.

Mead, G. R. S. *Orpheus.* 1896. Reprint, London: John M. Watkins, 1965.

Megas, George A. *Greek Calendar Customs.* Athens: Press and Information Department, Prime Minister's Office, 1958.

Melton, J. Gordon, ed. *The Vampire Book: The Encyclopedia of the Undead.* Detroit: Gale Research, 1994.

Miklosich, Fr. *Lexicon Paleoslovenico-Graeco-Latinum: Emendatum auctum.* Vindobonae: Guilelmus Braumueller, 1865.

Miller, Elizabeth. *Dracula: Sense and Nonsense.* Essex: Desert Island, 2000.

Miteva, Neli. "Ethnocultural Characteristics of the Population in the Thracian Lands in the 4th–6th cc." *Byzantino-Bulgarica* VIII (1994): 241–52.

Moretti, Franco. *Signs Taken for Wonders: Essays in the Sociology of Literary Forms.* Trans. Susan Fischer, David Forgacs, and David Miller. London: Verso and NLB, 1983.

Murray, Margaret. *The Witch-Cult in Western Europe.* Oxford: Clarendon Press, 1921.

Nasta, Mihai. "Les rites d'immortalité dans la religion de Zalmoxis: Syncrétisme et/ou contamination." In *Actes du IIe Congrès International de Thracologie,* 337–53. Bucharest: Editura academiei republicii socialiste Romania, 1976.

Nilsson, Martin P. *Greek Folk Religion.* Philadelphia: University of Pennsylvania Press, 1972. Originally published as *Greek Popular Religion* (New York: Columbia University Press, 1940).

Nirenberg, David. *Communities of Violence: Persecution of Minorities in the Middle Ages.* Princeton, NJ: Princeton University Press, 1996.

Nock, A. S. "Cremation and Burial in the Roman Empire." *Harvard Theological Review* 25 (1932): 331–41.

Obbink, Dirk. "Dionysus Poured Out: Ancient and Modern Theories of Sacrifice and Cultural Formation." In *Masks of Dionysus,* ed. Thomas H. Carpenter and Christopher A. Faraone, 65–88. Ithaca, NY: Cornell University Press, 1993.

Obolensky, Dmitri. *The Bogomils: A Study in Balkan Neo-Manichaeism.* Cambridge: Cambridge University Press, 1948.

Oinas, Felix. "East European Vampires." *Journal of Popular Culture* 16 (1982): 108–14.

————. "Heretics as Vampires and Demons in Russia." *Slavic and East European Journal* 22 (winter 1978): 433–41.

Pascu, Stefan. *A History of Transylvania*. Trans. D. Robert Ladd. New York: Dorset, 1982.

Pelikan, Jaroslav. *The Emergence of the Catholic Tradition (100–600)*. Vol. 1 of *The Christian Tradition: A History of the Development of Doctrine*. Chicago: University of Chicago Press, 1971.

———. *The Spirit of Eastern Christendom (600–1700)*. Vol. 2 of *The Christian Tradition: A History of the Development of Doctrine*. Chicago: University of Chicago Press, 1974. Phoenix, 1977.

Perkowski, Jan. *The Darkling: A Treatise on Slavic Vampirism*. Columbus, OH: Slavica, 1989.

———. "Dualist Elements in the Spiritual Life of Bulgaria's Minorities: The Alevi, the Nekrasovtsy, and the Paulicians." *South East European Monitor* (Vienna) 1, no. 2 (1996).

———. "On the Legend of Demir Baba, the Iron Father." *Zeitschrift für Balkanologie* 34, no. 2 (1998): 1–8.

———. *Vampire Lore*. Indianapolis: Slavica, forthcoming.

———. "The Vampires of Bulgaria and Macedonia—an Update." *Balkanistica* (Sofia) 12 (1999): 151–62.

———. *Vampires of the Slavs*. Cambridge, MA: Slavica, 1976.

Pócs, Éva. *Between the Living and the Dead: A Perspective on Witches and Seers in the Early Modern Age*. Trans. Szilvia Rédey and Michael Webb. Budapest: Central European University Press, 1999.

Polidori, John William. *The Vampyre*. London: Sherwood, Neely, and Jones, 1819.

Polignac, François de. *Cults, Territory, and the Origins of the Greek City-State*. Trans. Janet Lloyd. Chicago: University of Chicago Press, 1994.

Popkonstantinov, Kazimir, and Otto Kronsteiner. "Starobâlgarski nadpisi." Die slawischen Sprachen 36 (1994): 113–26.

Popov, Dimitâr. "Zalmoxis (le dieu aux différents noms)." In *The Thracian World at the Crossroads of Civilizations*, vol. 1, *Proceedings of the Seventh International Congress of Thracology, Costanta-Mangalia-Tulcea, 20–26 May, 1996*, 571–91. Bucharest: Romanian Institute of Thracology, 1997.

Popov, Račko. *Butterfly and Gherman: Bulgarian Folk Customs and Rituals*. Trans. Marguerite Alexieva. Sofia: Septemvri State Publishing House, 1989.

Porter, J. R., and W. M. S. Russell, eds. *Animals in Folklore*. Totowa, NJ: Rowman and Littlefield, 1978.

Postan, M. M., ed. *The Cambridge Economic History of Europe*. Vol. 1, *The Agrarian Life of the Middle Ages*. Cambridge: Cambridge University Press, 1966.

Puech, Henri-Charles. *Sur le manichéisme et autres essais*. Paris: Flammarion, 1979.

Puech, Henri-Charles, and André Vaillant, eds. and trans. *Le traité contre les Bogomiles de Cosmas le Prêtre*. Paris: Imprimerie nationale, 1945.

Puhvel, Jaan. *Comparative Mythology*. Baltimore: Johns Hopkins University Press, 1987.

Quispel, Gilles. "The Origins of the Gnostic Demiurge." In *Kyriakon: Festschrift*

Johannes Quasten, ed. Patrick Granfield and Josef A. Jungmann, 1:271–76. Münster Westf.: Verlag Aschendorff, 1970.

Ramsland, Katherine. *Piercing the Darkness: Undercover with Vampires in America Today.* New York: Harper Paperbacks, 1999.

Randisi, Robert. *Curtains of Blood.* New York: Leisure, 2002.

Rice, Anne. *Interview with the Vampire.* Paperback ed. New York: Ballantine, 1977.

Rice, Jeff. *The Night Stalker.* Paperback ed. New York: Pocket Books, 1973. Originally titled *The Kolchak Papers* (unpublished).

Ristelhueber, Réne. *A History of the Balkan Peoples.* New York: Twayne, 1971.

Rohde, Erwin. *Psyche: The Cult of Souls and Belief in Immortality among the Greeks.* Trans. W. B. Hillis. 1920. Reprint, New York: Books for Libraries Press, 1972.

Rose, Fr. Seraphim. *The Soul after Death: Contemporary "After Death" Experiences in the Light of the Orthodox Teaching on the Afterlife.* Platina, CA: St. Herman of Alaska Brotherhood, 1995.

Rudnyćkyj, Jaroslav B. *Etymological Dictionary of the Ukrainian Language.* Winnipeg: Ukrainian Free Academy of Sciences, 1962.

Runciman, Steven. *A History of the First Bulgarian Empire.* London: G. Bell and Sons, 1930.

———. *The Medieval Manichee: A Study of the Christian Dualist Heresy.* Cambridge: Cambridge University Press, 1947. Reprint, 1955.

Rush, Alfred C. *Death and Burial in Christian Antiquity.* Washington, DC: Catholic University of America Press, 1941.

Russell, Jeffrey B., ed. *Religious Dissent in the Middle Ages.* New York: John Wiley and Sons, 1971.

Ryan, Alan, ed. *The Penguin Book of Vampire Stories.* New York: Penguin, 1987.

Ryan, W. F. *The Bathhouse at Midnight: Magic in Russia.* University Park: Pennsylvania State University Press, 1999.

Rymer, James Malcom. *Varney the Vampire, or The Feast of Blood: A Romance.* Book 1. Berkeley Heights, NJ: Wildside, 2000.

Said, Edward W. *Orientalism.* New York: Vintage, 1979.

Sanders, Irwin. *Balkan Village.* Lexington: University of Kentucky Press, 1949.

———. *Rainbow in the Rock: The People of Rural Greece.* Cambridge: Cambridge University Press, 1962.

Schevill, Ferdinand. *The History of the Balkan Peninsula from the Earliest Times to the Present Day.* Rev. ed. New York: Harcourt Brace and Company, 1933.

Schneider, Kirk J. *Horror and the Holy: Wisdom Teachings of the Monster Tale.* Chicago: Open Court, 1993.

Segal, Robert A. *The Myth and Ritual Theory.* Malden, MA: Blackwell, 1998.

———. *Theorizing about Myth.* Boston: University of Massachusetts Press, 1999.

Senf, Carol A. "A Response to '*Dracula* and the Idea of Europe.'" *Connotations* 10, no. 1 (2000–2001): 47–58.

————. *The Vampire in Nineteenth-Century English Literature.* Bowling Green, OH: Popular Press, 1988.

Senn, Harry. *Were-Wolf and Vampire in Romania.* Boulder, CO: East European Monographs, 1982.

Shinedling, Abraham I. "Burial and Burial Customs." In *Universal Jewish Encyclopedia,* ed. Isaac Landman, 594–602. New York: Universal Jewish Encyclopedia, 1939–43.

"A Short Treatise on the History, Culture, and Practices of the Hermetic Order of the Golden Dawn," compiled by Fra. A.o.C., Het-Nuit Lodge, OSOGD, version 1.1 (2002). http://www.osogd.org/library/biscuits/history.html (accessed October 18, 2003).

Silver, Alain, and James Ursini. *The Vampire Film from "Nosferatu" to "Bram Stoker's Dracula."* Rev. ed. New York: Limelight Editions, 1994.

Smith, Jonathan Z. *Map Is Not Territory: Studies in the History of Religions.* Chicago: University of Chicago Press, 1993.

South, James B., ed. *Buffy the Vampire Slayer and Philosophy: Fear and Trembling in Sunnydale.* Chicago: Open Court, 2003.

Sperber, Dan. "Is Symbolic Thought Prerational?" In *Between Belief and Transgression: Structuralist Essays in Religion, History, and Myth,* ed. Michel Izard and Pierre Smith, trans. John Leavitt, 245–63. Chicago: University of Chicago Press, 1982.

————. *Rethinking Symbolism.* Cambridge: Cambridge University Press, 1975.

Spinka, Matthew. *A History of Christianity in the Balkans.* Chicago: American Society of Church History, 1933.

Stahl, Anca. "Animal Sacrifices in the Balkans." In *The Realm of the Extra-Human: Ideas and Actions,* ed. Agehananda Bharati, 443–51. The Hague: Mouton, 1976.

Stoianovich, Traian. *Balkan Worlds: The First and Last Europe.* Armonk, NY: M. E. Sharpe, 1994.

Stoyanov, Yuri. *The Hidden Tradition in Europe: The Secret History of Medieval Christian Heresy.* London: Penguin, 1994.

Sugar, Peter. "The Least Affected Social Group in the Ottoman Balkans: The Peasantry." In *Byzantine Studies: Essays on the Slavic World and the Eleventh Century,* ed. Speros Vryonis Jr., – . New Rochelle, NY: Aristide Caratzas, 1992.

Summers, Montague. *The Vampire: His Kith and Kin.* New Hyde Park, NY: University Books, 1960.

————. *The Vampire in Europe.* Wellingborough, England, 1980.

Swartz, David. *Culture and Power: The Sociology of Pierre Bourdieu.* Chicago: University of Chicago Press, 1997.

Tâpkova-Zalmova, V. "Sur les rapports entre la population indigène des régions balkaniques et les 'Barbares' au VIe–VIIe siècle." *Byzantino-Bulgarica* I (1962): 67–78.

Tashkovski, Dragan [Taškovski, Drajan]. *Bogomilism in Macedonia.* Trans. Alan McConnell. Skopje: Macedonian Review Editions, 1975.

Taussig, Michael. *Mimesis and Alterity: A Particular History of the Senses.* New York: Routledge, 1993.

———. *The Nervous System.* New York: Routledge, 1992.

Todorov, Tzvetan. *The Fantastic: A Structural Approach to a Literary Genre.* Trans. Richard Howard. Ithaca, NY: Cornell University Press, 1975.

Tournefort, Joseph Pitton de. *A Voyage into the Levant. . . .* London: D. Midwinter, 1741. Originally published as *Relation d'un Voyage du Levant* (Lyons, 1727).

Trevor-Roper, H. R. "The European Witch-Craze." In *Witchcraft and Sorcery: Selected Readings,* ed. Max Marwick, 121–50. Harmondsworth, England: Penguin, 1967.

Turner, Victor. *The Ritual Process: Structure and Anti-Structure.* The Lewis Henry Morgan Lectures, 1966. Ithaca, NY: Cornell University Press, 1969.

Twitchell, James B. *The Living Dead: A Study of the Vampire in Romantic Literature.* Durham, NC: Duke University Press, 1981.

Vakarelski, Xristo. "Des vestiges anciens, probablement thraces, dans la culture materielle des Bulgares." In *Thracia,* (Sofia) II (1974): 183–89.

Vambery, Arminius. *The Story of Nations: Hungary in Ancient, Mediaeval, and Modern Times.* London: T. Fisher Unwin, 1887.

van Gennep, Arnold. *The Rites of Passage.* Trans. Monika Vizedom and Gabrielle Caffee. Chicago: University of Chicago Press, 1960.

van Swieten, Gerhard. *Vampyrismus.* Ed. Piero Violante. Palermo, Italy: S. F. Flaccovio, 1988. Includes the text of the Italian translation *Considerazione intorno alla pretesa magia postuma per servire alla storia de' Vampiri presentata al supremo Direttorio di Vienna,* trans. Signor Barone (Naples: Presso Giuseppe Maria Porcelli, 1787).

Velkov, Velizar Iv. *The Cities in Thrace and Dacia in Late Antiquity: Studies and Materials.* Amsterdam: Adolf M. Hakkert, 1977.

———. "Les campagnes et la population rurale en Thrace au IVe–VIe siècle." *Byzantino-Bulgarica* I (1962): 31–66.

———. *Roman Cities in Bulgaria: Collected Studies.* Amsterdam: Adolf M. Hakkert, 1980.

———. "Thrakien in der Spätantike (IV–VI Jahrhunderts)." In *Thracia* (Sofia) I (1972): 213–22.

———. "Thrakien und die Thraker in der spät Antike." In *Actes du IIe Congrès International de Thracologie, Bucarest, 4–10 September 1976,*vol. 2, *History and Archaeology,* 445–50. Bucharest: Editura academiei republicii socialiste Romania, 1980.

Venedikov, I. "La population byzantine en Bulgarie au début du IXe siècle." *Byzantino-Bulgarica* I (1962): 261–77.

Veyne, Paul, ed. *A History of Private Life.* Vol. 1, *From Pagan to Byzantium,* trans. Arthur Goldhammer (Cambridge, MA: Belknap Press, 1992).

Vickery, John B., and J. M. Sellery. *The Scapegoat: Ritual and Literature.* Boston: Houghton Mifflin, 1972.

Vlasto, A. P. *The Entry of the Slavs into Christendom: An Introduction to the Medieval History of the Slavs.* Cambridge: Cambridge University Press, 1970.

Volta, Ornella. *The Vampire.* New York: Award Books, 1963.

Vulcanescu, Romulus. "The Thracian Hypothesis of Romanian Mythology." In *Actes du IIe Congrès International de Thracologie, Bucarest, 4–10 September 1976,* vol. 2, *History and Archaeology,* 399–405. Bucharest: Editura academiei republicii socialiste Romania, 1980.

Vulpe, Radu, ed. *Actes du IIe Congrès International de Thracologie, Bucarest 4–10 septembre 1976.* Vol. 2, *Histoire et Archéologie.* Bucharest: Editura academiei republicii socialiste Romania, 1980.

Ware, Timothy. *The Orthodox Church.* London: Penguin, 1963.

Watts, Alan. *Myth and Ritual in Christianity.* Boston: Beacon, 1968.

Wenzel, Marion. "The Dioscuri in the Balkans." *Slavic Review* 26, no. 3 (1967): 363–81.

———. "A Mediaeval Mystery Cult in Bosnia and Herzegovina." *Journal of the Courtauld and Warburg Institutes* 24, nos. 1–2 (1961): 89–107.

———. "Graveside Feasts and Dances in Yugoslavia." *Folk-Lore* 73 (1962): 1–12.

Weston, Jessie L. *From Ritual to Romance.* Mythos Series. Princeton, NJ: Princeton University Press, 1993.

Wilkinson, William. "An Account of the Principalities of Wallachia and Moldavia." In *The Origins of Dracula,* ed. Clive Leatherdale, 86–96. London: William Kimber, 1987. Originally published in London, 1820.

Wilson, Katharina M. "The History of the Word *Vampire.*" In *The Vampire: A Casebook,* ed. Alan Dundes, 3–11. Madison: University of Wisconsin Press, 1998.

Wolf, Leonard, ed. *The Essential "Dracula": The Definitive Annotated Edition of Bram Stoker's Classic Novel.* New York: Plume, 1993.

Yerkes, Royden Keith. *Sacrifice in Greek and Roman Religions and Early Judaism.* New York: Charles Scribner's Sons, 1952.

Zečević, Slobodan. "Les douze jours." *Makedonski folklor* (Skopje) 8, nos. 15–16 (1975): 51–54.

Index

Text design by Jillian Downey
Typesetting by Huron Valley Graphics, Ann Arbor, Michigan
Text font: Adobe Garamond
Display Font: HTF Requiem

Claude Garamond's sixteenth-century types were modeled on those of Venetian printers from the end of the previous century. Adobe designer Robert Slimbach based his Adobe Garamond roman typefaces on the original Garamond types, and based his italics on types by Robert Granjon, a contemporary of Garamond's. Slimbach's Adobe Garamond was released in 1989.

—courtesy www.adobe.com

HTF Requiem is a family of types created by the Hoefler type Foundry in the 1990s. It was inspired by a set of inscriptional capitals in Ludovico Vicentino degli Arrighi's 1523 writing manual, *Il Modo de Temperare le Penne.*

—courtesy www.typography.com